American Heathens

JENNIFER SNOOK

American Heathens

The Politics of Identity in a Pagan
Religious Movement

TEMPLE UNIVERSITY PRESS
Philadelphia • Rome • Tokyo

TEMPLE UNIVERSITY PRESS
Philadelphia, Pennsylvania 19122
www.temple.edu/tempress

Published 2015

Library of Congress Cataloging-in-Publication Data

Snook, Jennifer Stephanie
   American heathens : the politics of identity in a pagan religious
movement / Jennifer Stephanie Snook.
       pages cm
   Includes bibliographical references and index.
   ISBN 978-1-4399-1096-2 (hardback : alk. paper) — ISBN 978-1-4399-1097-9
(paper : alk. paper) — ISBN 978-1-4399-1098-6 (e-book)   1. Paganism—
United States.   2. Group identity—United States.   I. Title.
   BL432.S66 2015
   299'.940973—dc23

                                                    2014044692

⊚ The paper used in this publication meets the requirements of the
American National Standard for Information Sciences—Permanence
of Paper for Printed Library Materials, ANSI Z39.48-1992

Printed in the United States of America

9 8 7 6 5 4 3 2 1

Contents

Preface

Despite the growing scholarly interest in Pagan studies, in-depth ethnographic research into paganisms is still relatively rare. This work is a small contribution that is also close to my heart. I not only research, write about, and teach about paganisms; I have been a practicing Pagan since my early teen years and a Heathen since age eighteen. My decision to research American Heathenry began as a matter of convenience, curiosity, and spiritual longing. Growing up, I had never belonged to a spiritual community. I had moved around too much and was too skeptical of the establishment. And my parents, both agnostics, did not encourage much spiritual pursuit.

As time went on, I came to understand Heathens as simply one group among many whose members were typical people, going about their mundane lives, who happened to embrace some eccentric interests and philosophies. As I began my work, I made fast friends with the Heathens in Colorado. I wrote my doctoral dissertation, earned my Ph.D., and continued my fieldwork, determined to fulfill the oath that I had made at a *blót* (ritual) in 2003—that I would honor the time that others had sacrificed to help me by publishing my work. Over the years, I became acquainted with other Heathens throughout the country, and I found that most of the literature that I had read about American Heathenry overlooked the more moderate voices of Heathens. These would be my primary informants in the first few years of my research.

Because place often influences the politics of its inhabitants, my earliest work, in Boulder, Colorado, focused on Heathens with liberal to moderate political sympathies. As U.S. politics became more divisive—a trend that started with the contentious presidency of George W. Bush and escalated with the election of Barack Obama—Heathenry, too, became more embattled. My moderate politics seemed surprisingly liberal compared with the politics of the people I came to observe. At times, my formal education proved to be a hindrance, a cause for mistrust and suspicion. Like other Americans, some Heathens began to post online partisan rants about Obamacare and social welfare programs. Others expressed vehement support for gun rights and asked that those who disagreed unfriend them. Strains of xenophobia, sexism, and racism seemed to permeate conversations increasingly frequently and in increasingly confrontational tones. The turmoil went on to poison the well of Heathen groups on social media, damage Heathen relationships, and widen political divides as Heathen groups organized opposing factions—those that espoused right-wing political beliefs and those that embraced more moderate views (often characterized by the opposition as representing the Left).

Yet these factions do not constitute the entirety of Heathen belief, community, and expression. The voices that speak up for human rights, religious tolerance, and human decency remain—even as some segment is consumed, with increasing vigor, by the currents of unwavering conservatism among American Heathens that other scholars have identified. Politics aside, American Heathens are, in the main, generous and caring people who are passionate about their faith, values, and communities. I hope that, for fellow Heathens, this book will serve as a glimpse of a larger perspective outside their own local communities.

I chose the topics in this book on the basis of twelve years of observation, emerging and recurring themes, and the concerns that many of my fellow Heathens shared with me and with one another. Certainly, Heathens are many and varied; tribes, kindreds, hearths, and garths are each unique; and it is difficult to generalize in a way that speaks to everyone's experience. There is always room to share additional American Heathen perspectives and cultures, and this endeavor I leave to future scholars.

I hope that those who find that some of their experiences conflict with elements of my analysis also find something of their own lives reflected in this work. I also hope that this effort to put our faith in its sociohistorical context, to highlight our strengths and also to gently, and in good faith, uncover our weaknesses, will provide the opportunity for further reflection about who we are or who we would like to become.

This book would not exist without the support of my graduate mentor, Leslie Irvine, and the continual feedback of other scholars and Heathens who have helped me by cross-checking data, reading drafts, answering questions, and sharing their lives and ideas. I extend heartfelt thanks to my partner, Ross Haenfler, for allowing me to interrupt him many times a day with a hundred questions and requests for help. I thank Kristen, the heart of Friedenhof, and Heathens in Colorado—Scott, Sin, Magni, Kaedrich, Rosa, Thorolf, and Becky—whose support and friendship have been invaluable over the years. Deep gratitude also goes to Destiny, David, Steven, Mark, Rod, Kari, and many more for keeping me connected and grounded. I owe a hearty thank-you to those who took time to help me collect images, among whom are Annie and Tana-Marie. To those kindreds who allowed me to crash their events and interrogate them online, I extend my gratitude. And to Michael Strmiska, for his many helpful comments, and my other scholar buddies—Thad, Jefferson, and Karl—I offer my thanks for being my fellow nerds.

American Heathens

1

Becoming Heathen

In 1997 I was a college-bound army brat, stationed with my family at the Army War College in Carlisle, Pennsylvania. One evening, while surfing the net in a tiny bedroom of my parents' home—a cozy white cottage in what the locals referred to as "smurf village"—I stumbled on an article titled "The Pentagram and the Hammer,"[1] a piece written by Pagan insiders that outlines the similarities and differences between Wicca and a Germanic reconstructionist belief system called Ásatrú. Although I had already dabbled in Wicca as a solitary practitioner within the confines of army life overseas, this particular publication was my gateway into Heathendom. In 1979 Margot Adler published "Drawing Down the Moon," juxtaposing her experience against conventional conversion narratives by describing the adoption of a Pagan identity as a gradual "coming home."[2] Since then, scholars have documented the dawning realization of countless adherents, experiences that each mirror this moment of epiphany.[3] As many Pagans have said over the years, and many Heathens have said to me since, I had "come home," and my story has unfolded like that of many others.

The tale of this research, and of my journey toward Heathenry, begins much earlier, and like many such stories, it begins with Wicca. Late in the summer of 1995, my best friend, Sarah, and I opened Scott Cunningham's book *Wicca: A Guide for the Solitary Practitioner* and, in my basement bedroom, awkwardly performed the scripted ritual to pledge that in a year and a day, the period required to reach the first stage of initiation into Wicca, we would dedicate ourselves to the Wiccan path. Like many tweens, we experimented with various identities. We diverged from the "normal" kids and became interested in what sociologists call "deviant subcultures."[4] Our experiment with the subcultural milieu began with heavy-metal music and vampires when we were twelve. Later, after consuming reams of heroic fantasy novels, playing Dungeons and Dragons, and finding the Society for Creative Anachronism, I became more genuinely interested in the occult. In the eighth grade I met a socially awkward thirteen-year-old girl named Susanne who claimed to be a witch. Despite her fanciful and often ridiculous assertions regarding her mystical abilities, something about her interests sparked my curiosity. Later, one boring afternoon, while I was leafing through the "R" volume of an old set of encyclopedias, I came upon an illustration of strange-looking symbols called "runes" and their history and use as an Old Norse alphabet. This obscure and magical knowledge fueled my developing sense of difference, and Susanne and I quickly learned how to use these symbols to write notes to each other in class. Despite their boorish misuse as playthings, the runes piqued a deeper interest in Germanic magical and religious practices.

In high school, I worked at the now-abandoned U.S. Army Europe library in Heidelberg, Germany, which stocked a variety of books on witchcraft, from Starhawk's *The Spiral Dance* (1979) to Israel Regardie's *The Golden Dawn* (1937). I spent much of my time at this job perched on step stools, lost in the stacks with my nose in a book, my tasks forgotten. Wicca, I had learned, was a religion that focused on magical concepts, nature, the elements, and communion with the Goddess and her Consort—a fundamentally gender-egalitarian religion that exalted the feminine. Modern Wicca began as a reconstructed Pagan mystery religion, introduced in the mid-twentieth century in southern England. It crossed to the United States, flourished there, and then returned to Britain and other parts of the world, transported by feminism and concerns over religious ecology.[5] It has no central authority, no hierarchy, and many divergent branches, each an offshoot of Gardnerian Wicca, founded by Gerald Gardner in the 1950s. To us, as kids, it meant the practice of a wide variety of cursory spells from how-to books and a new appreciation for nature. We called ourselves witches. We felt extraordinary and empowered to magically shape our own lives, contrary to the heavy control and the Cold War paranoia of barbed-wire fences, armed guards, and military rigidity surrounding us. Our isolation from other actual Wiccans or any alternative communities meant that we lacked a mature understanding of what we were getting into. Many traditional Wiccans consider self-initiation contradictory, but we did not know that at the time. We knew that whatever "it" was, it was exciting, but most importantly, it meant rebelling against the conservative social and religious culture of the military institution we had been a part of since birth. In this military community, the public face of Wicca consisted of disparaging letters to the editor of the *Stars and Stripes,* the tones of which gave a nod to the Satanic Panic ongoing since the 1980s. The basis or motivation for these letters was unclear, but they were timely in that they appeared in the newspaper just as we were developing our new Wiccan identities. These letters and a general public ignorance about alternative religions only increased our determination. I snipped them from the paper and carried them in my wallet as reminders of my social context. In one sense, they were my first connection to real-time expressions regarding Paganism. Mostly, however, they reinforced my sense of otherness and alienation. Our newfound religious experimentation gave us a feeling of greater closeness to our natural surroundings and provided us with a spiritual underpinning with which to challenge the conformity of the other kids at school. It was a powerful secret that brought us together and gave us a tangible reason for feeling like aliens.

As is standard in the military, Sarah moved away a year later, and I never saw her again. I continued my exercise in spiritual experimentation by myself, but—as I would hear later from other Heathens—something about Wicca did not fit. It did not feel grounded or authentic enough for me. I was interested only in my Germanic roots, in the gods of my ancestors about whom my mom, a German "foreign national," as we said overseas, had read me stories at bedtime. Wicca was polytheistic, asserting that all gods and goddesses are manifestations of "the one" great being, like a gem with a thousand facets—a reflection of the monotheism I found baffling. It focused on magic, elements, and spell casting that our sense of the romantic begged us to believe in, but that my skepticism would not allow. Wicca, in its 1990s manifestation as a nature-based Goddess religion, felt very nurturing, soft, and feminine, but my patriarchal military upbringing and my awareness of my Germanicity led to interest in something that I interpreted as more firm, profound, and epic. It was then that I began to identify as Heathen.

My identity and my interest in American Heathenry became more firmly rooted in my consciousness when my family was stationed in Washington, D.C., where I met David and his friend Matt, both of whom were into the black-metal scene. Because of his long hair, black clothing, and combat boots, I sensed a kindred spirit in David, who quickly became a friend and my doorway into the music scene. Black metal, as I learned, was a dark, harsh, fast, and screeching style of music that originated in Scandinavia, and many of the bands that created this genre were intricately connected and involved with aspects of their own native spirituality, referred to in the modern age as Ásatrú. This music was another aspect of my growing Heathen identity, although it was regrettably entangled in the 1990s with the Satanic Panic in Norway (imported from the United States) and an array of anti-Christian church burnings and interband homicide. Many black-metal bands sang about ancient Heathen mythology, culture, Vikings, medieval sagas, and epic battles. Although I was disturbed by the arson, the underlying anti-Christian, pro-Pagan protest spoke to my disenchantment with Judeo-Christian religion. My friends regularly reinforced my Heathen identity as they made reference to the ties between Ásatrú and black metal, referring to a range of my behaviors as "very Heathen" and thereby enforcing and constructing what it meant for me to "do" Heathenry.

Traditionally, research in the sociology of religion has focused disproportionately on empirical studies of American Protestantism and has neglected non-Christian religious experiences and practices.[6] In the early 2000s, sociologists of religion have turned increasingly to the cultural analysis of religion as it is experienced through the sacralization of daily life, analyzing religious cultural tools and symbolic boundaries.[7] Much of the early literature that focused on new religious movements (NRMs) regarded them as significant only in that they were "symptoms of a broader social malaise."[8] These analyses overlooked the complexities involved in the construction of religious identities that NRMs offer to their members. In so doing, the literature on cultural analysis of religion—and my contribution to it—is further revitalizing the field by diverging from traditional approaches and focusing instead on an intersectional investigation of religion as a source of symbolic legitimation. It responds to the scholarly call for more work among sociologists of religion to "proceed with a fundamentally different understanding of the nature of religious authority and religious identity in the late modern world than the one articulated by market and secularization-dominant approaches" while acknowledging that religious identity is always "inherently fluid and intersectional, with boundaries that are actively made and defended (or blurred and changed)."[9] Social scientists have also researched the many ways in which people's religious beliefs influence their political worldviews.[10] This book, however, offers insight into how dominant political currents can influence the shape of NRMs—a relationship in reverse—and how this influence plays out through the microinteractions and identity work of movement participants. By the term *political,* which I employ throughout this book, I am referencing a system that moves beyond people's individual preferences to ideas that tap into larger structures of power and inequality. The feminist rallying cry of the 1960s and 1970s "The personal is political" reflected the idea that people's personal choices and ideas are influenced by social structural and institutional considerations.[11] For second-wave feminists, women's personal lives were brought into the public arena to challenge massive structural inequalities and gendered oppression. Exclusion and exploitation were not individual acts, but were shared under patriarchy. In 1959 C. Wright Mills articulated the idea that personal attitudes and beliefs often have a structural component, and he distinguished between "personal troubles" and "public issues" as a way of explaining the impact of social, political, and historical context on individual experience.[12] American ideas of meritocracy, for example, undergird the assumption that poverty is a product of laziness rather than being rooted in wider structural obstacles. Put simply, people's personal ideas often reflect wider systems of oppression and dominance. In this book "the political" refers to concepts that reflect differential opportunities or identities that are part of a broader system of power and the perpetuation of inequalities. I hope that by focusing on these many variables, this project will assist with an intersectional perspective on religion's role in an ever-changing world.

Mapping the Neopagan Landscape

The relationship between American Heathenry and other Neopaganisms is complex, as I learned in the pre-Google age while perusing the "Metaphysical" section of various chain bookstores. What I found was very little information on Heathen practice and a plethora of New Age advice and instruction on astrology, Runology, UFOlogy, tarot, and witchcraft, as well as dozens of hip, up-to-date spell books for the modern dabbler in the occult. Commercialized and targeted to specific audiences, these books symbolize the marketability and self-help mentality of the New Age and the personal and self-driven postmodern spirituality that has come with it. Do you want to become a witch to wow your friends at school? *The Teen Spellbook: Magick for Young Witches, Be a Teen Goddess: Magical Charms, Spells and Wiccan Wisdom for the Wild,* and *Silver RavenWolf's Teen Witch: Wicca for a New Generation* will help you with that, complete with the *Teen Witch Kit: Everything You Need to Make Magick!*[13] Do you need help with your career, finances, or love life? Jen McConnel is there to help you with *Goddess Spells for Busy Girls.*[14] Or, if you need immediate spiritual assistance with your career or workplace, follow the modern trend of knowledge seeking and Google for instant guidance from websites with free spells and rituals written to satisfy your every need. Perhaps you are interested in learning more about the art of candle magick, a practice involving concentration, visualization, and willpower. Google.com's book search lists over 3000 results for "candle magick," including *A Little Book of Candle Magic, Mastering Candle Magick: Advanced Spells and Charms for Every Rite,* and *Candle Magic for Beginners: The Simplest Magic You Can Do* or, in 2014, *Candle Magic: Simple Spells for Beginners to Witchcraft.* If you are in a hurry, there is *Wicca Candle Spells: Simple Magic Spells That Work Fast.*[15]

Whatever the purpose of these books, one thing is clear: they are aimed at an audience whose spirituality, sense of empowerment, and alienation are intimately intertwined. They speak to those who seek a new approach to religion apart from traditional religious institutions and as readily available as handbooks in the spiritual marketplace. This pattern of interest and involvement in New Age spirituality indicates an increase in religious pluralism, an acceptance of alternative religious views, and a decline in participation in traditional religion.[16] For scholars of NRMs, the variety of explanations for the decline of the power of traditional Christianity in Europe and the United States has been exhausted by decades of debate and microscopic investigation. Max Weber outlined these changes early in the twentieth century, referring to "disenchantment" rather than secularization to highlight their effects not only on the social and organizational level but also on a subjective intellectual level. Disenchantment, he argued, refers to the knowledge that there are no mysterious forces at play; rather, we can "master all things by calculation."[17] Consequently, "the bearing of man has been disenchanted and denuded of its mystical but inwardly genuine plasticity."[18] Later, other scholars echoed Weber's prediction, positing that this "disenchanted world in which we live" is due, in part, to "the decline of the community . . . the increasing fragmentation of modern life, [and] the impact of multicultural and religiously plural societies," along with "creeping rationalization and the influence of scientific worldviews." Together, these have "led to a situation in which religion is privatized, far less socially important, and far less plausible than it used to be in premodern communities."[19] Postmodernism has also undermined our search for metanarratives, particularly those that stress certainty in the world, human emancipation, and social progress. The postmodern condition is one in which everything becomes relative, and quests for overarching myths, narratives, or frameworks of knowledge are easily abandoned. The acceptance of traditional or dominant forms of religiosity is on the wane as modern life has eroded the formerly held belief in ideas about inevitable human progress and a future full of divine significance and purpose.[20] More to the point, perhaps, is the declining influence of ascribed identities, which, in the case of religion, leaves people free to pursue personal and individualistic religious concerns.[21] Weber's prediction that increased rationalization would lead to the end of religion has not yet been fulfilled. Despite the argument that secularization has changed the pattern of religious life, most contemporary scholars have been reluctant to claim that a decline in traditional religion means that God is dead. Rather, we have traded in the traditional, institutional religion for privatized, personal spirituality.[22]

Indeed, it seems that there are no aspects of modernity or postmodernity that cannot be said to have a hand in the birth of the NRMs that I discovered in those bookstores. We have filled much of the resultant black hole with a variety of social networks, subcultures, and other forms of community, a trend that has earned a fair share of attention by religious studies scholars. The growth of new religions is, at least in part, enhanced by the breakdown of religious monopolies and the growth of the spiritual marketplace.[23] New religions are evidence of secularization[24] as dominant religions lose their authority and religion undergoes the privatization that leads to spiritual seeking and the development of religious movements like Paganism(s).

Under the umbrella term *Neopaganism,* scholars and practitioners alike have captured the myriad modern Pagan faiths into one large container. Most Neopaganisms are exceptionally diverse and inclusive. Many Pagans identify their practice as eclectic and choose not to adopt any single tradition.[25] Although the groups sometimes demonstrate extreme differences from one another, their proximity and similar temporal origins have, to a large degree, rendered them inseparable. They are part of the cultic milieu, defining themselves in relation to one another while delving, in many cases, into the same tomes for answers to their origins and practice.[26] Many have a specific pantheon of gods and spirits central to their tradition, while others worship any and all gods to whom their particular needs and desires apply. Some are hard polytheists, who believe that each god is an independent, unique individual; others are soft polytheists, who view all gods as manifestations or facets of one central deity. Most Neopaganisms are centered on the cycles of the earth and the workings of animals, plants, and humans and their relationship and interconnectivity with the cosmos.[27] Others are more cultural, focusing on ancestors and community building with a less politically inspired ecological focus despite the reverence of the spirits of land and place. In the last few decades, ethnic groups around the world have, like Heathens, turned increasingly to a revival of the pre-Christian religious systems of their ancestors. These folk religions vary, however, from the development of romanticized and generic paganisms that focus on, for example, the magical Celticity of practitioners' (often imagined) Celtic forebears to a more politically charged focus on a particular peoplehood. The place of reconstruction also matters greatly to the outcome of a particular pagan project. In Eastern Europe, "the issue of national identity is strongly emphasized while magical practices are de-emphasized." To these communities, "the necessity of a return to pre-Christian national-tribal traditions" is paramount.[28]

In the United States, Paganisms are many and varied. Even among those Paganisms under the umbrella of "Germanic," the origins, goals, and philosophies of each particular tradition have led to significant schisms and differences. Scholars who study American Heathenry often distinguish between Odinism and Ásatrú, viewing Odinism as a highly politicized right-wing movement and Ásatrú as having greater ideological variance and a closer relationship to the wider Pagan movement.[29] Both, however, can be traced back to a variety of overlapping and mutually influencing movements during the early nineteenth century. As a reaction against the industrialization movement and the increasing rationalization of society, the highly emotive Romantic movement espoused folk art, folklore, an idealistic focus on early Germanic culture, and a renewed interest in the natural world. From this, and from the Esotericism prevalent in mid-twentieth-century Europe, grew the Völkisch movement. Born of romantic nationalism, the Völkisch movement championed the affirmation of white identity in opposition to modernity, immigration, multiracialism, liberalism, and multiculturalism. Out of this zeitgeist came the veneration of antiquity, a fantasy of medievalism and romantic epics, and a variety of *Deutschgläubig* (German Faith) movements throughout Europe, including the Germanische Glaubens-Gemeinschaft (1907), the Deutschgläubige Gemeinschaft (1911), and the Germanenorden (1912). During the Third Reich, Jakob Wilhelm Hauer, a professor of religious studies, devised the influential German Faith Movement (Deutsche Glaubensbewegung) as a countermovement to replace Christianity with an essentially German folk religion. After the Nazis appropriated Germanic antiquity, however, many of these precursor movements died, but the influence of the Völkisch focus on white identity and the connection, and conflation, of Heathenry with neo-Nazis and white supremacy continued. These movements of revitalization set the stage for a second wave of interest in Germanic antiquity during the countercultural activities of the late 1960s and early 1970s.

Situated in the sociopolitical upheavals of the 1960s and 1970s, contemporary Ásatrú developed alongside of, and in response to, other Neopagan NRMs as an outgrowth of the era's New Age spirituality movement, influenced by new waves of feminism, male liberation movements, the civil rights triumphs, and changing racial awareness.[30] The new Pagan movements ultimately sought to revive ancient non-Christian and typically polytheistic, pantheistic, or animistic belief systems situated in a more political climate than their nineteenth- and twentieth- century precursor movements. Because of a renewed interest in folklore and historical research, some Pagans began to look closely at their Scandinavian, Anglo-Saxon, or Germanic heritage as a foundation for spiritual practice. Partly as a reaction against the New Age, but spirited by the same protest against modernity and similiar ameliorating reenchantment processes as the earlier movements, in 1972 and 1973 Heathen organizations developed simultaneously across the globe. In Iceland, the Icelandic government recognized Ásatrúarfélagið (Ásatrú Association), led by farmer-poet Sveinbjörn Beinteinsson, as a religious organization. The recognition came on the heels of a dramatic volcanic eruption that destroyed hundreds of homes and captured the attention of the international media, bringing Iceland, and Ásatrú, to the public's attention worldwide. In 1973, a month after the eruption was declared over, Beinteinsson held the first public outdoor *blót* (ritual) since the conversion to Christianity in 1000 C.E. The next year in England, John Gibbs-Bailey and John Yeowell founded the Committee for the Restoration of the Odinic Rite, which later became the Odinic Rite. In the United States, Danish anarcho-syndicalist Else Christensen (1913–2005) began publishing *The Odinist* newsletter. Christiansen's writings influenced the formation of Ásatrú groups in Europe and the United States, with varying levels of attention to her political motivations. Sidestepping Christensen's focus on racial ideology, Stephen McNallen, an active-duty American soldier at the time, produced *The Runestone* and began the Viking Brotherhood, which later morphed into the Ásatrú Free Assembly, the first national Heathen organization in the United States. Yet the circumstances of Heathenry's creation, as a movement influenced by Neo-Volkism, in a country still mired in the struggles of Jim Crow racial ideology made its divorce from racial concerns difficult.

In the next few years, differing ideas about how to approach racial exclusivity and whether to allow white supremacists membership caused a schism, and the Ásatrú Free Assembly splintered into the Ásatrú Alliance and the Ring of Troth, now known simply as The Troth—a history thoroughly outlined in Mattias Gardell's book *Gods of the Blood*.[31] In 1994 McNallen revived the Ásatrú Free Assembly, now known as the Ásatrú Folk Assembly (AFA). Other organizations came and went, each with its particular sociopolitical leanings or preferred practices.[32] Many still adhered to Völkisch ideologies, preferring racial politics and exclusivity over other aspects of faith. White supremacists, neo-Nazis, and Aryan prison gangs co-opted the movement to pursue their own political agendas, using Heathenry in the same manner as the Nazi Party—as a platform for the fantasy of a "pure," epic, heroic, and ultimately dying race, threatened on all sides by the nonwhite "other," which was leading to the degradation of traditional morals and values. Other groups purposely and vehemently positioned themselves against such ideologies, focusing instead on the apolitical reenchantment born of scholarship, spirituality, and the fantasy epic. The distinct Heathen groups that emerged were Ásatrú, Theodism, Fyrn Sede, Odinism or Wotanism, and Irminism. These groups vary in their region of ancient origin in northern Europe, in their structure, and often in their sociopolitical leanings. The followers of these faith systems came to call them "Heathenry," a term used to demarcate them from other Neopagan religions whose sources are more modern. In the United States, however, much of Germanic Paganism came to be known generically as Ásatrú. Ásatrú is an Icelandic translation of the Danish word *Asetro*. It means "belief in the Aesir," the gods of Germanic tribal peoples, among whom Thor, Odin, Freyja, Freyr, Frigg, Tyr, and Heimdall are the most popular. In Iceland, it is the largest non-Christian religion. In this book I prefer the term *Heathen* to describe all these groups because it is inclusive of all varieties of Germanic paganism.

Although Heathens revere the forces of nature, Heathenism is not a nature religion in the usual sense of the term. Heathens and other historically based reconstructionist groups are dissatisfied with the term *Neopagan* and differ markedly from their Neopagan peers. Reconstructionist Paganisms go to great lengths to stress their independent roots. Germanic, Celtic, Hellenic, Egyptian, Slavic, Baltic, and other Paganisms often avoid association with the term *Neopagan,* arguing that not only has it been co-opted by Wiccans, in particular, as synonymous with their faith, but also *Neo* implies that the faith is new and modern. *Modern* implies inauthentic, made-up, and New Agey, along with other politically charged assumptions, such as effeminate or liberal. Instead, reconstructionists claim ownership over their faith tradition as an "indigenous" ethnic right passed down by their forebears. Ideologically, Neopaganism is decidedly individualistic, allowing for free interpretation and invention and engaging in cultural appropriation, or "cultural strip mining,"[33] a practice that reconstructionists typically find irritating. American Heathenry, in contrast, is ethnocentric, paying close attention to historical research and the written lore of northern Europe and drawing strict boundaries of authenticity around what beliefs and practices can be considered legitimately Heathen. Based on the tribal models of ancient peoples, Heathenry remains incredibly diverse and decentralized, often lacking even a sense of oneness with other adherents who identify as Heathen.

American Heathenry 101

Ten years after my first experiences with Heathenry in the flesh, I stood outside a campground dining facility, a log cabin on a concrete slab, waiting my turn to be called inside for a seat at the solemn ritual of *High Sumbel*. It was surprisingly swampy and warm for a summer evening on my visit to this northern state, less of a contrast from the Mississippi weather I had left behind than I had hoped. Nearby me were dozens of members of local and regional Heathen groups that were already bonded to one another in familiarity and friendship. I was an interloper—the Heathen-turned-researcher stranger—watching them chatter as they clustered around one another in kindred groups. Each participant wore a pendant, sometimes many, variants of Thor's hammer in bronze, silver, or pewter. Mjollnir, as Thor's hammer is called, is the primary symbol worn by most American Heathens to indicate group belonging. Heathens wear their symbols in the open, often remarking that colleagues, family, or other outsiders interpret the symbol as a sailor's anchor—hardly a threatening icon in the popular imagination. To many Heathens, it symbolizes strength, perseverance, and protection—a tool with which the god Thor defended humans and gods alike from the baleful forces of frost giants and other enemies of Asgard. Nearby, a group of women dressed in shawls, long skirts, and handmade cotton shifts exchanged stories, laughing and chattering in the shadow of the shelter's floodlight. Some nearby men wore tunics or bits and pieces of reenactor's garb, each waiting in the dark to be called in. To a certain degree, I was reminded of the aesthetic of a Renaissance fair, but the occasion felt more reverent and significant. It was similar to my other experiences among Heathens, although this time no one was wearing chain mail. Inside the hall, members of the Twelve Lakes Kindred,[34] the group hosting this annual event, milled about, arranging the tables to seat themselves at the front of the hall and their guests in one long row down the length of the room. On each table they placed a crisp white tablecloth, a floral centerpiece, bowls of snacks, and pitchers of water.

Once the Twelve Lakes members concluded setting up, their *Thule,* a lawspeaker—in charge of clarifying and maintaining protocol and the taking and keeping of oaths—stepped outside to call us in from the dark. Dressed in a Viking-style tunic with decorative trim, he called our names. Waiting guests enter the hall by order of rank—a reflection of their significance in friendship and obligation to the hosts. He called each kindred, who entered together, punctuated by couples and an individual here and there. Mostly, those individuals present were unaffiliated—guests, merely—and stayed outside to straggle until last, to sit at the end of the table, symbolically marginalized. I was fortunate enough to be a guest of the women-in-shawls, a high-status group in this area. We got seated toward the front of the room. Inside, the space once used by summer campers and Boy Scouts had been transformed into a chieftain's *hof.* On the stone wall above the long table reserved for the hosts hung a variety of brightly colored kindred banners of those groups in attendance. Sewn as quilts or painted onto fabric, the symbols, runic writing, and images of animals, weaponry, or other iconography reflected a scene of medieval heraldry. The largest quilt, central on the wall, was that of the host, an intricate work of Twelve Lake's motto in runes surrounding a large central bindrune,[35] the symbol of their group. On the table beneath, drinking horns of mead, a honey-wine symbolic to Heathens for its historical importance to Germanic peoples and its role as an elixir of poetry and inspiration. On a small wooden podium, other odds and ends awaited their purpose in the night's ritual. Once we were ushered in and our hands were washed in scented water and dried on clean white cloths, we took our assigned places. Hans, the chieftain, stood, his embroidery-trimmed tunic belted at the waist, and welcomed us to the hall. Beside him, Thordis, his wife, in her reconstructed Viking apron gown, took up a large drinking horn of mead to approach each group's leader in welcome. Heathens derive the practice of drinking from a horn from the lore and historical scholarship. In the Icelandic epic poem *Lokrur,* for example, the god Thor drank heartily from a horn that, unbeknownst to him, contained the vast sea. Historically, the Viking and medieval Scandinavian elite used drinking horns during ritual functions, while those of lower status drank primarily from bowls. Fulfilling the duty of Valkyrie for the ritual, Thordis had the sacred obligation to pass the horn among the speakers, a practice preserved in *Beowulf,* in which Queen Wealhtheow presents a cup to the visiting Danes.[36] As we watched, Thordis exchanged words of friendship and, with others, words of encouragement or welcome. Down the row of tables she walked, speaking to kindred leaders, each in turn. To the Three Oaks Kindred,[37] a local group with whom the men in her kindred had quarreled, she offered tearful words of reconciliation for past grievances, suggesting that although the men might have injured friendships, the women were here to repair them. The solemn moment moved many in the hall to tears or, at the sight of such emotion, awkward fidgeting. When Three Oaks Kindred accepted the apology, Hans and the rest of the Twelve Lakes Kindred thumped the high table with their fists—a Heathen applause, taken up by the hall's guests to great vibration. I could feel the thunderous pounding from my heels to my teeth, a powerful expression of support and camaraderie. The rest of the ritual involved each participant sharing words of thanks, blessing, encouragement, or prayer with the horn in hand before passing it back to Thordis. Most thanked the host out of ritual obligation before sharing poems and songs about gods and ancestors, offering gifts to one another or to the hosts, and toasting friends, friendship, and community. The ritual lasted into the early hours of the morning. At this time, we brought to bear the sociopolitical purpose of this ritual among the ancient Germanic tribes and among the current Heathens present there. Now, as then, the ritual of *Sumbel* is a game of politicking, of socializing, cementing bonds of peace and friendship and forming new relationships—all under the weight of public scrutiny. To many there, what is spoken over the horn passes into the Urd's well, where the Norns sit and weave the destiny of all humankind. The words spoken into the well affect our *wyrd,* the interconnected web of obligation. The words said there transcended the profane, enveloping us all in feelings of goodwill—an expression of Émile Durkheim's "collective effervescence."[38] This, and many experiences before and after, offered insight into the power of local community, the Heathen perspective, and its anachronistic aesthetic.

As a unit of analysis, Heathenry is decidedly complex. It is in every way subcultural, but it is also a religion, a category that is itself challenging to define. Like other scholars whose work on religion requires clarification, I work under the understanding that Heathenry, like other religious groups, is a cultural system. According to Clifford Geertz, religion can best be understood as "a system of symbols which acts to establish powerful, pervasive and long-lasting moods and motivations in men by formulating conceptions of a general order of existence and clothing these conceptions with such an aura of factuality that

the moods and motivations seem uniquely realistic."[39] Indeed, Heathenry provides such a conception to its adherents and is simultaneously spiritual and
cultural. As a cultural system, it provides for its adherents ethnic identification—a
system of meaning tied to heritage, place, and daily practices with historical
significance.

Although the origin of the "old way" is lost in antiquity, at its peak, it cov-
ered all of northern Europe. It was more than a religion; it was a custom involving political, social, and cultural beliefs and practices, a complex blending of the
sacred and profane. It was not called a "religion" by the people who practiced it;
it was just "the Way." Specific practices and beliefs varied across family and tribal
groups and across time and space. Much like today, there was no central authority, no dogma, and no assumption by its practitioners that it was the only way.
In various forms, across various tribes, Germanic belief and practice changed
after forcible conversion to Christianity. In 1000 C.E. Iceland was peacefully
converted to Christianity, and a Heathen king ruled Sweden until 1085 C.E.
Conversion-era Scandinavian law codes prohibited "Pagan" behaviors, indicating
that there, in fact, Pagan practice was commonplace enough to warrant punishment and control. Although Christianity brought with it a formalization of
nations and religious practice unknown before, the old way was maintained
through customs and folkways in everyday life.[40] It was at least another hundred
years before Christian monks in Iceland recorded tales of their Heathen forebears, known to us as the Icelandic sagas, told through a Christian lens, the
stripping away of which proves arduous for modern Heathens. In addition to the
sagas, Heathens draw heavily from the *Poetic Edda,* a collection of ancient Icelandic poetry detailing Germanic cosmology, the experiences and philosophies
of the gods, and the end of the world, and the *Prose Edda,* which illuminates many
of these same stories. Although some Heathens take these texts at face value,
many more consume them with a critical and analytic eye, paying close attention to the material evidence unearthed by archaeology, reading academic jour-
nals and scholarly news sites, and interpreting various linguistic evidence to
piece together contemporary understandings of the realities of Germanic belief.

With the success of Marvel's *Thor* movies, released beginning in 2013, popular culture was awash with increased interest in Norse mythology. Fans of the
gods as portrayed in the films spawned a new generation of pseudo-pagans
across the Internet. Before this focus on the might and adventure of the comic-
book universe, actual Heathens had been working on defining their customs
since the 1970s. The project of reviving ancient beliefs and customs and adapting
them to the modern world is central to what it means to do any form of reconstructionist Paganism. From ancient Egyptian worship to Hellenic and Celtic
reconstructionism, the project of reviving ancient faith is a process of discovery
and world construction, an ongoing and self-conscious effort to unearth ancient
concepts and practices and adapt them to a postmodern context. The reconstructionist project is an exercise in desocialization—redefining familiar concepts and
introducing alien ones that, to ancient Heathens, were common sense. Specifi-

cally, Heathens often reference *Landvaettir* (land spirits) of the forest, earth, and streams, often represented as trolls, gnomes, elves, and fairies, give offerings to them, and invoke them. To some Heathens, interaction with the *Landvaettir* is the bulk of daily ritual, more than interaction with the gods, which may occur only during special rituals or occasions. Despite such spiritual ecology, Heathens are not necessarily green activists or spectacular environmental stewards. Their relationship with nature in many ways reflects the de facto daily practice, resource usage, waste production, and energy consumption of the average person for whom nature has little spiritual significance.

In addition to land spirits, the Germanic deities include a variety of beings concerned with the cycles of nature and natural phenomena, such as thunder (Thor), fertility and the harvest (Freyr, Sif), and the sea (Njord), and another group of gods affiliated with human capacities and reactions, such as love (Freyja), wisdom, and war and justice (Odin, Tyr). To most Heathens, the gods are complex and imperfect. Some Heathens understand them to be real, present, and distinct individuals. To others, they are abstract representations of fundamental needs, not necessarily "real" in the sense that they have the capacity to materialize or interact with us. To some, the Germanic gods are part of a pantheon of deities; to others, the idea of a pantheon is historically questionable, a construction of the Christian Snorri Sturluson's attempt to unify locally specific folk beliefs to create a Norse equivalent of the Greek myths. Some Heathens maintain an agnostic approach to the existence of the gods, focusing their humanistic energies instead on the sociocultural aspects of American Heathenry. Unlike the Ásatrúarfélagið, Iceland's state-recognized Heathen organization, American Heathens have no central authority. There are national Heathen organizations, but there is no obligation to join them. There are hundreds, perhaps thousands, of Heathen kindreds spread out across the country, ranging from family groups with a handful of members to large tribes with dozens of members. Each of these groups is autonomous and maintains its own particular philosophical and political beliefs, goals, ritual structure, and customs (often called *thew* or *sidu*). Although the landscape of American Heathenry is diverse and diffuse, my research has identified many common patterns and problems, beliefs and values.

American Heathenry in Scholarship and the Media

The early and intimate relationship between Germanic Paganisms and racism has influenced the media's perceptions of Heathenry. It is a catchy and controversial theme, prompting even the *New York Times* to refer to Ásatrú as a racist religion that promotes violence to maintain superiority over the "mud people."[41] Consequently, Heathenry's relationship to questions of race and racism continues to dog adherents. The white supremacist presence in American Heathenry has attracted the attention of the Southern Poverty Law Center, which helps track and prosecute cases involving hate groups and white supremacists. At least two such cases brought Ásatrú public attention: the 1984 case of convicted felon, white supremacist, and self-proclaimed Wotanist David Lane and, more recently, the 2013 case of Evan Ebel, a right-wing Heathen who jumped parole to murder Colorado chief of prisons Tom Clements in his home. In reaction, The Troth released a statement to the media in an attempt to counter the claim that Ásatrú is a race-based religion. For the first time since the Kennewick man fiasco,[42] when Stephen McNallen of the Ásatrú Folk Assembly fought with Indian tribes for the right to claim the remains of a prehistoric "ancestor," Ásatrú entered the national discourse.

Because of these ongoing ties to white nationalism, previous research has focused overwhelmingly on a fringe element within American Heathenry for whom whiteness is central to the question of who gets to be Heathen. This has led to a range of interpretations by academics, watchdog groups, and hate groups alike, perpetuating the stereotype of American Heathens as racist and focusing on Heathens' connections to white supremacist organizations and racial ideologies, a critique shared by Michael Strmiska and Baldur A. Sigurvinsson in their work on Heathenry in 2005.[43] Apart from this focus on race and other isms, self-published manuscripts by Heathenry's lay community are on the rise, providing subjective glimpses into the how-tos and wherefores of Heathenry as a lifestyle. Studies conducted by academia, however, are significantly sparse. In fact, academia has produced only one peer-reviewed publication on American Heathenry, from the field of anthropology, that provides a window into the apolitical religious and spiritual lives of Heathen practitioners. In 2001, anthropologist Jenny Blain published the results of her ethnographic study of *Seidhr* practitioners in the modern Heathen community, titled *Nine Worlds of Seid-magic*.[44] In her ethnographic work, she discusses the reconstruction of *Seidhr,* pre-Christian oracular shamanism, a practice involving trance-induced journeying of one's soul into the underworld and, at other times, performances of visions and interactions with deities or deceased ancestors. Despite the fact that Blain's work is perhaps the only positive illustration of Heathenry produced by academia, its focus is decidedly singular.

Aside from the focus on Heathenry as a racist movement, other scandals among Heathens have attracted the attention of the media as a sideshow, a spectacle of discredited weirdos in garb. Although many Heathens are public about their religious identification, wearing a hammer openly—a safe practice in most instances because of its obscurity in comparison with the Wiccan pentacle—many Heathens choose to keep their faith private. Indeed, Neopagans in general tend to remain closeted during their first years of participation, although this trend seems to be changing as public tolerance of alternative lifestyles grows. Yet the news is awash with reports of Pagans of all faith traditions losing their jobs or custody of their children or experiencing difficulty with the law upon revealing their religious status. In 2013, two stories made headlines when two prominent Heathens ran into trouble with the law. In one, New York City councilman Dan Halloran, the first aetheling or king of a Theodish Aett in New England, was charged with heading a bribery scheme to rig the mayor's race. Earlier articles had focused on Halloran's religious affiliation—The *Queens Tribune* ran a piece titled "Pagan 'King' Has Council GOP Nod."[45] The *New York Times* cited Halloran's religion as a "point of contention,"[46] while the *Village Voice* asked, "Grand Ol' Pagan: What Does the Republican 'Heathen' Running for New York's City Council Actually Believe?"[47] His downfall in 2013 created shockwaves throughout the Heathen blogosphere and on social media. In another high-profile case, Kansas City Police Department veteran Mark Stinson was fired from his job, accused of stealing tens of thousands of dollars from his elderly mother. Local news reports made sure to note that Stinson was a "Heathen religion chieftain,"[48] although his status as a disgraced cop stole the headlines. In both cases, Heathenry was scrutinized as a sideshow and used to discredit the men and add to their public shaming, to the ire of Heathens around the country.

The Influence of "the Political"

In the late spring of 2011, when I was working on my research, I submitted an application for membership in the Ásatrú Folk Assembly (AFA). Among questions such as "Have you ever been convicted of a crime?" and "Have you ever been hospitalized for a mental illness?" was a less innocuous question requesting the reason for joining. First, a potential member must read the AFA's declaration of purpose and affirm that he or she is in full agreement before issuing an explanation and attesting that the membership request is "free from deceit." After explaining thoroughly and in good faith my other organizational affiliations and my position as a researcher, I submitted my application. Finally, I thought, I would have an opportunity to get to know the people of the AFA, an organization whose media attention and leadership have led to the notion that it is an organization of thinly veiled white supremacy. I would be able to interview members themselves, a group most likely as diverse in belief and practice as they are in location across the United States. I was delighted when I received my AFA pin, membership card, and access to the online discussion board. Two months later, everything changed.

Among the AFA's stated purposes is the seemingly most important and all-consuming focus on "the preservation of the Peoples of the North," explained as "Northern European peoples" whose "cultural and biological" survival and welfare are of utmost import. In mitigation of the assumption that this is all about white folks, the declaration goes on to laud the "promotion of diversity among the peoples and cultures of the Earth," a call to take a stand against "the melting pot" of "global monoculture" and instead to protect the identities of "cultural and biological groups."[49] When it occurs, this kind of biological essentialism of groupness—as in *Europeanness*—can manifest as a focus on whiteness, an obsession with racial purity, and the fear that white people are quickly becoming a minority. It does not acknowledge that cultural and biological groups of people change over time and across space, or even that there is cultural and biological evolution. Although the sentiment—resistance to the McWorld and the disenchanting cultural pastiche produced by global capitalism—seems to be a call for enlightenment, the call for cultural preservation is a call for the halt of cultural exchange. Taken further, this ideological perspective can have such effects on society as the prohibition of racial intermarriage, racial isolation, and ultimately the takeover of a North Dakota town by white supremacists seeking to develop an all-white village.[50] The loss of privilege and dominance is portrayed as a loss of culture and identity, and religion is seen as "biological"—a shout-out to McNallen's earlier works on so-called metagenetics in which he argues that religion is not merely ancestral and inherited as a cultural system but genetic and therefore unique to each "people."

In late July I received a notice that the AFA had received "word" that I had joined under false pretenses. I was a suspicious entity, and my membership was under investigation, a process that for weeks led to the interrogation of my friends and me and the scouring of my dissertation, available online for a fee. I was asked to explain the meaning behind sentences and phrases copied from my work—to account for my political beliefs and defend my purported "liberal agenda" as part of the "academic elite." I was accused of having "multicultural" leanings, although I never received an explanation of what exactly this meant. I was asked to explain, line by line via an e-mail exchange with a member of the AFA's board of directors, my understanding and defend my position regarding each of the AFA's stated declarations of purpose. At times, I considered replying "Never mind anyway," but instead, I decided to endure the exercise. After days of exchanges, my inquisitor, finally satisfied that my position as an academic would be a welcome challenge to the sentiment of anti-intellectualism growing in the AFA, and that my work could in fact vindicate them, suggested that my membership be maintained. With relief, I looked forward to hearing from the McNallens, both of whom oversee the organization from the top down. In June I received an e-mail that, after due consideration, my membership had been terminated and that I was better suited to membership in The Troth.

During the process, I was not asked questions about my experiences as a Heathen for a decade and a half, my beliefs regarding Heathen theology or morality, my knowledge of the lore—the foundational texts of Heathenry—or my understanding of the cosmos. I was simply interrogated about my political beliefs, asked to defend the concept of "white privilege," and accused of being liberal. Although the AFA's tax-exempt 501(c)3 status forbids it to engage in political activities, its position was clear. I had joined a religious organization whose membership presumably run the gamut in political belief. I was ousted from a political organization with religious overtones, whose leadership, months later, was accused of sending envoys to a conference of white supremacists for recruiting.[51] During my time on the AFA message boards, a member asked the group, "Can you be a Liberal and a Heathen?" The general sentiment among the exchange of fifty-two replies was "Not really." Liberals, it seems, hold traditional American values "in contempt," the same values that provide a foundation for Ásatrú as it should be, the same values professed by the Christian Right as central to what it means to be a good Christian—such values as monogamous family ties, respect and support for law enforcement and the military, patriotism as "love of country," and respect for nature. To this, Heathens add a love of "folk" and idealized anachronistic northern European "culture"—but not modern northern Europeans, because they are socialists. The argument, in the end, established that liberals disdain all good American values, liberal Heathens are never folkish Heathens, and Folkism is the only legitimate way. The other guys are "Universalists," lacking strong core values, and they do not do "real" Heathenry. Although these arguments seemed to me, at the time, examples of isolated right-wing enthusiasm, they have cropped up time and time again. On Facebook, Heathens post regularly with disdain on hot-button political issues and culture wars, increasingly on the side of the Libertarian and Republican Right. Political ideological battles are no longer simply exercises in philosophy; they are at the roots of deeply held beliefs and identities and have shaped American Heathenry in fundamental ways (see Figure 1.1 for this data).

Yet, despite such testaments that conservatism is key to real Heathen values, both Americans in general and Heathens in particular are much more politically complex. A survey of 687 Heathens, 65 percent of whom were between the ages of thirty-one and sixty, a life period during which people tend to have established political identities, indicated a complex array of values. They favored

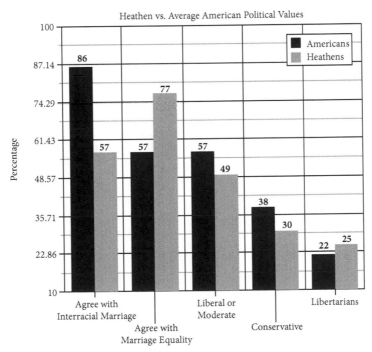

Figure 1.1. Heathen political values compared with average American political values.

marriage equality (77 percent), were more likely to identify as "liberal or moderate" (49 percent) rather than conservative (30 percent), and yet were less likely than average Americans to favor interracial marriage (57 percent versus 77 percent). Among those who identified as "folkish" (40 percent), 25 percent were against interracial marriage, compared with 2 percent of their nonfolkish peers, and 13 percent were against marriage equality, compared with 2 percent of those who did not identify as folkish. Although the folkish identity seems to indicate a trend toward conservatism in social matters, a majority of those Heathens who identified as folkish supported these "liberal" social agendas or simply "don't care." In the past, scholars and the media have argued that folkism is a product of prisons, but my survey indicates that although folkish Heathens have served time in prison over twice as often as their nonfolkish peers, only 5 percent of the folkish Heathens I surveyed have ever been behind bars. Only 6 of the 687 Heathens surveyed identified as "White Nationalist," compared with Democrats (6 percent), Independents (7.7 percent), and Libertarians (22 percent), and there were slightly more socialist Heathens (7 percent) than Republicans (6 percent).[52]

My experience with the AFA and with Heathens around the country has illuminated the intimate role that dominant political polemics and identities play in the Heathen project. My experience in this regard is not unique. Michael Strmiska writes in "Becoming a Pariah" that, for American Heathens,

> The world of the Vikings was a Paradise Lost, a confirmation that the best kind of society was one of rugged individualism and minimal central authority in which men were strong warriors who protected their families and their private property and were willing to die for honor and freedom, a society in which no one had any responsibility for anyone outside their own family or clan. It was as if the political world view of small-town, conservative, fundamentalist Republican Americans had been repackaged in romanticized Viking terms, substituting Thor for Jesus, the Edda for the Bible, Old Norse for Latin, but keeping much else the same. The precarious existence of medieval peasants scratching out a bare livelihood on the edge of starvation had been elevated into the American Dream, and the endless feuding and warring that had undoubtedly caused immense suffering in medieval Northern Europe had now been shown to be the glorious forerunner of American military excellence.[53]

After sharing his political views with other Heathens, he was quickly shunned and rendered persona non grata. This incident and other evidence have led me to the conclusion that Heathenry (like all religions) is intimately connected to "the political"—to how its adherents conceptualize and enact various identities (gender identity, political identity, ethnic identity) and how they patrol the borders of these identities in order to maintain a sense of authenticity and legitimacy and to protect what it means to be "Heathen" and not something else. For many Heathens, American political currents influence religious expression, belief, and purposes as they are translated into spiritual conviction.

Researching American Heathenry

Late one evening in the autumn of 2002, I stood in a cramped living room in a small urban apartment, surrounded by college-aged strangers. I had arrived hours before to attend a Pagan ritual, a celebration of the harvest with people I had never met. I entered the small gray space, its mismatched furniture and sparsely decorated periphery punctuated by a small bookshelf turned altar, on the surface of which were carefully arranged the many tools, statues, and symbols necessary for Heathen devotion. Rather than stand alone in the awkward and alien space, I offered the hosts my help preparing for the upcoming feast, decorating the apartment with baskets of gourds and sheaves of wheat. The members of the small group of Pagan practitioners, Heathens of the Anglo-Saxon variety, arranged a feast of potluck dishes in the kitchen as we all waited for the last of the guests to arrive. They were at the periphery of this community, harassed into attendance by Einar, the headman and de facto *Gothi* (priest) of the informal local group. As we prepared, guests continued to arrive in various styles of dress: Gothic, grunge, 1970s witchy hippy, or T-shirts with Celtic designs or heavy-metal band logos. One enormous bearded man sported studded leather bracers.

After the last guest arrived, Einar marked the beginning of the ritual by lighting candles at the rear corners of the room, shuffling from one candle to another to the quiet sounds of our sniffles and throat clearing. Surrounded by flames, we looked on quietly, breaking the silence with fidgets and coughs, as he lit the candles and incense on his altar—a modest setup of a central offering bowl and its miniature duplicate, a pine sprig, a tiny cauldron, a drinking horn, and idols of the god Thor and the goddess Freyja. Wandering throughout the now-congested room, he switched off the lights, powered down the computer, closed the blinds, and started some gentle instrumental music. Having never practiced with this group, I felt as though I was in for an experience—a meaningful spiritual connection with other humans as we communed with the old gods of our ancestors and cemented community bonds, or perhaps a New Age breathing workshop and guided meditation—I was not sure which. Turning to face us, he announced that we should begin. Those ten of us in attendance crowded together on opposite sides of the living room, taking a moment to shift furniture out of the way. Because our arrangement was awkward, I wordlessly ushered everyone together. After some snickering and jabs mocking me for the circle configuration a few perceived as a Wiccan arrangement, we stood shoulder-to-shoulder in front of the altar. Einar and his girlfriend, Halla, his ritual co-officiant, began with a "greeting," as it is called. Einar spoke:

In the time of the *eildrfaederas*, the Heathen Angles and Saxons of old, the month of September, what they called *Haligmonath*, marked the harvest of oats and grains. On this, the eve of the Autumnal Equinox, we gather as our forbears did to give thanks for a plentiful harvest, and celebrate the season and the bounty it brings. Though we do not work in the fields to bring in the harvest, others must do so on our behalf, for without their efforts, we would go hungry. And let us not forget, that while some labor on farms to bring us bread, we also reap our own personal forms of harvest this Autumn, each in his or her own way.

After fiddling with the incense that had gone out, Halla, cued by Einar's silence, took up the small cast-iron cauldron and began to chant:

Fire I bear around this sacred site, and bid all men make peace. Flame I bear to enclose, and bid evil spirits to flee. Thunor make sacred, Thor make sacred, Thunor make sacred this holy site. Fire I bear around this sacred site, and bid all men make peace. Flame I bear to enclose, and bid outlaws fare away. Thunor make sacred, Thor make sacred, Thunor make sacred this holy site. Thunor make sacred, Thor make sacred, Thunor make sacred this holy site.

As Halla returned the cauldron to the altar, Einar filled the drinking horn with mead. He offered the horn to Ulfrich, his best friend and a central player in the group. Approaching the altar, Ulfrich raised the horn in the air and in an booming voice proclaimed:

Hail Thunor, red-bearded warden of Heaven's bright halls! Hail to the Thunderer who brings the fall rains. May Oat-Crusher's keeper with all goodwill, bless those bairns that know him! Hail to Sib, the golden-haired Lady, bearer of the field's golden bounty! Goddess of plenty, look well on your folk, who give to the Noble-Ones praise!

Then, when the horn was returned to him, Einar spoke a common Heathen prayer:

Hail to thee Day, hail ye Day's Sons! Hail Night and Daughter of Night!
With blithe eyes look on all of us, and send to those sitting here speed!
Hail to you, Gods! Hail Goddesses! Hail, Earth that givest to all!
Goodly spells and speech bespeak we from you,
And healing hands in this life.

Einar took a swig of mead from the horn and poured the remainder into both small and large bowls on the altar. The small bowl he offered to the gods on the altar; the larger had a later purpose. Filling the horn anew, he handed it back to

Ulfrich, who murmured a prayer and passed it on to the man in the Celtic-knot T-shirt. He held it up toward the ceiling, improvising a prayer to the gods for prosperity. He took a drink and handed it to his neighbor, a young Goth woman with a sullen expression who likewise requested peace and prosperity. Around the circle it continued until finally it reached Einar, who set the horn on the altar. Taking up the large offering bowl and the pine sprig, he walked around the circle, sprinkling mead with the bough on each of us, and to each person he said, "May the blessings of Thunor and Sib be with you." At last, when each of us had been blessed, Einar set aside the bowl, its mead imbued with our words and wishes, as an offering to the gods and land spirits to be emptied into the ground outside. He spoke: "We stand now in fellowship with the Holy Ones, to whom we dedicate this feast. Let us bring forth the bounty of the hunt, of field and forest, and rejoice in the company of hallowed folk. Let's eat!" The room erupted in cheers and smiles—now hallowed, we could attend to our hunger. As we ate, the conversation turned to a celebration of community—a feeling of peoplehood and camaraderie that would come to pervade the discourse of Heathen gatherings around the country. This was one of my first experiences among Heathens, and it provided me with a framework with which to begin thinking about Heathenry as an intersectional religious project.

Before this, however, it had taken five years from the moment I began to identify as Heathen for me to encounter another Ásatrúar face-to-face. In the interim, while I was in college, I struggled with how to create and maintain a Heathen identity in the absence of a physical Heathen community. My identity as "other" became increasingly salient the more it was, again, socially imposed, as classmates introduced me as their "Pagan friend." The Internet was still new technology to me, and my presence or participation in Heathenry online was negligible. Without guidance and the demonstration of boundaries, my new identity as Heathen was tenuous and untried. I felt like a poseur. It was not until graduate school that I solicited a regional Yahoo! group e-mail list, which, before the ubiquity of social media, was the modus operandi of social networking. Within days I received word from a cheerful young man who would become my first Heathen friend and research participant. As I have illustrated, my first experiences with Heathen ritual and community were humble gatherings in people's living rooms. From one house to the next, from one weekend to another, I recorded field notes with feverish enthusiasm. As I continued to learn about Ásatrú, I was struck by the anachronism of this community because the people in it toiled at blacksmithing, brewing, spinning, and weaving, almost obsessed with the fantasy epic and its aesthetic. Heathens had dubbed it "the religion with homework" and were studious in their attention to Norse mythology and Germanic history, reading Tacitus, Bede, and multiple translations of the Eddic poems and Icelandic sagas. I also became perplexed by the complex interplay of "the political," primarily ethnic and gendered identities with the collective reconstruction of Heathenry and the priceless yet troublesome role of virtual technology as a foundation.

Having had little experience at first with real-life flesh-and-blood Heathens, I did not have many expectations. As I met and interviewed Heathens, I became more Heathen. As I observed them and worshipped with them, I discovered my own way of being. They became my teachers in faith and scholarship as I studied their lives, behavior, beliefs, and words. It did not take long before I became more comfortable and familiar with the community's dynamics in group relationships, locations, norms, values, customs, and the various political leanings of geographically dispersed groups, located coast to coast, rural and urban. I have been a member, a friend, and a confidant, but my training as a sociologist was most salient, making me ever an outsider, critic, and distant observer.

My research took me into a variety of settings, both public and private. On a micro scale, Heathens assemble in semifixed or unstructured groups (which Ásatrúar primarily refer to as "kindreds," although sometimes as "tribes"), each of which is independent of the others and free from any central authority, although they may have affiliations with a national organization. Some groups choose at least one member who is responsible for the organization and management of group events, while others are more democratic and egalitarian. The lack of a central authority makes it difficult to approximate the population of modern American Heathenry as a whole. In the mid 1990s, Jeffrey Kaplan's research on the Heathen community provided him with the rough estimate that Heathens number 500 in "committed adherents . . . with peripheral members perhaps swelling to a maximum of 1,000."[54] In December 2013 Karl Seigfried, author of the popular *Norse Mythology Blog*, completed his months-long "Heathen Census." Over 16,700 Heathens in ninety-eight countries answered the one-question survey about their country of origin, 7,878 in the United States alone. On the basis of the sample of replies from Iceland, Seigfried estimates that there are likely far more Heathens in the United States than answered his survey.[55]

In contrast to the formality and scope of the *High Sumbels* I experienced later in my research, my first ritual experiences were decidedly lower key. For weekly or monthly observances, Heathens usually congregate in nonpublic spaces, holding ritual *fainings* or *blóts* (pronounced "bloats") in the homes or yards of participants. A large portion of my research has therefore taken place in people's living rooms, which have often been small and sometimes chaotic spaces. On an annual basis, Heathens from around the country hold, "moots," or gatherings of regional or national groups, as well as holiday festivals. Typically, these events occur at state parks or other public campsites. Since 2002 I have attended at least two dozen *blóts* at over a dozen locations and eight regional moots in five states. I have held *blót* with Heathens in the woods on a mountain, under a sheet-metal pavilion in the center of the heartland, in a log cabin in the forest, and by the waterside down in the Bayou—in Oklahoma, Pennsylvania, Minnesota, Kansas, Colorado, New Mexico, and Mississippi (see Figure 1.2).

I kept track of the increasing number of books on American Heathenry by Heathen authors, as well as community publications such as the out-of-print

Figure 1.2. Eric of the Hridgar Folk (Texas) leads an early morning *faining* to Thor, bidding those gathered safe travels home. (Photo by the author.)

Mountain Thunder published in the early 1990s, the Ásatrú Alliance's 2013 publications of *Vor Tru,* and the 2010–2013 volumes of The Troth's magazine *Idunna.* In the early years of the twenty-first century, I digitally recorded fifty semistructured informal interviews with participants both face-to-face and over the phone. During these interviews, I questioned participants about their religious and subcultural experiences as children, their pathway to Heathenry, their experiences within the community regarding gender, definitions of Heathenry as an ethnic folkway, and current and ongoing events concerning the Heathen community, as well as their experiences with technology. Later I switched from formal interviews to digital communication via Facebook, which from 2011 became the primary communication venue by which to schedule events, keep track of friends, discuss Heathen lore, and hash out political polemics. From these discussions I learned that Heathens' lives mirror one another in many ways. They shared a common experience as the "loner" or the "weird" kid growing up with friends who were also unusual. They were the gamers, the geeks, the metalheads, the Goth kids, and the poets. Although a couple of them claimed to be "social butterflies" or pretty average, most were not. Most claimed an early interest in mythology or fantasy fiction—a draw to the fantastic, the epic, and tales of swords and sorcery—and many were involved somehow in role-playing games (Dungeons and Dragons) and medieval reenactment.

Most Heathens are white and middle-aged, and there are still more men than women, although that trend seems to be changing as American Heathenry abandons the last vestiges of its Viking Brotherhood origins. Throughout my work I have interviewed Heathens who earn their living performing odd jobs, as well as those who are unemployed. I have spoken to Heathens with careers in massage therapy, medical training, entertainment, information technology, nursing, government service, graphic design, and veterinary medicine, as well as those seeking advanced degrees in law, English, or other liberal arts. I have interviewed former military personnel and college professors, lawyers and high-school teachers. As I gathered data, I began to notice patterns in what Heathens discussed and how particular social variables or concerns affected their beliefs and behaviors. Using grounded theory methods,[56] I constructed a theoretical framework. As I began to analyze my data, I realized that documenting the lives and experiences of Heathens while maintaining confidentiality and anonymity would prove difficult. With the rise of digital media, Heathens have become ever more aware of one another. People who have never met in person nevertheless know a lot about each other's personal lives. It was therefore difficult for me to write thick description of particular individuals, to divulge their personal lives and ideas, without the understanding that in a community so small (though widespread), anonymity was not guaranteed. My descriptions therefore err toward the simplistic at times, and at other times, when I could have shared more about a person's beliefs, location, profession, or other interesting details, I chose not to.

This study, with all its various sources, is a blending of ethnographic methods and research roles in an endeavor to "engage with real life in all its glory and mundane horror."[57] It is informed by insights from feminist methods in that it involves reflexivity, with recognition of the interactional nature of the relationship between my informants and me.[58] As I tell the stories of the people whom I have met throughout the years, I also draw on my own experiences in the context of a wider body of literature and theory.

Throughout this book, I uncover the power of political polemics and sociohistorical context in the development and trajectory of Heathenry as a new religious movement, in which all identities are political and all politics matter. In Chapter 2, I discuss ongoing community concerns and conversations, starting with where many Heathens begin with the Heathen project—disassociating from Christianity as a central component of neophyte identity formation. Yet the formation of group identity requires distinction not just from the norm but from other competing elements of the cultic milieu. As scholars have noted previously, the emergence of the "fluffy bunny" sanction within Neopaganism provides adherents with a discursive tool with which to construct authenticity.[59] Fully embraced, this stereotype provides Heathens with a powerful tactic for developing distinctions between their group and other Neopagans, primarily Wicca, from which many Heathens transitioned. American Heathenry's relationship with Wicca is particularly complex, involving intricate gender and political stereotypes and assumptions that serve to devalue Neopaganism while perpetuating larger social inequalities.

In Chapter 3, I offer a glimpse into the world of Heathen meanings, rituals, and philosophy as I explore reconstructionism versus Neo-Heathenry as a growing area of contestation where adherents vie for legitimacy and authenticity in the negotiation of what constitutes real, historically minded Heathenry. As participants construct the meaning of correctness, they also politicize and deconstruct taken-for-granted elements of Heathen belief and practice, such as the hammer rite, the Nine Noble Virtues, and the Loki conundrum. In keeping with realities among ancient Germanic tribal peoples, reconstructionism has led to a focus on the local and the reworking of community and equality and to a meritocratic understanding of *worth* and a further depoliticization of exclusionary practices. This chapter offers American Heathenry as a lens through which we can understand our embeddedness in social structure and dependence on political frameworks for meaning making.

In Chapter 4, I discuss the various shapes that Heathen collectivities can take across time and space. In this chapter, the impact of social media is particularly important because it undergirds Heathen networks of communication and provides the primary source for contemporary value making. This chapter builds on the work of previous scholars who have attempted to articulate the impact of communication technology on new religious movements. I argue that the Internet has led to the development of various forms of American Heathenry, from formal organizations, diffuse groups, and local tribes to cyber-Vikings, ultimately leading to the proliferation of Heathenry and the simultaneous and increasing alienation of its members as Heathens have become trapped by the phenomena of online hostility, bullying, and flame wars that have assisted in the further deconstruction of community.

Chapter 5 takes on the topic of gender, resistance, and ownership, tracing the sociohistorical development of American Heathenry alongside the men's movement, feminism, and female-spirituality movements. I outline how Heathen women base their conceptualizations of gender and equality on the romanticized notion of the relative historical freedom of Old Norse women within ancient societies while focusing on daily realities in the here and now. I discuss whether the reframing of traditional oppression as empowerment creates social change and equality or reinforces existing inequalities.

Chapter 6 provides a challenge to previous literature, which conflates American Heathenry with white supremacy. In it, I situate historically the construction of whiteness while arguing that Heathen experiences with race and ethnicity are nuanced and complex. I pay close attention to how Heathens justify, legitimate, and reinforce politically contentious social boundaries around the term *race* in the construction of American Heathenry as an ethnic folkway while also deconstructing the folkish versus universalist identity battlefield.

Chapter 7 begins by offering a historical outline of the social and economic forces that influenced the birth of NRMs, and Neopaganism among them, as well as those forces that had a hand in the birth of American Heathenry. I discuss the complexities and problems of American reconstructionist faith, Heathenry's ongoing obsession and trouble with Wicca(ns), and what happens when Heathens go virtual. Then, I examine how Heathen men and women challenge and reproduce gender inequality, as well as how they negotiate the complexities of racial framing and whiteness. Lastly, I revisit my own experiences as a researcher and a Heathen after fourteen years of field work that ultimately redefined my identity and my relationship with the movement.

Throughout the book, terms familiar to Heathens but perhaps foreign to others are italicized. See the Glossary of American (Heathen) Terms.

2

Fleeing the Cross and the Pentacle

*Resistance and Opposition in the Maintenance
of Collective Identity*

*Eyvind was then haled before the King who offered him baptism in like
manner as he had offered other men baptism, but to this Eyvind answered,
"Nay." Then with fair words the King bade him be baptized and gave him
many good reasons therefore, and the Bishop spake after the same fashion
as the King, nonetheless would Eyvind in no wise suffer himself to be
persuaded. Then did the King offer him gifts, and the dues and rights of
broad lands, but Eyvind put all these away from him. Then did the King
threaten him with torture even unto death, but never did Eyvind weaken
his resistance. Thereafter caused the King to be brought in a bowl filled with
glowing coals, and had it set on the belly of Eyvind, and not long was it ere
his belly burst asunder. Then spake Eyvind: "Take away the bowl from off me
for I would fain speak some words before I die," and accordingly it was done.
Then the King asked: "Wilt thou now, Eyvind, believe on Christ?" "No,"
answered he.* —OLAF SAGA TRYGGVASSON, stanza 83

Overseas, everything from the States came to us on delay. When I began
experimenting with Wicca in 1995, it was in secret. I was an army brat
living in a military community dominated by conservative Christians,
still consumed with anxiety over the Satanic Panic of the 1980s. As most Wiccans
do, I wore a pentacle—a five-pointed star within a circle—under my clothing
and out of sight. To me, it was a symbol of magic, mystery, empowerment, and
defiance. I had been taught to think critically and resist peer pressures; "You are
your own person" was my mother's mantra. Consequently, given such parenting
and this community environment, I was an austerely rule-abiding and consci-
entious social misfit. The community's open hostility toward alternative religions and philosophies fueled my intense feeling of alienation and otherness. In
fact, were it not for this hostility, my Pagan identity would have been stunted.
Since my friend Sarah had moved away, I had not met another Pagan, so my
identity was constructed only in resistance to what I felt was religious oppression.

I remember very clearly the blistering anger that I felt at dominant religious
institutions (Christianity, in particular) for casting me as somehow alien, but my
feelings were not unique. I had been poring over books on witchcraft and had
become steeped in the Neopagan metanarrative. This grand story was the source

of much of my antipathy; it is the fundamental Neopagan myth that holds the modern Christian church responsible for all the historical atrocities committed against Pagans. Members produce this narrative in response to the "decline of the perception of a legitimate past" by creating a "new," subculturally nourished, historical truth.[1] The bitterness produced by this myth was palpable, as though the chaplain himself was somehow personally responsible for the "burning times" of Wiccan nightmares or the forced conversion of Germanic tribes that inspires Heathen teeth gnashing. At times, my identity as *not Christian* was stronger and more salient than my identity as Pagan, particularly as a novice. In more recent years, through my exposure to various Neopagan and Heathen groups and philosophies, I have come to believe that this not-Christian identity is central to what it feels like to be Pagan and is taken for granted by members of both communities as part and parcel of affiliation. This is the case regardless of the prior denomination of the practitioner and includes members whose natal faith was Judaism. I use *Christianity* in the remainder of this chapter to refer to my informants' prior affiliations because Christianity is the most common, and I use the term *mainstream* to refer to dominant religious currents in the United States, in particular, Christianity and Judaism.

My decision to adopt a Pagan faith was part of a growing trend. Since the 1960s, there has been a transformation of religious faith into private and individual practices outside mainstream religious institutions.[2] Although some scholars argue that the process of secularization has affected the authority of traditional religions, it has not deleted religion entirely. Religious expression has merely changed forms, offering members that join NRMs "lite" institutions that function as "anchors for the self."[3] Although many of the perspectives discussed in studies of NRMs furnish great insight into religious change, affiliation and disaffiliation, alternation,[4] and NRM membership, the discussion itself could benefit from more ethnographic or microlevel accounts by NRM participants that illustrate how members frame their own spiritual experimentation and, most important, how this experimentation affects individual and collective identity.

Scholars of religion have focused overwhelmingly on structural causes and effects of NRMs and various generic processes. Yet it may be helpful to begin conceptualizing NRM involvement as similar to subcultural belonging, regarding participation in terms of collective and individual identities, and paying close attention to the intricacies of boundary maintenance and negotiation. Studies in the early 2000s have argued that the study of boundaries in a variety of social groups captures the fundamental social processes of relationality.[5] These symbolic boundaries are "conceptual distinctions made by social actors to categorize objects, people, practices, and even time and space. They are tools by which individuals and groups struggle over and come to agree upon definitions of reality."[6] They separate people into likeness and difference and generate feelings of group membership essential to collective identity.[7] How people join these religions, as opposed to mainstream faiths, is also different. Early literature on the conversion process suggests that those undergoing it experience a "radical personal change."[8] Later works, however, argue that people are free to approach religion as consumers, finding one that suits them and adopting it (or merely some of its elements) as they see fit[9]—epistemological individualism articulated in religious terms.[10]

This chapter begins the journey through this book where all Heathens necessarily begin—with both the disassociation from mainstream faith and the resistance to competing Neopaganisms. Although Heathens are increasingly born into their faith, it is only forty years old—a fledgling religion with primarily deliberate participants. In the following pages I outline the intricacies involved in Heathens' ongoing disaffiliation with mainstream and other Neopagan religions as a key element of identity maintenance. This is not a new phenomenon; theories of social differentiation have already focused on how group members create symbolic subcultural boundaries to cognitively separate themselves and their collectivity from those who are different. By doing so, members maintain and construct authenticity, which is key to group identity.[11] In keeping with David Snow's observation that members' accounts are "social constructions" that signify current orientations,[12] I highlight members' experiences as indicative of community-endorsed identity narratives. Members' reasons for disaffiliation reflect much of the literature that reports participants' leaving "as a gradual and voluntary phenomenon that reflects disillusionment with both the social and emotional dimensions of religious commitment."[13] In other words, members' accounts of switching religions are necessarily connected to their rationale, which not only highlights aspects of Heathen identity, both collective and individual, but also engages participants in identity-boundary maintenance through community-sanctioned, repetitive narrative.

Not Like Them: Constructing Identity
Through the *Not-Self*

Hilda, a forty-year-old medical billing specialist, describes her parents as a lapsed Catholic and a Methodist who did not take her to church when she was growing up. Her dad had once been divorced, and before Vatican II the Catholic Church would not allow him a second marriage. So her parents married as Methodists but continued to attend Catholic services for a while—a disconnect Hilda's mother could never reconcile. "We couldn't get married in this church, my husband isn't welcome here, but they'll take our money?" After a while her parents stopped taking her to church, and she tried out the Baptist faith of her friends. When she was thirteen, her father died, and for the next few years she neglected church entirely. When her grandmother came to live with her family, Hilda began attending Catholic services with her and started going to catechism.

Yet "I just could not reconcile the Catholic Church's teachings and stances on women and birth control," she says, "and I'm like, 'This just doesn't make sense.'" After identifying as an Atheist for a few years, she discovered Barbara Walker and Feminist Spirituality and became what she describes as a "Goddess worshipper." At twenty-three, Hilda met a Wiccan; they traded stories and books and had discussions about "folk magic." After a few more years of solitary practice, Hilda began attending public Wiccan rituals. Something did not sit right, however. "I kept feeling really embarrassed," she says, "but I didn't say anything." A year later, she moved in with a Wiccan roommate and confessed, "Some things I'm willing to accept," she recalls, "and some, I'm just like 'you're full of shit' to be blunt—it's like, please, you're just pulling this out of your ass." I asked her to clarify.

> Oh, God—like Mercedes Lackey's book series Diana Tregarde being based on reality—you know, she had these psychic powers and she was a witch. There were all these demons and monsters and things, and she was a guardian who helped protect humanity, and before I knew it some of the people that I was hanging around with were claiming that they were guardians and they were here to protect humanity, and I'm like "You can't even keep a job at Burger King." You know? "You can't focus long enough to finish your G.E.D. You're still living at home."[14]

The ongoing so-called psychodrama in the Wiccan community, a common theme in Heathen narratives, was unappealing to her. After discovering, with a friend, *Northern Mysteries and Magic* by Heathen author Freya Aswynn,[15] she felt as though she had finally found something that "made sense." She began to devour every Heathen text and bit of lore she could find. She started to study the runes and began seeing them everywhere—in dreams and at the grocery store—and finally had a peculiar vision about a stranger she later identified as Odin. About six months later, she says, "I decided, 'Alright, I'm not Wiccan anymore,' so, I oathed to Odin, and that's pretty much been it." In interactions that followed, she had to learn how to be un-Wiccan: how to draw a Thor's hammer instead of a pentacle during ritual, and how to interact in a kindred instead of a coven. She developed a Heathen identity, a large component of which was a constant reminder not to be too Wiccan.

In addition to the "not" self, there are other striking contradictions and intricacies that coalesce as Heathen identity. There is a paradox of sorts in Heathens' disaffection with both mainstream and other forms of Neopagan religion and the embrace of a rather moralistic religious worldview that echoes that of traditional Christianity. Heathens frame much of this paradox as an alternative to what they feel is dogmatic reproach and oppression, viewing Heathenry as a more meaningful way of doing it better without hypocrisy. Christianity, as Heathens see it, is by and large a world-rejecting monolith whose major focus is that of redemption, salvation, and the hope of a rewarding afterlife. Heathens mark this concentration as irrelevant to them, rejecting notions of guilt, sin, or shame. They place little emphasis on an afterlife, choosing instead to focus on the here and now as a maintenance and continuation of *luck* and *Ørlög* (see the Glossary of [American] Heathen Terms). At the same time, they also actively reject behaviors associated with other Neopagan religious groups, particularly Wicca, whose ways are seen as hedonistic and undisciplined. Their disassociation and differentiation between their own group and other groups (both mainstream and alternative) is a method by which they create an "us" and construct "them" as the other. A critical dimension of collective identity formation involves the establishment of boundaries as groups come to distinguish between themselves and outsiders.[16] In order for people to act collectively and maintain we-ness, they must come to a common understanding of their experiences.[17] Collective identity can be defined as a group's perceptions of its distinctiveness from other groups and its preferred practices, rituals, and interpretive frameworks.[18] These components form a unity of "individuals, events and ideas through time and space"[19] that collectively form a "we" and allow for the identification of a "they."[20]

Most participants experienced the same pattern of becoming Heathen: rejecting the mainstream, spiritual seeking and experimentation, dabbling in or associating with Neopaganism, and ultimately rejecting Neopaganism and settling into the Heathen identity. What is striking, however, is not the process per se but rather how identities are negotiated and collectively maintained throughout the various stages, which most Heathens have experienced. Even those few Heathens who have not shared in this experience benefit by association; the abundant discussion regarding the differences between "us" and "them" are telling. While other NRMs often involve rituals associated with affiliation and membership,[21] joining Heathenry seems to involve, primarily, the gradual, casual adoption of a Heathen identity. Membership, or association with other Heathens, is often an event that happens later, after a person has already researched Heathenry and begun settling into the identity.

Resisting Oppression: Opposition to the Mainstream

*The king ordered Raud to be brought before him, and offered him baptism. "And,"
says the king, "I will not take thy property from thee, but rather be thy friend, if
thou wilt make thyself worthy to be so." Raud exclaimed with all his might against
the proposal, saying he would never believe in Christ, and making his scoff of God.
Then the king was wroth, and said Raud should die the worst of deaths. And the
king ordered him to be bound to a beam of wood, with his face uppermost, and a
round pin of wood set between his teeth to force his mouth open. Then the king
ordered an adder to be stuck into the mouth of him; but the serpent would not go
into his mouth, but shrunk back when Raud breathed against it. Now the king
ordered a hollow branch of an angelica root to be stuck into Raud's mouth; others
say the king put his horn into his mouth, and forced the serpent to go in by holding
a red-hot iron before the opening. So the serpent crept into the mouth of Raud and
down his throat, and gnawed its way out of his side; and thus Raud perished. King*

Olaf took here much gold and silver, and other property of weapons, and many sorts of precious effects; and all the men who were with Raud he either had baptized, or if they refused had them killed or tortured.
—OLAF SAGA TRYFVASSON stanza 87

Overseas in Germany, in the care of the patriarchal and paternalistic U.S. Army, I was immersed in the Old World of medieval castles, cathedrals, churches, and cobblestone squares. I found profound inspiration in the romantic history and folklore of the Rhineland; it was in every way a meaningful part of my teenage identity and growing consciousness. I needed magic to be real. While my friends were hanging out at parties, drinking, and doing mischief, I was in my basement bedroom reading spell books and leafing through the *Malleus maleficarum,* a medieval guide to the hunting, identification, and execution of witches, written in 1486 by Heinrich Kramer, a German Catholic clergyman. This text and the 1608 *Compendium maleficarum* provided agents of the Inquisition with instructions on how to identify, torture, and persecute alleged witches. For an angsty teenager, these texts contributed to an early critique of gender inequality and a keen awareness of the historical context that led to unthinkable carnage. When I was growing up in Germany, religion was at once ubiquitous and unassuming, important but reserved. In the nearly total institution of the heavily Republican, conservative military environment, however, the Christian Right had planted a seed, and many of my friends were keen churchgoers, quick to pass judgment on deviant religious others. For an emotional fifteen-year-old experimenting with my new Wiccan identity, the grand narrative of forced conversion and Christian oppression led to many hours of hand-wringing and writing dark poetry while pondering the historical atrocities committed against Pagans. The images of women burned at the stake consumed me, and at the time, I experienced it as a fundamentally gendered phenomenon, the silencing of women through murder by the patriarchy of the church. But my story is not unique.

Heathen narratives of exiting Christianity and finding Heathenry are, as noted in earlier studies of NRMs,[22] retrospectively reinterpreted to fit their new "member" and "ex" identities. I asked my informants to relate their familial experience with churchgoing and their first run-ins with Neopaganism or the occult. As they often explained it, abandonment of mainstream religion was almost always attributed to some failing of the church, which was perceived as hostile, currently and in retrospect. Even for those who have never identified as Christian, the process is very much the same. The narrative of forced conversion and Christian brutality replaces that of the "burning times" of Wiccan discourse, highlighting the differences between Heathen theologies and Christian concepts of god and nature. Each year, Heathens (and other Pagans) continue this narrative by arguing the Pagan origins of Christian holidays. Easter, they assert, is actually a holiday meant to celebrate fertility (hence the eggs and rabbits) and the goddess Eostre during a holiday named Ostara. Christmas is

Yule, complete with the Nordic traditions of decorating an evergreen and gift giving. Santa and his eight reindeer are actually Odin and his eight-legged steed Sleipnir. St. Patrick's snakes are a metaphor for Pagans, driven from Ireland by the Catholic Church. The list continues ad nauseam. Although scholars have confirmed many of the points made by Heathens in this regard, some arguments are fast-and-loose revisionist history effective in bolstering the narrative of persecution. Anti-Christian resentment becomes a built-in component of Heathen expression and identity. In his blog, Stephen McNallen highlights the pattern of these feelings upon affiliation with Heathenry:

> I went through a stridently anti-Christian phase in the years immediately after I decided to follow Ásatrú. I was young and brash and angry because I had been cheated of my heritage. Now, I am older and somewhat less brash. I still feel the loss of our traditional culture, and I still honor the martyrs of our faith who fell before the steel and fire of Christians. I certainly believe that Christianity is a faulty faith, a foreign imposition on European soil, a way that has done us great damage.[23]

McNallen's story parallels the experience that many Heathens have upon entrance into the community. As one of American Heathenry's founders, he has had over four decades to settle into his Heathen identity, and disassociation from the mainstream is less of an imperative. Heathens like blogger Alfarrin interject critiques of Christianity into a focus on history, discussing the work of scholars and asking, "Were the Viking attacks self-defense against Christianity?"[24] While McNallen attempts to disarm the Heathen metanarrative of forced conversion, which incites bitter historical references to atrocities committed centuries ago, saying that he finds it hard to "blame the Catholic or Baptist down the street for what Charlemagne did," many of his peers continue to hold a grudge. The ongoing discourse surrounding Christianity as the oppressor, both historical and modern, includes both community-sanctioned practices and personal narratives. The practices include days of remembrance devoted to Heathen heroes such as Raud the Strong and Eyvind Kinnrifi, both of whom were tortured to death when they refused to convert to Christianity. Another practice involves a ritualized blessing, a Heathen revision of an old Irish saying, "May you rest for nine days and nights in Valhal before the White Christ even knows you're dead!" or more tongue-in-cheek parodies, such as this parody of the Lord's Prayer by an unknown author that circled Facebook:

> Allfather, who art in Asgard, Many be Thy Names, Thy kingdom come, the Norns fate be done, in Midgard, as it is in Asgard. Give us this day our daily Mead, and Forgive not those who trespass against us, and lead us not into mindless conviction, but deliver us unto your wisdom. In Odin's name I *blót,* for ever and ever.

This jab at Christianity also illustrates ongoing resistance to the perceived blind conviction and lack of critical thinking and rationality among followers of Abrahamic faiths. It is juxtaposed to Heathenry's emphasis on wit, research, homework, and science, illustrated by a Facebook posting by a Heathen who said, "The Lord is not my shepherd, for I am not a sheep,"[25] and another that remarked, "Jesus loves you. Odin demands you grow the fuck up." On an e-mail list, a Heathen neophyte asked his peers what they believed was the nature of the gods, how they manifested, and whether they were omnipotent. This complex discussion of Heathen theology was quickly informed by a member's posting of the following historical text, borrowed from a letter sent by Bishop Daniel of Winchester to Boniface to overcome the resistance of eighth-century Heathens to conversion:

Do not begin by arguing with them about the genealogies of their false gods. Accept their statement that they were begotten by other gods through the intercourse of male and female and then you will be able to prove that, as these gods and goddesses did not exist before, and were born like men, they must be men and not gods. When they have been forced to admit that their gods had a beginning, since they were begotten by others, they should be asked whether the world had a beginning or was always in existence. There is no doubt that before the universe was created there was no place in which these created gods could have subsisted or dwelt. And by "universe "I mean not merely heaven and earth which we see with our eyes but the whole extent of space which even the heathens can grasp in their imagination. When they maintain that the universe had no beginning, try to refute their arguments and bring forward convincing proofs; and if they persist in arguing, ask them, Who ruled it? How did the gods bring under their sway a universe that existed before them? Whence or by whom or when was the first god or goddess begotten? Do they believe that gods and goddesses still beget other gods and goddesses? If they do not, when did they cease and why? If they do, the number of gods must be infinite. In such a case, who is the most powerful among these different gods? Surely no mortal man can know. Yet man must take care not to offend this god who is more powerful than the rest. Do they think the gods should be worshipped for the sake of temporal and transitory benefits or for eternal and future reward? If for temporal benefit, let them say in what respect the heathens are better off than the Christians. What do the heathen gods gain from the sacrifices if they already possess everything? Or why do the gods leave it to the whim of their subjects to decide what kind of tribute shall be paid? If they need such sacrifices, why do they not choose more suitable ones? If they do not need them, then the people are wrong in thinking that they can placate the gods with such offerings and victims.[26]

The original intent of this letter was to offer advice to Boniface on how to more easily convert the Saxons and Frisians. Some Heathens have used it as a window into what their ancient forebears believed, in part so that they can reconstruct these beliefs and also so that they can clarify, once again, exactly how Heathen notions of the gods and universe differed then, and differ now, from Christianity. The comparison of theologies—the omnipotence and nature of the gods, the origin of the universe, the motivation behind right action—assists Heathens in demarcating clear boundaries between themselves and their natal faiths. That their foci are so divergent as well—a noted disinterest in questions of an afterlife, for example—is in keeping with what we know about the theological concerns of ancient Germanic tribes and remains crucial to contemporary Heathens as a boundary marker. The image of the church in the Heathen imagination, fraught with inflexible demands, judgment, guilt, and shame, is often cited as one of the reasons for exit from Christianity, which they frame as oppressive, dogmatic, and hypocritical. Alvis, a forty-one-year-old environmental protection specialist from the Midwest, recalls his experience with his church:

> The dissonance between the hypocrisy that I saw in the way Christianity was acting out and ostensibly what the faith was supposed to be about, and even internally within their holy documents, within the Bible, you know, you'd see "Okay, Jesus says this, but the Apostles say this other, totally opposite sounding or feeling message." And when you questioned the minister or priest about it, they had no really good answers, except "It's all a matter of faith."[27]

To many Heathens, mainline Protestant denominations are highly routinized and disenchanting. Standing at *blót* around a burning bonfire, chanting runes, and sharing a horn of mead to the sound of a resounding "Hail!" offer them a magical, mystical, and deeply moving experience that highly rationalized church services did not. To Alvis, "faith" was an ungrounded and irrational answer, or nonanswer. His peer, Brand, a young father, dabbling hypnotherapist and aspiring author, was attracted to the empowerment he says he felt after experimenting with the runes, Old Norse symbols used in divination, after ongoing attempts to develop a personal relationship with the god of the Catholic Church. Because runes are presented as occult symbols in metaphysical stores and are appropriated by a variety of Neopagan groups, they are an accessible gateway to a *magical* religious alternative and, as such, are clearly in opposition to Judeo-Christian teachings. Later, after more experience with alternative Neopagan philosophies, Brand began to feel that a monotheistic view of the world was not just alienating; it was "dangerous": "The sort of disregard that Catholicism and Christianity has for the world around, I mean the world is irrelevant, if not dangerous and evil to most Christian perspectives and that's just something I couldn't share."[28]

Criticism of monotheism is not unique to Heathenry; it is part of the discourse of difference in most Neopagan pantheistic or polytheistic faiths. Heathens take issue with many aspects of Abrahamic faith and do not hesitate to criticize its macrostructures that they view as problematic. A popular criticism of mainstream faith is the contradiction between the teachings of Christ and the actions of Christianity, both historic and current, a Christianity that is defined and treated as one large entity rather than separate denominations. Like Brand, Ivor, a middle-aged tech guru at a city museum, spent his life very active in his natal church. He played the church organ for years and became very active in church youth-group activities. After what he now recognizes was a rather frivolous falling-out with his pastor, he began to question his faith and eventually left to explore new avenues. In retrospect, he notes that there is something very fundamental about his early religious experience and the beliefs of the church that he finds troubling. He recalls:

> I was raised to believe that if it's not, you know, Christian, God, Jesus, that sort of thing, then it is of the devil. Even in a fairly liberal Protestant denomination. You know, the attitude is still underlying everything. So I spent about a year really, really examining what I believe about life and the universe and everything, and Christianity as a whole, what I came up with was really when it comes down to it, Christianity does believe that we are born in sin and corruption, we will die in sin and corruption without the grace of God, who was the one who created us in sin and corruption in the first place. So this particular paradox kind of broke me.[29]

Brand's and Ivor's accounts of alienation from their natal faiths are in line with the accepted narratives of church failings. Egil's experience with religion was slightly different. He became Mormon when his mother converted after her second marriage. He now believes (like other Heathens who have experienced Mormonism) that even though he never felt connected to the beliefs or to "God," the intense sense of community offered by the church was alluring. Despite his lack of connection, he did not directly question the existence of God until much later, after a painful divorce and separation from his family.

> I just didn't feel that Christianity was answering the questions that I had or, I wasn't getting any feedback. And this disturbed me greatly, because I had always been taught, you know, "All you gotta do is pray, God will answer your prayers." I was—I kept knocking on the door, and nobody was answering.[30]

It was then that he started to experiment with a variety of alternative religions, beginning with inquiries into Buddhism and culminating in his discovery of Heathenry. His feelings about Christianity have become stronger now that his absence and disassociation from it have been incorporated into his current and very salient Heathen identity. He believes that people have been "poisoned" by Christianity, a perspective frequently shared by other members. He argues that mainstream religion teaches us that

> everything on this earth is wrong, is evil, stems from Satan, because where was Satan cast out to? He was cast out here to Earth. So anything that is Earthly in nature, whether it be . . . any kind of pleasure must be denied and must be considered, um, evil. And that's how the Christians teach us. Look at, look at the seven cardinal sins, most of those are just— most of those, some, you know, of the cardinal sins are just—you know, if it feels good it must be wrong. . . . Nature is bad, Nature is evil, there's bad things in nature. Christianity has removed us from our natural place in this world.

Everyone I talked to experienced negative or conflicting feelings about Christianity, particularly if it had been their natal faith system. Many of them had been very dedicated to and active in their church. Many of the Heathen women I spoke to expressed a sense of disappointment and alienation from Christianity's patriarchal foundation. A few echoed the Pagan tagline "A religion without a Goddess is halfway to Atheism" and expressed distress at the lack of female spiritual leaders (discussed further in Chapter 5). In an introductory booklet printed by the Germanic Glaubens-Gemeinschaft (Germanic Faith-Community), Geza von Nemenyi expresses a criticism common among U.S. Heathens:

> In Heathenry women do not only have equal rights with men, they are considered to have a better contact with the Gods than men. Christian-patriarchal thoughts, like the following quotation from Thomas of Aquinas, "Woman relates to man as the imperfect and defective relates to the perfect," or the Bible-quote from Ephesians 5:24 "As the Church is subject to Christ, so also should wives be subject to their husbands in all things," are completely alien to Heathen thought.[31]

The pamphlet continues by contrasting Heathenry to various biblical passages that speak about the subjugation of women, a gendered distinction that receives its fair share of airtime, if not contrasting action. To others, like Heathen blogger Alfarrin, Christianity paints a problematic picture of the human spirit, which to him finds spiritual harmony with the divine "through the combination of deeds, places, treasures, things, beasts, kindreds, families, emotions, songs, and our sacred histories." He writes:

> In that wholeness, the other Gods are to be found, emerging as they will . . . and most importantly, emerging as we make them able, through

our deeds and our understanding. Unlike the Christian faith, which presents humans as sinful, fallen, and helpless without divine grace, able to do nothing without the church and the god of the church except be condemned to hell, the Heathen way tells us that humans are literally *capable of the Gods.*[32]

These common experiences of alienation and separation from Christianity and other Abrahamic religions have created the space for a common and ongoing dialogue among the Heathen community regarding "us" versus "them." This was illuminated on a variety of occasions. In an online blog, Vidars Gothi encourages new Heathens to keep peace with their Christian relatives, warning them that rejection and religious confrontation are expected. "Keep reminding yourself that they aren't Ásatrú because they don't know better, but you may not be able to convince them of that. Try to agree to disagree and keep the peace. Christianity has no problem with tearing apart a family if there are non-Christians there."[33] Those who have close relationships with members of Judeo-Christian faiths are often reluctant to interrupt the open disdain expressed in public forums, either online or in person. When people enter into disagreement online, as they inevitably do, one of the most popular social controls is to argue that a belief or practice is a "Christian holdover." This is not unique to Heathens, however; most Pagans experience an element of anti-Christian resistance—just as subculturists position themselves in opposition to the mainstream, Pagans do so on the religious front. On occasion, however, as the community matures, popular figures settle into a Heathen identity with no further need to disassociate from the mainstream and begin to condemn anti-Christian sentiment as immature and unproductive. Yet to many Heathens, appearing to support Christianity is still dangerous to perceptions of authenticity and loyalty, despite the fact that many Heathen values are in keeping with mainstream Protestant ethics.

Negotiating Authenticity: Opposition to the Alternatives

In the late 1960s Garman Lord began to study Wicca. Like most Wiccans in the early years, he found himself seduced by the narrative of the "Old Religion" as a European tradition that had survived underground for centuries. He was told that the secrets and answers to all his questions had survived unburned in a *Book of Shadows*—a Wiccan book of secrets, spells, enchantments, and histories. Later he came to realize that this ancient book was, in fact, nothing of the sort. In his recounting of these events, written in *Theod* magazine to a Heathen audience decades later, he remarks that the discovery of the illegitimacy of this text was "a crushing spiritual blow."[34] To satisfy his disappointment, he set up a panel of "wise men and wizards" called "the Witan" and began a new Anglo-Saxon coven. Four years later, in 1976, spiritually unfulfilled, unemployed, and with few members participating in his group, he called on Heathen gods for the first time, and they came. After he began to interpret Wicca as "all BS"—baseless and without historical foundations, citations, or a concrete focus on recovering a "folk" mentality—he began Theodism, a major branch of American Heathenry. At the beginning, his biggest challenge, he argues, was "getting rid of the old Wiccan connections." Members of his new group, no longer identifying as Wiccan, found themselves "constantly being drawn into Wiccan crisis situations, sorting out Wiccan politics," furthering the Heathen stereotype of Wicca as eternally embroiled in dramatic and unstable interpersonal turmoil. At the same time, he and his comembers "started forming strict rules; our 'theod' was not a 'coven,' and Wiccans were not allowed into it. Yet, all through the summer of '77 and '78, breaking loose from Wicca was like finding your way out of a trackless swamp."[35] Throughout its history, Theodism, like all Heathenry, sprouted groups and offshoots that would later crumble, reform, or dissipate. Yet all of them, to some degree, built reactions against Wicca as part of their identities.

Whatever forms a group might take, members engage in the collective construction of agreed-on, negotiated group identity.[36] Studies of subcultures have argued that collective identity among members is produced not only in resistance to the mainstream but also in reaction against other subcultures. Others have called for a break in the traditional focus on macrolevel targets of subcultural resistance and for a more inclusive study of the micro- and mesointeractions that affect subcultural identity.[37] They distinguish this identity from other types of selfhood, defining it as cognitive belonging to a group, though not necessarily intimately or with feelings of attachment. It is less interpersonal than personal or social identity, having more to do with one's identity as belonging to a group and the internalization of group norms, values, and boundaries.[38] This collective identity is "expressed in cultural materials—names, narratives, symbols, verbal styles, rituals, clothing, and so on," the essence of which involves a shared sense of "one-ness" or "we-ness" in contrast to some sets of others.[39] This essence is "anchored in real or imagined shared attributes and experiences among those who comprise the collectivity and in relation or contrast to one or more actual or imagined sets of 'others.'" Identity is not a "thing" but rather a process of identification, and all identification necessarily occurs through interaction with others; to both "be" and "not be" something, under any circumstance, makes us who we are.[40]

During their first major identity shift from Christianity, the Heathens I spoke to experienced a profound sense of separation that grew stronger the more they engaged in spiritual seeking and experimentation. Many practitioners who leave a mainstream faith struggle through the seeking stage to discover that few NRMs offer them the structural familiarity and comfort that they had been socialized to appreciate. Most of them, however, did not follow a straight path out of Christianity and into Heathenry but instead stopped at the most accessible Neopagan fork in the road: Wicca. NRM scholars often lump Heathenry together with other Neopagan religions, a fact relentlessly vexing to Heathens as they struggle to disengage from Wicca and construct a separate, authentic subcultural identity. Because of the overlapping influence of Heathenry's position in the cultic milieu, leaving Wicca is more complicated than exiting the church. Heathens have gone to great lengths and lengthy discourse to delineate quite emphatically the difference between themselves and Wiccans. As Arlie Stephens explains in a short piece of commentary on the difference between Wicca and Heathenry, "Wiccans (especially relative newbies) often think that all pagans are basically similar to Wiccans, with perhaps a different pantheon or some minor changes. Heathens, on the other hand, often feel like they are sharing a (neo-pagan) tent with a (Wiccan) elephant."[41]

Unni, like Egil, introduced earlier, became Mormon and remained part of the church into adulthood. At the same time at which she was becoming disillusioned with Christianity, she began working at a metaphysical bookstore that was frequented by members from a variety of NRMs. Like most Heathens, she came first to Wicca because the plethora of literature and trinkets available for practitioners heightened its visibility. She recalls: "[Wicca] just never seemed fulfilling, or—they focused way too much on just the Goddess aspect of things, and that was to me just as bad as focusing—on the Christian side—on God, you know, there was no balance."[42]

The criticism of Christianity as "halfway to Atheism" because of its lack of focus on the feminine finds its opposite here, in a common criticism of Wicca as gynocentric. In its focus on both male and female deities, members believe that Heathenry offers practitioners "balance." In this and other ways, it is distinct, Heathens argue, from less historically based Neopagan faith systems, particularly Wicca, which is seen as fuzzy (both fuzzy-feminine and fuzzy-incoherent) and therefore inauthentic. On a public Heathen discussion forum, one member posted a mocking description of "Wiccatru," a derogatory term used by Heathens to refer to Heathenry that has been "tainted" by Wiccan or New Age influence. The Wiccatru, he writes, are "like, OMG [Oh My God], when we called the four quarters Freya showed up and said she was totally like, earth power, and stuff. Then we chanted over our crystals to Sif and had a Vegan lunch. Then, whoah, we went off to protest something The Establishment was doing."[43] The feminization of various symbols or behaviors labeled "Wiccan" is symbolic of the normative mainstream devaluation of the feminine as a political tactic. Anything perceived as New Age (like Wicca, Veganism, or other politicized and feminized associations) receives the brand "liberal" politics, a relationship many Heathens take for granted. As Unni remarks, many Heathens think that Wiccans are "just a bunch of flaky people who can't make a commitment to anything." The basis for this belief is complex but involves foremost the disdain for Neopagans' appropriation of world cultures and religious traditions and the cobbling together of rituals and practices based on "what works." This, along with the association of Wicca with the hedonistic philosophies of the 1960s and 1970s, has created an image of Wicca as undisciplined and higgledy-piggledy. This incites panic and a mandate among Heathens to disassociate from anything remotely Wiccanesque. The consequences include harsh criticism and loss of legitimacy. Inga, a young massage therapist, explains:

I think the big thing is you don't want to show your fluffiness. Because if they don't know you and you say something fluffy, they immediately start attacking you. Whereas if they know you as a good and honorable person first, and then you start showing a bit of fluffiness, or what they consider fluffy, which it varies from Heathen to Heathen, but what they consider fluffy, then they might not attack you immediately.[44]

The word *fluffy* is ubiquitous in Heathen identity discourse and is another gender-coded term that implies effeminacy, inauthenticity, and silliness, also evoked by the words *woo* and *froo froo*.[45] Alvis, like most Heathens with a Wiccan past, recalls that his previous participation in Wicca was largely due to its accessibility. He remembers, "I enjoyed the structure of the ritual," but, he says, "Some of the people were definitely a bit uh, light and fluffy spiritually for me." I asked Eskel, a graduate student in religious studies, what *fluffy* means. He laughed and gave it a try:

"Fluffy" ooh. Making me define the vague stereotype. Hm . . . I think it's related, probably, from my perspective, to the polytheism versus more pantheistic perspective, whereas a Heathen is more likely to say "Oh, this relates to this, in this way," and try and, you know, show sources or something like that, not just for divinity, but for other parts of life. A more standard Wiccan perspective is "Oh, it's all the same. It's all part of, you know, divinity, it's all part of the Goddess, or the God" or something like that, which is more fuzzy, and less distinct, less articulate.[46]

Part and parcel of Heathen avoidance of Wiccanness is the queasiness caused by the introduction of ritualistic elements tainted by ceremonial magic or melodrama, which, nevertheless, some Heathens still appreciate. Brand, for example, has confessed a secret weakness for the dramatic. He revealed to me his desires to hold "high ritual," a rite involving scripted interactions, props, and a lot of drama. The problem, he said, was that high drama feels "contrived," or "froo-froo," as he calls it. More difficult, he admitted, would be collecting support for this idea among the highly suspicious and critical Heathen populace. I asked him why he thought his idea would not be well received:

It just seems that the Germanic tradition is very—cut and straightforward. This is what we're here to do, we're here to raise a horn, this is how we do it, and we do it. We don't beat around the bush, we don't come up with some froo-froo dance and song to pour out the horn, we just pour out the horn, say "Here's your offering. Thank you for things that you gave to us." That's been my experience with every Heathen ritual I've ever seen anymore, it's just been straightforward. We're not gonna song-and-dance that literally, we're just going to do it.

I asked, "Why? Because people would think it's 'froo-froo'?"

> Yah. People would think it's too froo-froo. There's a lot of Wiccans out
> there really into the spring drama high-ritual, doing a lot of ritualistic
> steps and there's a lot of people that have come to Heathenry through
> Wicca that don't want any part of that, and they're afraid of seeing, you
> know, this is a Wicca-ey thing, and we don't want any of that. We want
> to go straight back to the history books and thump our Eddas, and find
> out the way they did it a long time ago and we'll try to re-create that as
> much as we can without the froo-froo, without the pomp and circum-
> stance.[47]

Brand's suspicions were correct. After his unconventional *blót* honoring the
goddess of death, held in the cramped quarters of his living room, a few Heathen
participants looked rather uncomfortable. At her ranch in the country, I spoke
to Freydis (introduced in more detail in Chapter 5) about her feelings regarding
the ritual and the behavior of her fellow participants. Something, she said, had
gone horribly wrong. It was too histrionic. The chanting, guided meditation, the
Gothi's pausing for effect—it was, as Brand predicted, "froo-froo." The high drama
of the ritual led Freydis to label it "too Wiccan," and she would know; she had
been a Wiccan priestess for many years before she found Ásatrú. She explained
to me that she had expected that changing religions would result in a change in
ritual style and experience. Her disappointment was palpable. During the Hela
blót, a few participants began chanting during the guided meditation, a behavior
that, in itself, is not unusual. Heathens often *galder* (chant) the names and
sounds of runes in order to make manifest various energies and intentions. This
time, however, the chanting turned into unintelligible moaning—a sexualized
groaning with peaks and valleys that would have been a comical faux pas had
the Heathens nearby not looked so uncomfortable. Not a minute later, the
moaning devolved into panting. To Freydis, these sexual undertones and the
ecstatic expressions recalled a very "Wiccan" participatory style. To make matters worse, during the *blót*, one participant hailed the Archangel Michael and
another hailed the goddess Diana—perhaps the worst breach of etiquette imag-
inable. The incident immediately incited indignant sucking of teeth and audible
intakes of breath from nearby Heathens. Later we learned that not everyone
present was Heathen; the moaners who had behaved inappropriately were local
Pagans whom Brand had invited to attend. This was not the last time that something would occur during *blót* that violated community norms, nor was Brand
the only *Gothi* to be marked as weird for his dramatic ritual style. In subsequent
years the taboo against "foreign influence," as one Heathen called it, particularly
in ritual spaces, became even more severe. The cautionary tales in which people
had made inappropriate toasts to other gods became an ever-present topic of
laughter and derision.

It is not a secret to the community that Heathens spend so much of their energy disassociating from (and mocking) Neopaganism as a category; it is often conflated with Wicca, but eclectic Pagans are just as much the target. Even those whose experience with Neopaganism was limited to the brief perusal of sub-cultural how-to literature are still part of and privy to this discussion. Alfdis, a forty-eight-year-old world traveler and ex-soldier, recalls growing up in a household whose spirituality was already in line with polytheistic and animistic ideas. Although she found Heathenry later through spiritual practices that she notes are "not quite Ásatrú," she still identifies as Heathen and expresses the same ideas about Wicca. Like most Heathens, she spent time with Neopagans with whom she experienced a sense of likeness, primarily because of accessibility, before her discovery of the Heathen community. She explains:

> I've never been a Wiccan, I can't get into it at all, cannot wrap my head around that kind of stuff—no basis—has no foundation on which to firmly stand, but they were individuals who had a like mind. I didn't always agree with their hedonistic—or what I perceived to be their hedonistic tendencies, or their lack of scholarly pursuit or investigation into their own faith, but as I said—they were at least individuals who were not family members who were of like mind.[48]

Like Alfdis, Soren, a young college professor, is one of the few Heathens I interviewed who skipped experimentation with Wicca before joining Heathenry. A friend in college introduced him to Heathenry before his experience with it in texts or on the Internet. I mentioned this to him. Although he understands the current community discussion regarding Wicca and Neopaganism in general, he immediately identifies it as problematic and peculiar:

> SOREN: In Heathenry today there's an awful lot of disdain expressed for Wicca and Neopaganism, but still an awful lot of Heathens that seem to have come from there.
> AUTHOR: I think the two are connected.
> SOREN: Mmhm. What, sort of like Heathenry is trying to establish its own identity by establishing what it isn't? Reacting against something that it's perhaps closer to than it would like to admit?[49]

Soren's concise summary is merely one clear expression of a general knowledge among Heathens that they are a fledgling religion struggling to create their own niche in an overwhelming cultic milieu. The process involves a strict adherence to historical text and documented evidence about ancient culture, but it can also be rather forgiving. Nonetheless, the discursive element of identity and boundary negotiation is unrelenting. The process is not, however, without contradiction.

Boundaries in Contradiction

Despite such rigorous endeavors to generate unambiguous identity markers that will allow Heathens to discard the baggage of mainstream religion and demarcate themselves from Neopaganism, Heathens ultimately discover that boundaries are quite permeable in two major ways (see Figure 2.1). First, although mockery of Wicca is part and parcel of community discourse, practitioners unavoidably introduce Wiccan elements into Heathen ritual and practice because it is often their only experience with which to frame Pagan religious performance. In fact, even in their most personal expressions of religious experience, Heathens must maintain caution in overstepping the boundaries of what is considered acceptable and authentic.

Many of the contradictions and distinctions can also be tied to differences in political leanings. American Heathenry's national organizations are divided increasingly along these lines, as Kaplan argued in 1996.[50] In the 1990s The Troth was associated with "intellectuals," an association that has grown stronger, inviting the labels *progressive* or, by its foes, *liberal* and *elitist*. In contrast, the Ásatrú Folk Assembly and the Ásatrú Alliance are seen as conservative, with identities as working-class red-blooded Americans or, by their foes, racist, and

Figure 2.1. Members of Raven's Wolf Kindred (Colorado) display their "Heathen Pride" with patches of runes, Scandinavian heritage, and other Pagan identity markers. (Photo by the author.)

anti-intellectual. In many of its shared values, however, American Heathenry in general is more similar to Christianity than any other Neopagan group. Many of its American founders and popular personalities are former members of the military. The ideology of political conservatism finds many supporters among the Heathen community, particularly because of the community's emphasis on the warrior ethic and its consistency with many mainline conservative moral values. Wicca, however, finds itself in contrast to both Heathenry and Christianity as an increasingly feminist-centered, progressive spirituality. Alvis explains: "The Heathen community does have a conservative streak, okay, you're much more likely to find guns in the closet of Heathen home than a Wicca home. You're much more likely to find discomfort towards homosexuals or the sexually liberal in a Heathen home."[51]

Although most of the Heathens I interviewed are not overtly racist or homophobic, it was not unusual to hear them identify themselves as Libertarian and express many antigovernment sentiments. Early in my research, much of this sentiment manifested itself in behaviors that reminded me of survivalism, as when one man, whose family lived on a remote ranch, stockpiled firearms and spoke to me of black government helicopters and the dangers of the surveillance state. Likewise, Heathens do not hesitate to mock the liberal stance that Wicca takes toward sexuality and the body. Those on the periphery of Heathenry sometimes participate in subcultures with a noted Neopagan presence, such as BDSM or polyamory, to the chagrin of their more conservative peers. On the other hand, many also cringe at what they perceive as a Christian shaming of the body and seek to appreciate bodies and sexuality as a natural aspect of life, within limits. During a large event at a campground, the hosts posted a "no nudity" rule within the designated Heathen space despite the fact that the campground itself was clothing-optional, less a rule for Heathens than a warning for Neopagan outsiders. Community narratives abound about Heathen horror at open nudity and drug use by Neopagans at public festivals such as Dragonfest and the Free Spirit Festival. Despite Heathen paranoia over the label *Wiccan*, practitioners often recognize that because of the small sizes of their groups and their myriad foes, borrowing from or participating in activities with other Neopagans is often necessary. When the situation arises, however, Heathens make it clear that Heathen ritual is dedicated to Heathen gods, and other deities are not to be invoked. Like others who maintain a Heathen identity, Inga also honors her Celtic ancestors in worship, a practice known as *dual-trad*. To many Heathens, this poses an uncomfortable dilemma. As Alvis explains, one of the criteria for inclusion in the Heathen community is "Do we think this person belongs here or do they belong with the Wiccans?" He clarifies, "I think the community tries to get a sense of the person, you know, in an overt sense they're going to ask themselves, 'Does this person have the understanding that this is a mono-traditional,' this is a single Pantheon." I read between the lines and say, "Don't call on Diana [the Greek goddess of the hunt] in a *blót*." Alvis responds, "Exactly. You can maybe get away with calling some of the Vanir, okay, but I've had the sense that there are people in the Ásatrú community who aren't real comfortable with that. I may be totally wrong, but that's my sense. I think they look at whether this person will fit in with how they perceive the Heathen community to be, or with how they perceive the Wiccan Neopagan to be."[52]

The second way in which the boundaries of Heathen identity are rendered ambiguous is in its very relationship to Christianity. Although Heathens reject the institutional and structural force of Christianity, their own morals and values come to mirror that very system. In many ways, American Heathenry, including the sector with progressive political leanings, is a return to traditional conservative values. This contradiction is readily explained, however, by differences in commitment, a marker often used in negotiating subcultural boundaries to define who is a poseur and who is authentic.[53] According to Brand:

> I've always felt that Heathenry, you know, Ásatrú is not like people go to church, they get absolved of their sins and then they're done. And then they go back to drinking, and smoking, and fighting, screwing around, but they go back on Sunday and [*in a mocking voice*] "Oh, I'm a good person again, I'm a good Christian." But the Nine Noble Virtues, the ways of the *Hávamál* seem to be like a daily practice, that it's noble deeds, right action, good intent, that if you live every moment of your day that way, you're doing the right thing for whatever reason it is.[54]

Although Brand is critical of the perceived hypocrisy of the church, he clearly lists many Heathen values that echo those of traditional religion. Sunna, the *Gythia* (priestess) of a kindred in the Midwest, left the Minoan Tradition—an offshoot of Alexandrian Wicca—because it was "too skewed toward the feminine" and "not balanced enough in taking personal responsibility." To her, Heathenry encourages people to win renown and build reputation through honorable deeds. According to Thrain, "There are a lot of people in this country, especially in the South, I think, that—if they could do a relatively rational side-by-side comparison of Christianity versus Heathenry, there are a whole lot of Heathens in this world." Similarly, Valda claims that sometimes it is hard to tell the difference between Heathen practice and the religious system that she abandoned: "The thing that's frustrating for me is the focus is not on the Earth and natural . . . the natural world, but it's more on Lore and what the Lore can teach us. And I think the Lore is fine and dandy, but there's got to be more that you base your practice on. Otherwise, I don't see how we're any different than Christians with our Bibles."[55]

The contradictions present in the practice of Heathenry, in its incorporation of Wicca or Wiccan elements, and in its adherence to many mainstream religious values highlight the importance of differentiation as a discursive and ongoing identity practice. Heathens may be a lot more like Wiccans than they would like to admit, but the movement itself is only about forty years old, and the struggle to create boundaries and define itself as unique is essential to its survival.

Some NRM scholars have argued for marking a group's relationship to its host culture as a defining characteristic of NRM qualification.[56] Others argue that new religious groups should be defined as those groups that manifest a low level of alignment with dominant cultural patterns and social institutions of their host society at a given historical moment. In contrast, dominant religious groups are "groups that are most strongly aligned with dominant cultural patterns and social institutions," and intermediate "sectarian religious groups" exhibit a low alignment with dominant social institutions but demonstrate a greater alignment with dominant cultural patterns and values.[57] American Heathenry's values align with and perhaps surpass dominant cultural values, but it is not a sect.

Heathenry, specifically, is more difficult to classify. Members often frame it as an "ethnic" religion instead of a religion belonging to the rest of Neopaganism or Western Esotericism. In addition, its values are also remarkably socially conservative, in keeping with dominant cultural norms. Heathens use this conservatism as an identity marker to separate themselves from other, more countercultural Neopagan movements and to politicize Heathen identity. Heathenry also sets itself in contrast to many of the other New Age or Neopagan religions under Western Esotericism in that to Heathens, morality is not a subjective, relative truth. Actions and decisions create effects that are passed down, influencing each successive generation.

The essentialism that is imagined and expressed through the Heathen metanarrative illustrated in this chapter is part and parcel of identity politics. To imagine that rivals and oppressors are clearly demarcated as different allows Heathens to envisage a clear and legitimate boundary around Heathendom, or, in Heathen imagery, a moat of authenticity. The irony, and the ultimate failure of essentialism, is that in many ways, Heathens have come full circle. They have left behind a dogmatic system that they feel has offered only discouragement, threats, and rejection and has ultimately done them a disservice for a system that appears to be quite similar in its tenets. One major difference, however, is that there is no formal punishment for failure to comply with Heathen values, but high personal reward and community credit for appearing to achieve them. There is no divine mandate to help the needy and no threat of divine punishment. There is only community praise or community indifference.

3

Neo-Heathens and Reconstructionists

The Project and Problems of Constructing
a Heathen Nomos

Late one summer evening in a log-cabin meeting hall, forty Heathens gather around pub tables to hear Sven's history lecture. Scheduled first among the weekend's workshops, talks, and events, Sven's story covers the legendary Battle of Teutoburg Forest. Amid bottles of beer and horns of mead, we watch the images from his slide show projected on a white bedsheet hung from a rope across the front of the hall. With animation, he informs us that this battle was the "principal event that allowed our folkway to survive." For Heathens, lectures and lessons about ancient Germanic history, geography, and culture are in many ways religious experiences that offer insight into the conditions, philosophies, and cultural practices of the people they perceive as their pagan forebears. As the story unfolds, Sven begins the complex interweaving of idealized history and Heathen aesthetic, reminding us of the struggles of our ancestors and their heroic battles against oppression. With careful explanation, he sets the scene, flipping from slide to slide to detail the extraordinary training and discipline of the Roman army, foe of Arminius (Hermann) of the Cherusci, affectionately known as "Herman the German," Germany's first hero, in the year 9 C.E.

Hermann's story is one of reinvention, revitalization, and a complex political history. Sven's retelling of this battle is part of a larger pattern of mythologizing the story of Hermann in the reshaping of a German national consciousness. From the sixteenth century onward, when an account of the battle by the Roman historian Tacitus resurfaced in a German monastery, nationalists fashioned the Germanic leader into an icon to help them forge unity in the face of such perceived enemies as the Vatican, the French, and the Jews. In the nineteenth century and well into the twentieth, the story of Arminius was reinvented and turned into propaganda. Well into the evening, Sven is now relating the enslavement of Germans captured in Roman territory beyond the Rhine. "Your ancestors! In Slavery!" Sven yells. He continues: Hermann, who had been a hostage in Rome, had received Roman education and military training, and thus understood Roman tactics, formed a secret alliance of Germanic tribes, organized a rebellion, and led the Roman army into an ambush, resulting in Roman casualties estimated at fifteen thousand to twenty thousand. The Germans won the battle and took the remaining Romans as slaves. As Sven tells us that the captured centurions were "burned as offerings to Thor," his voice rises in excitement. The room explodes in shouts of "Hail Thor!!" and thunderous pounding on tables. After this battle, "no Roman would ever again cross to the east of the Rhine," Sven says, to which we all reply "Hail!!" Despite the dramatic effect of this assertion, the notion that Arminius drove the Romans out of Germania east of the Rhine is a fallacy. Only six years after the battle, Roman forces were back to devastating Germanic tribes and winning major battles. Yet this detail does not overshadow the powerful message of Hermann's victory. His story over, Sven reminds us that much of this country was settled by Germans, some of whom built a monument to Herman the German, a way for us "to remember our folk soul." Hans, the chieftain of a local kindred, asks us to donate to the fund for the preservation of the local statue. "If it weren't for Herman," Hans says, "we'd all be Roman." To Sven, the story of Hermann, divorced from its historical use as a tool used during the Third Reich to perpetuate nationalist ideologies, reinforces the idea of ancestral greatness, perseverance, and resistance to the oppression of dominant religion, part and parcel of the reconstruction of historical "truth" for contemporary Heathens.

In a media-driven culture increasingly enthralled with vampires, zombies, wizards, and hobbits as an antidote to the alienation of postmodern society, a hearkening back to the illusory magic and purity of the epic past reenchants our lives. By seeking to understand, through studious research, the worldview of the Old Norse before Christianization, some Heathens attempt to piece together Heathenry in what they view as its most authentic form, unadulterated by modern influence and interpretation. Since the early years of the twenty-first century, some Heathens have become increasingly involved in reconstructionism as a method for understanding historical Heathenry more deeply than a focus on the anachronistic and fantasy-epic razzle-dazzle of heroes or Viking raiders. Although the main base of support for reconstructionism within American Heathenry is found among kindreds in the northeastern United States, the discourse surrounding what is "real," academically validated Heathenry permeates groups around the country. Spread primarily through social media, the new wave of reconstructionism is a contrast and challenge to the popular current of "Neo-Heathenry," as its detractors call it, that has evolved over the years to incorporate elements of ritual and belief from other Neopaganisms.

Religion in the postmodern age frequently emphasizes individual religious experience.[1] This emphasis has created a Heathenry that many feel has become overpopulated with spiritual seekers and those for whom religion is fluid, personal, and less preoccupied with the rigors of historical research. Josh Heath, a young Iraq War veteran at the center of the mission to have Thor's hammer approved as a military grave marker, argues that "reconstruction in Heathenry is about understanding why the ancient Heathen peoples did what they did and applying that thought process to the building of religious ceremonies and customs (also known as *sidu*), today."[2] To his wife, Cat, a British-born former kindergarten teacher, the difference between those who emphasize reconstructionist methods and those who do not is that reconstructionists tend to be "more locally and community based (as opposed to playing on the national stage)," focusing on "building up traditions over the years that can be handed down to our children." During an interview with Dr. Karl Seigfried of the *Norse Mythology Blog*, Cat noted, "We also tend to stick to discussing subjects that can be backed up by sources, which admittedly can lead to the impression that we're somehow 'anti-UPG,' an impression that pervades the discourse of 'reconstructionism' throughout Heathendom."[3]

An unverified personal gnosis (UPG) is an indemonstrable personal spiritual experience. UPGs are often spiritual visions of the gods or religious interpretations of natural phenomena as somehow spiritually significant messages. These subjective experiences are often very powerful and meaningful for the individual involved, and revealing them to one another is one method by which Heathens share in the sacred. Disclosing them can be risky, however, because unlike adherents of other spiritualities with New Age elements, Heathens are hesitant to accept the idea that spiritual knowledge comes solely from listening to inner voices, or that spiritual revelations are relative and equally valuable. To Heathens, this smacks of Neopaganism and threatens the clearly defined, grounded, and historically legitimate tradition that they have been trying to create. The very name *UPG* is meant to counter this, to demonstrate to the listener that the narrator understands that his or her story is potentially unbelievable, but that the spiritual message and the experience itself are most important. The tone of UPG stories is usually very matter-of-fact and avoids dramatic narrative style or pomp that might be interpreted as New Agey, among the gravest of Heathen insults. Cat observes that "some of my most treasured UPG conversations have been with 'recons' at the end of a night of revelry and with a drink in hand,"[4] a comment that suggests that UPGs are acceptable only when they are framed within a "legitimate" scholarly context and understood as stories rather than as universal truths about the spiritual world.

As a method, reconstructionism emphasizes understanding the worldview behind the behaviors and beliefs of the ancients. To Bil Linzie, a pioneer of Heathen reconstructionism, being a reconstructionist requires that "one takes a scientific approach to Heathenry" in order to "understand how the makers constructed the thing in the first place and how they understood it, felt about it, and interacted with it after it was created." He writes, "Being a reconstructionist requires no belief. In fact, 'belief' can actually be a hindrance to understanding the data in hand—'belief' can interfere greatly with 'interpretation of the facts.'

To be a good reconstructionist, one must be able to step away from one's cultural background as well as spiritual background."[5]

Not all Heathens agree on the details. According to Josh Heath, "There isn't really such a thing as reconstructionist Heathenry; different Heathens have done differing levels of reconstruction." To Heath, reconstructionist Heathenry emphasizes "understanding and implementing a traditional worldview."[6] Although most Heathens are interested in and studious of histories of early northern Europe, the *Eddas,* the sagas, and archaeological research, the weight given to historical accuracy of belief or practice varies along a spectrum. After analyzing the content of dozens of discussions among Heathens regarding authenticity, as well as engaging in conversations of my own, I have found that different people have different ideas of what *reconstructionism* means, what counts as "authentic" Heathen practice or philosophy, and what is irrelevant fluff (often involving UPGs). Most Heathens are mindful of the *Eddas* and the sagas, and although many also pursue historical and archaeological research as a side interest, few spend as much intellectual energy analyzing the research of Old Norse religionists, historians, archaeologists, and linguists as those who identify as reconstructionists. The differences often lead to conflict. Arguments abound in online forums as individuals challenge one another's assertions or experiences as lacking historical or literary foundation. A new Heathenry forum on Facebook includes among its rules, "If you are stating something that is a UPG (Unverified Personal Gnosis) please state that it is so, so people do not argue with you about it."[7] Accusations of poor scholarship, demands for citations, and references to scholarly "proof" occur daily in interactions. This constant brawling often renders reconstructionism less a method than another politically laden identity category used to claim expertise, ownership, and control over the broader *Heathen* label—a war of authenticity that frequently escalates into bullying, name-calling, and hypermasculine one-upmanship on the Internet.

Although Pagan studies scholars have mentioned, often in passing, the contested nature of the eclectic-romantic versus the historically minded approaches to Paganism, few have gone further. Many have researched Eastern European paganisms, highlighting a historically mindful ethnic identity as pagans from Lithuania, Hungary, Russia, and other Baltic nations revive the pre-Christian aspects of their cultural heritage, often in the context of nationalistic ideologies.[8] These cases are based on paganisms whose practitioners can claim native identity and inherited ties to sacred sites. Ethnographic research into how American reconstructionist traditions alienated from their pagan "homelands" negotiate the gap between historical accuracy and practical concerns and how this divide creates two competing but overlapping religious movements remains unstudied. Although most pagan studies scholars share a tendency to group all pagans under a Neopagan canopy, the methods of religion creation, philosophies regarding "truth" finding, and different individual/romantic versus community/tribal foci have created two divergent movements.

Authenticity Wars: Innovation Versus Historical Accuracy

The distinction between Neo-Heathens and reconstructionists is in many ways another spectrum along which Heathens contest legitimacy, authenticity, and identity. It can also be understood as the tension between *construction* and *reconstruction*.[9] The former category applies to Heathens for whom religious devotion involves a creative adaptation of existing historically documented practices influenced by personal spiritual revelation and elements of other faith systems that seem just "Heathen enough." The majority of Heathens whom I have met fall within this type. They give studious attention to history but are less critical of the historical accuracy of existing Heathen practice, choosing instead to go with the flow of their particular community. They believe that historical accuracy is not as important as developing a meaningful spirituality tailored to their personal needs. Many choose to wear garb to Heathen ritual or events, a myriad of costumes drawn from various historical periods, some from early northern Europe, others a pastiche of items available—a costumer's version of interpretive dance. To those further along the spectrum toward hard-line reconstructionism, authentic Heathenry involves more than reviving a historical aesthetic or engaging in what some refer to, in a derogatory sense, as a "reenactor's" superficial focus on costuming and kitsch. Similar to other Heathen identity talk, the *Neo-Heathen* label, like that of *universalist,* is rarely a self-identifier; rather, it is a term most often used by reconstructionists to designate their perceived opponents as "other."

To be correctly and authentically Heathen, as many reconstructionists understand it, the pursuit of a deep understanding of the ancients' worldview is paramount. Why Germanic peoples practiced *Sumbel,* for example, rather than how, offers the most useful insight into societies' sociopolitical structures and social motivations. The journal *Odroerir,* written and edited by Heathens interested in pursuing a scholarly approach to their faith, offers readers a deeper historical perspective. Among its many foci, it dissects such practices as *Sumbel* and animal sacrifice and provides commentary on the suitability of the modern Heathen use of such trappings as drinking horns, historically limited to elites but now an omnipresent Heathen accessory. The authors of *Odroerir* aim to help Heathens untangle themselves from their socialization into a postmodern Judao-Christian culture in order to create a Heathen worldview anew. To Josh Rood, the presenter of a "Reconstructionism 101" workshop at East Coast Thing in 2012,

> Ásatrú is not a world-rejecting religion, it was an indigenous religion, and like most is inseparable from the culture in which it grows up. You cannot extract the religion from the pre-Christian Germanic peoples. It is bound within the culture, there's no compartmentalization of religion/ work/home/politics. It is all one and the same—we have no early Ger-

manic words before conversion that relate to religion. They didn't have a word—all words translate to "custom" or "the way things were done," or "knowledge." We must investigate the culture in which the system was contained, to understand the worldview of our ancestors to understand why they did what they did.[10]

The replacement of a current worldview with a wholly other and deliberately constructed rationale is difficult, to say the least, a challenge not lost on many Heathens. Modern Heathen reconstructionism is disturbed by, among other things, the disjuncture between concepts of politics and Heathenry's relationship to religion, time as linear, and ideas of rugged individualism. Erik, a forty-one-year-old who has been a solitary practitioner for eight years, problematizes reconstructionism at its core:

> The fundamental problem at the heart of the reconstructive enterprise is that there are no actual sources of Heathen worldview. There is not one Heathen written source. All the surviving sources are Roman, Greek, Arab or post-conversion Christian. When a reconstructionist cherry-picks the "Heathen" elements from the Icelandic sagas or interprets archeological objects as concrete and understandable representations of specific worldview concepts, they are really doing nothing different from the "Neo-Heathens" and "Wiccatru" they are so condescending towards. On one hand, they attack Snorri's Edda as unreliable and "Christian-influenced," on the other hand they literally re-enact rituals described in Snorri's saga-writing.[11]

There is a contradiction inherent in the attempt to re-create a unified Heathenry, one coherent version of the "truth" based on these sources whose foundation was to a great degree higgledy-piggledy. Ancient Heathenry, in its practice, comprised multiple sects and understandings of the gods and their relationships to humans that varied by time and place. Scholars who study Old Norse religion and material culture argue that "pre-Christian Norse religion is not a uniform or stable category. Instead there were profound chronological, regional and social differences in pre-Christian religious practice in Scandinavia."[12] The experience of belief as a unifying force was alien to the Old Norse, for whom warfare with neighboring Heathen clans was not uncommon. Tribes destroyed one another's sacred shrines to deities that, presumably, they themselves worshiped. Essentially, despite popular community myth, ancient Heathens did not share a unified understanding of the Heathen cosmos and culture. Religion was highly localized, although scholars of Old Norse "religion" argue that *religion* is not an accurate term for Old Norse belief, nor is *belief systems,* because there was nothing systematic about it. Rather, archaeologist Neil Price argues for the term *discursive space* to describe the fluid and ethereal assumptions of pre-Christian belief.[13] The Old Norse had "no pagan Norse 'orthodoxy,' no rules or moral overtones, no 'worship,' obedience to, or even approval of the gods, no consistent understanding of a spiritual complex, no consistent practice or means of interaction with it," rendering our understanding of the Old Norse religious worldview(s) problematic and scattered at best.[14] Some reconstructionists argue, however, that understanding one of the many pagan cults or tribal practices is better than nothing because it offers insight into a segment of ancient reality—each insight of which contributes, in whatever small way, to our growing knowledge.

The Heathen community today is rife with disagreements over varied political and religious views, which often lead to bad blood among members. As Heathens seek to uncover the worldviews, beliefs, and sociopolitical motivations behind ancient Heathen rituals and customs, definitions of Heathenry as an ethnic religion find firmer footing. As an ethnic religion, Heathenry would have encompassed all aspects of Old Norse action and consciousness. Today, however, the argument has different sociopolitical implications, discussed further in Chapter 6. Josh Rood argues this point in his introductory article on reconstructionism, published in the first issue of *Odroerir:*

> Heathenism is an ethnic religion. In order to reconstruct any of the ancient Heathen religions the adherent must thoroughly investigate the culture that they are entwined with. One must investigate the social structure, the language, the customs and the political system *not* to find *things* to reconstruct or *how* to do things. Rather, the adherent must seek to understand the "why" which shaped those systems and must try to comprehend the very *worldview* from which the investigated religion has developed. It is the worldview which formed the foundation from which Heathen practice, action, belief, and tradition developed amongst the pre-Christian Germanic people. The worldview produced the "why" and it is the worldview itself that we aim to reconstruct.[15]

It cannot be overlooked, however, that the "why" presumably would so radically differ from the needs, desires, and opportunities of contemporary Heathens that reconstructionists would likely be reduced to general notions of how to put ancient Heathenry into contemporary practice. For example, the Norse had different material resources and concerns regarding survival. Once reconstructionists develop an understanding regarding tribal/group beliefs about the land, or crops, or the next tribe over, held as a matter of survival, they must translate that "why" (however imprecise) into applications to contemporary relationships and concerns.

Also, a focus on cultural heritage rather than whiteness minimizes the racial implications of *ethnic*. Cat Heath argues that the common obsession with ancestry is misguided when the focus is on "a particular" ancestry. Instead, Heathens should explain "why we think our ancestors are directly important to us." She asserts, "No, it doesn't matter where your ancestors came from. If you lived in a

Heathen tribe in the old days, and you grew up there, you knew their way of life. You were a Heathen. Period."[16] The argument that the Old Norse determined group belonging by culture and language is a direct challenge to the politically and racially coded focus on ancestry. Yet, to the Old Norse, the political and religious landscapes were overlapping, one and the same. *Things* and *althings* were regional and national political assemblies with a religious foundation, presided over by the gods and functioning on their account. All religious life had political implications, and all political life was religious in nature. Modern Heathens, however, live in modern times in which the political landscape influences religious discourse in varied and often contentious ways. This presents an inescapable quandary in the attempt to re-create an authentic Heathen worldview because Heathen religion without Heathen politics is the separation of particles and the creation of something wholly new and immensely other.

During his "Reconstructionism 101" talk at the 2013 East Coast Thing,[17] Josh Rood offered the example of the alienation of the Amish—"other" in tension with and resistance to popular culture and socialization into civil society. To many Heathens, the long-term success of groups that are of society but not in it provides hope that competition with the Judeo-Christian underpinnings of Western society is possible. Yet the success of the Amish is in large part due to their physical isolation. To Heathens, who are part of mainstream society, consumers of popular culture, avid users of technology and social media, and in many respects average citizens working as nurses, software analysts, soldiers, teachers, and government workers, the challenge of the construction of a competing worldview is to make fundamental social change more than a mere exercise. The socially constructed meaningful orders that characterize the plausibility structures of American society are deeply embedded in rationalized systems of meaning, scientific thought, and relationships to technology that form much of our taken-for-granted reality. This disconnection has caused a new kind of division of authenticity within the community, separate from the more traditional regional or religious differences of Old Norse sects. To a certain extent, modern Heathens are echoing the instability of their ancestors, although this has less to do with any intentional or planned organization within the religion and more to do with human group dynamics. To the pragmatists, a replacement of their natal weltanschauung with a wholly Heathen worldview requires studious attention to historical detail. To the more cynical reconstructionist, it also requires resistances to consumerism, the perceived triviality of popular culture, and the usurpation of reality by Christian colonialism. According to a post by "Boar's Heart" on a Heathen message board, "Even for those not actually raised Christian, it must be recognized that Christianity and its core assumptions forms the basic Western/American worldview in profound ways. So . . . how does one get PAST all that?"[18] Our worldview, our socially constructed sense of how we live and move through the world, our languages, symbols, thoughts, and ideas are inseparable from who we are as a society, as a culture, and as individuals. Yet our socially constructed reality is an ongoing process. To sociologist

Peter Berger, culture, "although it becomes for man a 'second nature,' remains something quite different from nature precisely because it is the product of man's own activity. Culture must be continuously produced and reproduced by man. Its structures are, therefore, inherently precarious and predestined to change."[19]

To reconstructionists, reconstructionism is a process of making and unmaking reality. The difficulty is not lost on many Heathens, although the process continues. As Josh Rood remarks:

> If it is a religion, then on what terms is it being reconstructed? Is the religion being ciphered out of a vague understanding of an entirely foreign culture like broken jewelry out of sand and wired together to the shape and understanding of a modern American with a Judeo-Christian background? If this is the case, then one can not claim that the end result of this process is a reconstructed religion when it is really a modern construct bearing the *surface appearance* of its original form. The original spiritual framework has been lost. . . . The reality is that the spiritual framework, which we label as "Heathenry," is inexplicably bound to the culture and locality from which it developed and cannot be separated. The very idea that religion and culture can be separated is in fact, inherently "unHeathen."[20]

As Rood indicates, the reconstructionist goal since the early years of the twenty-first century has been the reconfiguration of the Heathen "worldview," a concept central to the reconstructionist project and reminiscent of what Berger referred to as the "nomos."[21] The project requires that the "Judeo-Christian background" that Rood references be replaced with an alternative reality, a new order under which Heathen children will receive socialization into an alternative and wholly Heathen worldview. In the meantime, reconstructionism has become an identity among its most ardent supporters, serving as a powerful tool for the construction of, as Rood calls it, the "unHeathen," providing a framework for authentic belief and behavior. On the religious front, to Boar's Heart, the problems are many:

> As Morpheus said to Neo, "See how deep the rabbit hole really goes."
> Here be some rabbits that I see going unquestioned, even among Heathens, ALL THE TIME. While not all of them are peculiar to xtianity, they are certainly part of the Western xtian worldview:
>
> 1. Duality—the existence of a separable, eternal soul.
> 2. A "special" afterlife of some kind, with preferred and feared destinations.
> 3. A personal, individual relationship with deity.
> 4. "Everything happens for a reason."

5. Cosmic brownie points for being a "good little ____."
6. The idea of deity as omnipotent, omniscient, omnipresent, or focused on you.
7. The notion of one really, really TRUE universal Truth.™

There's probably lots more, but I'd say that recognizing and thinking through these seven is probably an awfully good start on shedding one's draugrtrú cultural roots and beginning to Think Like A Heathen.

Draugrtrú is a modern Ásatrú term borrowed from the modern Icelandic term *draugr* (undead) and the Old Norse suffix *tru* (true), used to indicate one's troth or belief. Some of the more sarcastic Heathens use the term specifically to refer to Christians because Christians believe in Christ, an "undead" God—which Boar's Heart argues is an impediment to "thinking like a Heathen." To accomplish this goal, rather than remove themselves from society, Heathens engage in studious research, contemplation, and discussion, unearthing and separating what scholars of Old Norse history and religion have documented as "probably happened" from those truths unverified by the academy. As Boar's Heart notes, the Heathen concept of the soul differs significantly from that of Christianity, as does the understanding of the afterlife—a concept considerably less important to Heathens than their this-worldly behavior and tribal *gefrain* (reputation or renown). Likewise, some Heathens have rejected notions of determinism, of religious compensations for "good" behavior, and of the omnipotence of the gods. Instead, they view the gods as rather imperfect beings whose concern for human affairs is rather limited.

Further illustrating the separation of Heathen worldview and theology from that of other world religions, in a Facebook group, members suggested that Heidelberg University theology professor Theo Sundermeier's distinction between traditional primary religions and secondary world religions can be used to understand Heathenry in an attempt to clarify to other Heathens the difficulty of the reconstructionist project.[22] To Sundermeier, "Traditional religion and society interlock: religion is a constituent element of a society." It sustains society, in which "primary experience of the world and religious experience are two sides of the same coin." Primary religions are ancestral, cultural, and rooted in community, providing the foundation for a people's taken-for-granted sense of the way the world and the cosmos function. It is principal in that "it makes a total claim, and permeates a person's whole life." It is handed down, "informed by the life-cycle and the annual cycle of nature," and fundamental to the identity and preservation of a people. In this way, primary religion is "inescapable."[23] Religions of this kind include those of the ancient Norse, the Egyptians, the Babylonians, Greco-Roman antiquity, and traditional African religions. "Secondary religions, by contrast, are those that owe their existence to an act of revelation and foundation, build on primary religions, and typically differentiate themselves from the latter by denouncing them as pagan, idolatry and superstition."[24]

Secondary religions view primary religions as "survivals" that need be "overtaken by the progress of civilization."[25] To Bil Linzie,

> "Religion," in our modern sense of the word, is an ideal divorced from culture, from landscape, from language, and from worldview. A term that I have often used in the past is "modular religion" as opposed to "ethnic religion." A modular religion is a religion which can be easily imported and exported across cultural boundaries. The most common modern example of a modular religion is Christianity. . . . The concept is completely self-contained, essentially, complete with its own rules, laws, axioms, and corollaries, i.e., a module. A modular religion stands in direct contrast to an ethnic religion such as the indigenous religions of Africa, Australia, Alaska, and Greenland. Anthropologists over the past 150 years have been entertained, fascinated, and frustrated by how closely bound religion-culture-worldvew in these regions are to landscape-occupation-environment.[26]

Secondary religions are based strictly on holy books that require interpretation, are separate from one's indigenous traditional faith, and, in the Heathen experience, vilify primary religions as "pagan" (i.e., illegitimate and enemies to be fought). In providing this explanation, Heathens frame their faith as indigenous, ancestral, traditional, and authentic, but problematic in the loss of its connection to land, heritage, and an unbroken nomos. They continue to contrast it with the "artificial" competing worldview of interloping universalist Abrahamic faith systems.

Late one afternoon, at the same event where Sven shared the story of Herman the German, Liza began her scheduled workshop on the body-soul complex of the Old Norse. Over the quiet hum of mosquito-repellent fans and the stink of bug spray and camp sweat, we sat huddled over our pens and legal-size handouts. Liza, her threefold posterboard taped with images representing various parts of the soul, instructed our group of twenty in philosophical lessons of how "the ancestors," in this case, a generic reference to old Scandinavia, understood the soul and its connection to human behavior, inherited and lived. At least one scholar of Old Norse religion has noted the difficulty of tracing the conception of the soul "sufficiently clearly to receive any impression of a consistent whole, since as usual we are limited to isolated fragments here and there, often misunderstood and imperfectly remembered."[27] A veteran educator at a cultural center, Liza began with the assertion that the Old Norse had a concept of *soul,* a body-versus-spirit dualistic separation critiqued by others in the Heathen community as a Christian import or a crossover from Western mysticism or Qabbalistic or ceremonial magic. Liza presented the central term on the handout, *Lich,* our physical bodies that connect us, through DNA, to our ancestors in a very literal sense. Other soul-parts include the *Feorh,* or tree soul, our ubiquitous spirit shared with all living things; *Odr,* battle frenzy, divine consciousness or inspiration; *Ond,* "livingness" or breath; and *Hamr,* the skin of the soul. Liza's chart included more aspects of the body-soul complex than most scholars typically identify, such as *Aldr,* length of life; *Maegin,* spiritual brightness; and the *Fylgia,* our spirit guardian inherited from our ancestors. As she spoke, she took questions from her Heathen audience. She fielded a question about *Ørlög,* which she explained as the "sum of past deeds," and offered advice on how to heal the damage done by alcoholism, abuse, or the unsavory deeds of our family members. A woman nearby asked her about our *hamingja,* or store of *luck,* and whether this, too, might fall victim to the deeds of our ancestors. Liza confirmed that it might indeed, and she reminded her questioner that the common Western concept of a soul as a singular essence separate from the body was foreign to ancient Germanic tribes. In order to repair the damage done to our *luck,* we must engage in positive, affirming, helpful, and beneficial action. The message about right action was moving to a few people nearby, who nodded and murmured approval. It reminded me of the many occasions on which I had felt as though the conservative ethic of Heathen behavior demanded a return to personal accountability and self-help, where personal responsibility was sanctified and structural context was irrelevant. To many Heathens, the reconstruction of the body-soul complex is a crucial component of the Old Norse worldview, an understanding of which can help alleviate the perceived contamination by our socialization into a contemporary Judeo-Christian perspective. Yet the conversation regarding separation of body and spirit suggests that the soul is of primary spiritual importance, while the body is banally insignificant—a world-rejecting philosophy not in keeping with Heathenry's world-accepting weltanschauung. Liza's audience, eager for the challenge, took studious notes. Nobody asked her for a detailed list of her sources; all accepted her scholarship as legitimate. Although a few soul concepts receive references in the sagas, many are of ambiguous origin—a problem of modern knowledge production as lay scholars cite one another rather than original literature or scholarly sources. When her seminar was completed, the rest of us left our wooden benches and wandered off into the campgrounds, our knowledge increased but our lives, on a macro level, still very much unchanged.

To the Old Norse, fate and *luck* were inexorable and essential concepts for the shaping of human life. Such understandings of how the world works are alien to us in that the Old Norse believed in life as somehow inescapably ruled by outside forces. The modern emphasis on the individual and the pop-psychological influences telling us that we are the creators of our own destiny are pervasive and inexorable elements of our socialization. The essentially individualistic search by modern Heathens for meaning diverges significantly from Old Norse ideas of fate and *luck.* Furthermore, it conflicts with the very structure of Old Norse Heathenry, which was fundamentally a community or folk religion obligating individuals to focus outside themselves. Although there were personal means of expression and personal piety, there was generally a lack of emphasis on "I" or "me" and individual feelings; rather, there was a concern with how the local group related to the gods.[28] An individual was important only in relation to how he or she featured in the collective. The idea that the Old Norse were just as fervently individualistic and antihierarchical as modern practitioners is a romantic fallacy perpetuated through modern discourse. The opposing formats and worldviews of modern individualism versus ancient collectivity are another incompatibility between the Old Norse and modern Heathens that impedes the accuracy of Heathen reconstruction.

The (De)Construction of Community and Equality

As Heathens hearken back to a more epic, anachronistic, and pure age of ancestors and heroes, they inevitably construct a sense of peoplehood. To be part of a lineage, whether real or imagined, is to feel connected with a folk and grounded in a cultural heritage. On countless occasions Heathens have expressed this belief with toasts to, hails to, or discussions regarding "the folk." Others have suggested that Heathens, though strangers, support one another in times of trial. In one particular case, the arrest of a high-profile Heathen chieftain resulted in simultaneous rallying cries of "Support a fellow Heathen" and denunciations by others of the notion that just any Heathen is worthy of support. The implication, in addition to a further rift in community sentiment, is that one person's Heathen is very possibly another person's illegitimate poseur. The concept of an Ásatrú people that groups such as the AFA champion requires a unified and relatively cohesive faith system—a reworking of the universalism that so many conservative Heathens reject as a Christian construct in regard to one-size-fits-all religion—and a liberal one in regard to the acceptance of racial diversity. Instead, many Heathens treat Ásatrú as one faith, with small variations but nonetheless shared rituals, norms, values, and gods.

Social psychologists have long argued that identities involve not only the construction of both similarities and difference but also the formation of emotional communities. Traditional organic community is no longer a reality. Today, *community* can mean everything or nothing; it is whatever members make it. Reflective of Herman Schmalenbach's concept of the *Bund*,[29] Heathen community, like most community, is based on the *feeling* of similarity with others, a shared member identity, and a "desire to share a sense of commitment and belonging with others who are seekers after some kind of expressive alternative to the conditions of modern life."[30] Reconstructionists resist the idea of a broader peoplehood because the Old Norse and Germanic tribes had no such concept but rather understood themselves as separate families, villages, or tribes. The idea of one cohesive community and the peoplehood that it implies runs counter to a reconstruction of ancient sociopolitical tribal boundaries. To be of a community or a people implies shared experience, background, and belief. Instead, reconstructionists have revived a "glocal" response to the myth of unity, basing their growing tribal traditions on local *wights* and creating local cults and customs that distinguish them from other Heathens for whom collective identity encompasses a global Heathenness. Heathen holidays celebrating the changing of the seasons hold little relevance for kindreds in areas like New Mexico or Arizona, for whom the climate is more static than in the plains states. Glocalization thereby serves as a means of merging the notion of globalization with that of local considerations. The practice of Heathenry throughout the world illustrates the effect of globalization on the religious marketplace. Yet the tailoring of Heathen ritual, values, and norms to suit contemporary local customs and geography illustrates its glocalization. Heathenry is not homogeneous. As it is transported across the globe, it is necessarily influenced by local political, economic, and social ecology.[31] Thus Heathenry in Norway is shaped by different historical, political, and social events, is embedded in distinct cultural traditions and knowledge, and is not the same Heathenry as that found in the United States. Further, the Heathenry of New England differs in its focus and sociopolitical traits from that of Berkeley, Florida, or New Mexico.

In reviving the Old Norse focus on the *innangard* (inner yard), with an understanding that the *utgard* (outer yard) encompasses a wide variety of people who are not "your" people, Heathens have begun a debate on the nature of equality. Partly political, partly ethical, the notion of who is equal to whom centers on the nature of personal responsibility and accountability, divorcing the individual from the structural constraints facing those society has deemed "less than." Rather than focus on the effect of poor education or class limitations on an individual's ability to achieve a particular goal, Heathens, like many Americans, have revived a personal-accountability model that sidesteps socioeconomic conditions and blames each person for his or her shortcomings. In effect, Heathens have engaged in a reversal of C. Wright Mills's classic argument,[32] insisting on a public issue's return to the realm of personal troubles. In this way, Heathens may argue that not all people are created equal because not all people have earned equal standing in a community. They have not achieved renown through good deeds, gifting, or making themselves useful to others. If they have not, the argument goes, they are inferior to those who have, social context aside. This *innangard* construct has a common second use when it is deployed to shun others with whom someone disagrees—labeling an ideological opponent as an outsider with no right to question a group's *thew* (group norms, or customs, also referred to as *sidu*). This happens regardless of the legitimacy of the opponent's point and even in cases where a group's claim to authentic practice falls flat in the face of academic evidence to the contrary. To avoid being made wrong by scholarship that suggests, for example, that the term *blót* is not etymologically related to the term *blood,* and therefore the idea of *blót* as blood sacrifice may not be historically accurate, groups may simply brush it off as the ravings of someone whose opinion does not matter because he or she is *utangard.*

The notion of earned worth is certainly not new; it is a fundamental part of American rugged individualism and pop-psychological explanations of individual failings. It provides Heathens legitimacy in their reasoning about who gets to be Heathen—that is, a racialized exclusion, because people of color are frequently framed as "other" and less virtuous.[33] This framing of race is nothing new (and is discussed further in Chapter 6), but for Heathens, that each person is equally capable of making a positive contribution to a community, obeying the law, and adhering to right action, is rendered, through reconstructionism, into a more authentic way of viewing society. We do not have to be our brother's keeper if our brother is not worthy of such attention, nor are we obligated to accept people into our communities merely because they are called to Heathenry. Instead, the meritocratic focus on personal worth helps define the limitations of tolerance.

Heathen Practices: Creating a Socioreligious Foundation

The chill sets in at eight o'clock on a windy late summer evening, and those of us assembled outside the hall—a sheet-metal pavilion big enough to park three semis—wait for the *High Sumbel* to begin. Loitering in a grassy field, more than a hundred of us wait to be called on. People mill about, laughing, chatting, and gathering straggling kindred members or unaffiliated friends into their groups. Those closest in friendship to the host kindred will be seated closest to the high table at the front of the hall. One by one, kindreds are called from the field and led to their seats. Earlier in the day, my fledgling kindred had taken an oath—a solemn vow of commitment and elective kinship to one another, written and officiated by a well-known *Gothi* in attendance. After a while, we are finally seated toward the back. Our worth unproven, we disappear in the background of the crowded hall. *Sumbel* begins with the chieftain of the host kindred welcoming us to the hall and, with arms outstretched, raising his voice to the sky in a welcome to gods and ancestors that they might hear our words and watch over us. The Valkyrie carries the horn from person to person so each can hail a god in prose or poetry. At the end of each turn, the hall erupts in collective cries of "Hail!" creating ripples in my water glass, and the horn moves on. The kindred seated next to us pays us little attention. Two hours later, the horn is only halfway to my table, and it is getting colder. On into the night, many men stand and present gifts, with flourishes and applause, to other men of note, a decidedly traditional and gendered gesture. Few kindreds in attendance are led by women, and those few who boast women leaders are small hearths, almost always families. The ritual of gifting, often cited by Heathens as encouraged in the *Hávamál*, obligates a person to return a gift with a gift. Among the Old Norse, public gifting cemented social and political relationships, created bonds of family and community, and allowed for displays of status. The ritual continues until the early hours of the morning. By then, I have already returned to my tent, where the darkness is pierced by distant hails and table-thumping applause.

When Heathens engage in ritual observance, it usually takes the form of a *blót* or *Sumbel*. *Blót*s (pronounced "bloats") vary from private, individual prayers and offerings of food and drink to one or more deities to large-scale community events. The origin of the term *blót* is debated; some scholars and Heathens argue that *blót* is etymologically related to the word *blood*,[34] while others argue that it simply means "blessing." Yet among reconstructionists, blood sacrifice is an increasing part of authentic *blót*, a practice that, as discussions on Facebook indicate, perplexes and distresses many Heathens in the United States and the international community. The conversation over animal sacrifice, hashed out in both face-to-face and virtual spaces, ultimately returns to the necessity of sacrifice—the killing of animals for food in general and an assault on vegetarianism as un-Heathen. The political connotations of meat and meat eating, a cacophony of symbols tied to masculinity and class consciousness, and of its converse, vegetarianism, as a symbol of the effeminate elite find their way into the discussion of blood sacrifice without fail. Yet most Heathens forgo the practice, seeking instead to honor the gods with a symbolic sacrifice of material items, to abstain from chosen behaviors, or to honor the gods with offerings in keeping with the newer emerging definition. In the Midwest, *blóts* without live sacrifice are sometimes called *fainings*, although *blót* remains the term most often used (see Figure 3.1).

Figure 3.1. Members of various local tribes gather for a ritual to celebrate the summer solstice. Scott of Mjodvitnir Kindred (Colorado) blesses those present with a sprinkle of mead at the end of a *faining*. (Photo by the author.)

*Blót*s often honor a specific deity or have a specific purpose at regular cycles throughout the year, in tune with the change of seasons or community needs. Many Heathens engage with the gods in a casual, though solemn, approach that lacks the ceremonial magic or pageantry of many Neopagan rituals.[35] In contrast to the religious significance of *blót, Sumbels* are sociopolitical drinking rituals. To most Heathens, "*Blót* is about the community's dedication to a reciprocal gifting relationship with our gods. *Sumbel* is about reaffirming the *frith*-bonds between members of that community and the passing of the horn symbolically represents the weaving of those bonds."[36] Both ritual forms involve the sharing of a drinking horn of mead (honey-wine) or other fermented beverage. Although the styles and organizations of these rituals vary greatly according to a group's *thew,* they usually hold true to these two forms.

From research and the lore, Heathens have gleaned other Old Norse concepts that have been adopted into the modern Heathen worldview. One example is the modern Heathen understanding of *luck* and its relationship to action, similar to concepts of karma. To Heathens, a person's *hamingja* or "repository of good *luck* and fortune"[37] is responsible for the current of a person's life.[38] In American Heathenry, *luck* is not happenstance; it is inherited, lost, or gained and affects intimately the currents and trajectory of a person's life. A person may enact certain rituals to acquire *luck* or have such circumstances visited upon him or her that *luck* is lost. *Luck* may also be passed down through generations. In addition to *luck,* the forces of nature are personified in a multiplicity of beings believed to interact and interfere with the human routine. Specifically, Heathens often give offerings to, and invoke *Landvaettir* (land spirits) of the forest, earth, and streams, often represented as trolls, gnomes, elves, and fairies. On the darker side of things are what some consider "baleful *wights,*" among which are the Jotnar. Jotnar are giants, engaged in a constant state of war with the Aesir and representing chaos and destruction. To many, the worship or veneration of baleful Jotnar is taboo. Gods and ancestors are central to the Heathen focus. The Germanic pantheon includes a variety of deities concerned with the cycles of nature and natural phenomena, such as thunder, fertility and the harvest, and the sea, and another group of gods affiliated with human capacities and reactions, such as love, wisdom, war, and justice. To most Heathens, the gods are complex and imperfect. Some Heathens understand them to be real, present, and distinct individuals. To others, they are abstract representations of fundamental needs. Regardless of a person's stance on the nature of the gods, Heathens typically expect one another to adhere to principles of right action in regard to their tribal group, and to limit the introduction of foreign practices. Yet spiritual expression can be decidedly personal. For some Heathens, daily practice is limited to wearing a hammer pendant or chatting on Facebook with Heathen buddies. For others, it involves complex daily rituals, morning and evening meditation, or food and drink offerings to the land spirits, house *wights,* or gods. For Sunna and her family, daily practice involves a combination of poems and interpretive rituals beginning with "greeting the divine." Sunna's young daughter began to open each day by greeting the trees, a practice that her parents amended with the prayer spoken in *Sigrdrífumál:*

> We do this together every morning. We each take turns reciting what we have put together and then adding whatever is moving the person for that day. We recite, "Hail to Day / Hail to the Sons of Day / Hail to Night and her Daughters / Hail the Aesir and the Vanir / The Alfar and the Disir / The Vaettir of this land / The Elves and the Dwarves / And the All giving Earth / Watch us this day and see us as ones who are Tru / Guide us on our path and protect our family.[39]

In addition to larger philosophical and socioreligious worldview construction, Heathens have a proclivity to engage in anachronistic hobbies or enterprises. In my 2012 survey, 60 percent of Heathens said that they practiced a "Heathen hobby." They brewed, blacksmithed, carved wood, cast jewelry, spun wool, wove, embroidered, kept bees, engaged in storytelling, and wrote skaldic poetry, among other pursuits. They often did so while reflecting on their connection to the gods and their real (or imagined) ancestors, experiencing their faith through being in the moment with their projects. At Heathen gatherings, workshops about brewing—beer and ale, with an emphasis on mead—seem to be a requirement for the schedulers. Every regional gathering I have attended has seemed to include a veritable gauntlet of drinking horns, offered up by strangers and friends alike as samples and boasts of the giver's brewing skills. Mark Anderson, a home brewer from New England, believes that in addition to providing a feeling of connection to the past, home brewing is a powerful way to experience community. At a regional gathering, he was struck by the variety and quality of home brews, as he reported in *Odroerir:*

> There seemed to be a real sense of pride in this homemade beer and mead, not only by the individual brewers, but by the community as a whole. . . . Folks were very hospitable when it came to sharing their beer and mead. It was as if a significant part of the pleasure derived from brewing and mead making came from sharing it with other Heathens and the socializing/bonding that went along with it. . . . Home brewing is an integral part of our culture and highly valued by the Heathen community. Becoming a proficient home brewer is one way that an individual can gain a good reputation.[40]

Earning a reputation as a proficient home brewer within the local or regional community is one way in which Heathens, in a spiritual sense, gain renown and *luck*. At one gathering alone, my first hour consisted of unsolicited samplings of meads flavored with strawberries, chocolate, lavender, raspberries, and a variety of flavored ales with promises that bacon-flavored liquor was in the making. Other Heathens focus on reconstructing ancient methods and recipes for baking. Linzie, for example, writes in closing his introduction to *Odroerir*:

> Shortly, I'll leave here and go home to eat a sandwich of homemade Leberkaes, and homemade mustard on homemade sourdough bread— I'll be participating in my own cultural heritage, the fruits of my research. Perhaps after that I'll knock off a few tunes on the old dulcimer knowing that I am actively contributing to my cultural heritage which extends all the way back in the archaeological record to the faint beginnings of germanicity.[41]

At one gathering, I lay awake in the dark of my tent late at night, kept up by the banging of a hammer on an anvil, the clank, clank, clank emanating from the smithy-on-wheels assembled next to my camp. Other workshops related to crafts commonly seen at Renaissance festivals keep Heathens engaged in activities that the Old Norse or ancient Germans practiced out of necessity. To Heathens, however, these exercises take on a spiritual component. They are a way of honoring the ancestors through imagined ties to their daily activity by transforming profane hobbies into sacred callings.

Heathen Fluff: Contested Realms of Authenticity

The movement toward a more staunch reconstructionist approach in American Heathenry leads to struggles over what is or is not authentic or legitimate Heathenry. Throughout the debate Heathens argue about the nature of deity, regarding concepts of gods, mysticism, and spirituality influenced by New Age movements as "Neo-Heathenry," a less-than-authentic version of Heathen practice that contributes little to the advancement of historical "truth." Beneath the surface, the marking of Neo-Heathenry as inauthentic, fake, and Wiccan dominates Heathen discourse and veils the politically coded claims made by each side. To reconstructionists, the terms *Wiccatru* and *Neo-Heathen* are meant as derogatory accusations of inherent poseurism and, worse, of liberal New Age politics. Furthermore, the reconstructionist discourse surrounding American Heathenry as ethnic, as traditional, and as rooted in a darker, more ancient and primal worldview is a cover for a general conservative antipathy toward political or religious progressivism. Even among groups that do not self-identify as reconstructionist, this bristling at liberalism is the mainstay of Heathen politics. In the Midwest, for example, at a large regional event, vegetarianism provided no end of fodder for jokes, jabs, and commentary stereotyping liberals. Although such identity politics undoubtedly intersect with experiences of social class and various forms of cultural capital, among many Heathens, liberal identity markers are in direct contrast with authentic Heathenry. Political beliefs frame the distrust of Neopaganism in many ways, but the stereotyping of Neopaganism is at the heart of the struggle for Heathens trying to create wholly Heathen beliefs and practices.

As Bil Linzie remarks, the influence of Neopaganism and popular culture on Heathen reconstruction did little to aid in its historical accuracy. By the mid-1990s, "there were a number of Heathen 'customs' which had become accepted as historical fact." For example,

> The Hammer Rite, the eight-fold calendar, rune-casting/reading, seidr as neo-shamanism, the pop-American form of reincarnation, old-souls, walk-ins, even UFOs. Nigel Pennick had published his book on runic astrology and everyone else seemed to be jumping onto the bandwagon.... Back in '95, modern Heathenry looked no more like historical Heathenry than did Catholicism, Wicca, or Buddhism. At the time, creating elaborate rites had become far more important than historical fact. Both common sense and historical fact had become a burden to creativity.[42]

Influenced heavily by community politics and a popular distaste for anything Wiccan, Heathen opinion regarding borrowed material leads to comments like this, posted on a blog: "So today we mostly have Wiccatru instead of Ásatrú, following a Wicca sun circle that has nothing to do with the Germanic lore at all."[43] Other reconstructionist groups face the same struggles. Within Kemeticism (Egyptian reconstructionism), practitioners face patterns of infighting—like Kathryn Fox's subjects in her classic article "Real Punks and Pretenders"[44]— over who is doing it right. In "Kemeticism Is like a Fandom," Devo notes, "Recons hate the fluff. Everyone dislikes eclectics. Someone will judge you because you're Kemetic Orthodox, which obviously means you're a mindless drone. If you're not posting two pages of sources for each of your points, you're obviously not hardcore enough to have any say in the matter."[45] Writing for *Imbolc Magazine,* David Thorne argues that Celtic reconstructionism "began partly as a reaction to the populist approaches to Celtic Spirituality such as Celtic Wicca and Celtic Shamanism [sic], which seek to put a Celtic veneer on essentially non-Celtic religious and cultural practices." Like reconstructionist Heathens, Celtic "Reconstructionists have gained a somewhat unfair reputation for being anti-Wicca due to their insistence that Celtic spirituality should be rooted in [Celtic] culture, rather than grafted on to practices and beliefs from outside the culture." According to Thorne, "CR is not opposed to Wicca per se. However, our insistence on authenticity in our practices and critical attitude toward cultural misappropriation has on occasion led to dissent among those who see our position as a judgment on the worth of more eclectic spiritual practices."[46] Yet, as I discuss in Chapter 5, the "othering" of Wiccans is symbolic in other ways, connected to issues of gender, power, and political identity.

During Heathenry's early years, historical scholarship on Old Norse or ancient Germanic tribal practices was limited to the basics: Tacitus, Bede, the Icelandic sagas, and other manuscripts recorded by Christians or outsiders to ancient Heathen customs. The common denominator for the original sources of Eddic poems and other Icelandic texts is oral tradition. "As many scholars have stressed, oral tradition is both changeable and rich in variation. An extant text is therefore just one possible variant of a narrative," rendering all sources of Heathen reconstruction historical fiction and further complicating Heathen interpretations of Old Norse literature.[47] The details of how to do Heathenry were extrapolated from these same limited sources, a fragment of the available scholarship on the subject, which, until recently, remained untranslated and inaccessible. Adherents coming out of Wicca, Christianity, or both, often with an eye on the indigenous ritual practice of Native Americans, felt the need to develop equivalent rituals to demarcate the sacred from the profane. Others, influenced by Wicca and ceremonial magic, reenchanted the runes and used them as a system of divination. Other practices evolved with limited or no adherence to historical fact.

The mystical practices under the Heathen umbrella provoked skepticism from reconstructionists and others who remained suspicious of the Wiccan—and therefore feminine, liberal, and less authentic—influence. The history, performance, and influence of these practices, viewed by some as questionable at best, provide insight into how Heathens negotiate the myriad details of legitimacy and collective identity. Others, like Steven Abell, writing for the religion blog *Patheos,* critique reconstructionist methods, arguing that "the problem with the Hard Recon position is that there really isn't much to go on. When putting together a shared ritual for a Heathen gathering, what is there to do? And is that enough?"[48] Those who focus on reconstructionist methods are well aware of the criticism. In Josh and Cat Heath's interview for Karl Seigfried's blog, Cat Heath expresses her concerns:

> Reconstructionist Heathenry is very misunderstood, and—as someone that's often associated with it—I tend to find myself having certain "accusations" leveled at me. Most of the time, these center around how we're all apparently "soulless" and just slavishly following what them there dusty old books say, that we apparently don't have any of that UPG [Unverified Personal Gnosis, or mystical experience] stuff, and that we're all mean and intolerant.[49]

To many Heathens, whose entrée into American Heathenry often comes through Wicca, adapting Wiccan rituals to fit Heathen purposes is a simple solution. As Heathens grow increasingly critical of inauthentic practices, cultural appropriation becomes anathema, and Wicca becomes synonymous with fake faith, despite the stark variety of Wiccans and their own internal conflict between traditionalists and eclectics over issues of authenticity.[50] To eclectic Pagans whose faiths are influenced heavily by romanticism, Heathenry and other reconstructionist faiths seem inflexible and judgmental. According to the pagan blogger Wyrdwulf, reconstructionist "historic-rooted religions . . . often find themselves at odds with the majority Pagans over many seemingly separate issues," namely, theories of "romanticism and truisms." Because of reconstructionists' focus on "historic precedent," she argues, "these religions have structure, hierarchy, ethics and values. These structures may allow for personal experience and inspiration, but they are not as wide-open as the less-structured neo-romantic Paganism" and are thus a turnoff to many eclectic pagans because reconstructionism seems dogmatic and overly structured.[51]

The Hammer Rite: (In)Authenticity and Community Practice

An ever-present practice among Heathens, the hammer rite, developed by Stephen McNallen and Stephen Grundy, marks the beginning of ritual and consecrates sacred space. Wiccans cast a circle by raising energy through dance, sexual activity (real or symbolic), or chanting.[52] Heathen ritual openings typically lack such high drama or attention to "energies." During a Heathen rite, the designated leader begins to circle the sacred space with a hammer. For many, this takes the form of a short-handled sledgehammer inscribed with runes. Throughout the lore, Thor uses his hammer to protect the gods from destructive forces (Jotuns). Historically, the hammer was used to bless a bride on her wedding day.[53] In this way, it symbolizes protection, strength, and fertility to modern Heathens. The aesthetic of the ritual serves a principal sociopsychological function, to mark the ritual as sacred and holy and, in the Heathen mind, to call on the favor of the gods and *wights*. Holding the hammer aloft to the north, the leader invokes it, often in English, but frequently in broken Old Norse:

Hammer i Nordri	*(Hammer in the North)*
Helga ve' thetta ok	*(Make holy this ve' [holy space])*
Hindra Alla Ilska	*(Stop all harm)*

After proceeding to the east, the south, and the west and, in some cases, above and below, the ritual leader places the hammer on an altar, and the *blót* continues. I have witnessed this practice performed across the country at gatherings ranging from small *blóts* in people's living rooms to large regional events. On one such occasion on a sunny spring afternoon in the southern United States, I looked on with other Heathens as a *Gothi* from a neighboring kindred officiated the rite. Lifting aloft a giant hammer, constructed from a foot-long section of wooden two-by-four, capped with bolted metal plates on a thick, leather-wrapped handle painted with runes, he consecrated the four directions. The object, obtrusive because of its size, drew the attention of a Heathen elder nearby. With a straight face, she leaned over and whispered to me. As the *Gothi* shouted his booming invocation, she explained that the giant hammer and the myriad Heathen-themed accessories worn by U.S. Heathens are examples of the pomp and circumstance that strike some Scandinavian Heathens as odd and perhaps a little embarrassing in their ostentation. To her, whose connection to Heathenry is a product of her focus on her Norwegian heritage and the folk traditions taught to her by her grandmother, the ritual seemed like playacting and high drama. Other Heathens with Icelandic friends report the same sentiment.

Past analysis of sacred space, particularly in the works of Émile Durkheim and Mircea Eliade, has marked clear distinctions between the sacred and the profane. For Wiccans, a casting of a sacred circle is a complex ritual that demarcates mundane everyday space through the creation of a holy, clearly bound, and actively visualized globe of spiritual energy. To Heathens, the spiritual boundaries are less clearly delineated. Like Wiccans, Heathens practice religious ecology, which takes account of the natural world as part of, not separate from, the gods and *wights*. Although the ritual itself partly reflects Wiccan practice, it differs in that "one doesn't create an inside and outside, or even a 'ritual geometric shape.'" Rather, "The purpose of a Hammer Rite is to establish that a given 'space' is being used for ritual. It's the recognition that we're calling upon the gods and goddesses to be with us, as we exercise our will upon the universe."[54]

In the early years of the twenty-first century, Heathens began to take issue with this rite and other practices that were not attested in historical sources. Some Heathens have taken to hallowing an area by bearing a flame around its perimeter, citing the practice as historically verified in passages in *Landnamabok* and *Eyrbyggja Saga,* both Christian works of historical fiction. According to Wednesbury Theod, the lore offers multiple means of establishing sacred space: "1) Symbols placed around the area. 2) The building of fires at certain points and the erection of some symbol. 3) Circling the area with fire. 4) Use of ropes called in Old Norse *vébond,* tied to hazel poles called in Old Norse *höslur*."[55] In his early piece on Germanic spirituality, Bil Linzie offers a detailed alternative to the hammer rite reflective of Wednesbury Theod's first option, involving boundary markers and a declaration of purpose stated by the ritual officiant, followed by an announcement of special protocols and the punishments for not abiding by them. Once the officiant announces the declaration of purpose, those present agree (or leave if they do not) and light a fire, and the rite begins. In this way, participants mark the space set aside for ritual as inside the community by group law rather than by a mystical process.

The Nine Noble Virtues: Authenticity and Community Norms

Heathens cite the motto "We are our deeds" to explain how Heathens are to be judged by their community and descendants, adhering to the principles of right action. In many cases they also use it to excuse political ideologies perceived as potentially problematic. If Heathens judge an actor by her deeds, they are not as concerned with her thoughts or personal politics as long as they do not manifest themselves in any dishonorable behavior. A majority of Heathens regard the Nine Noble Virtues (NNVs) as a list of guidelines, distilled from the values outlined in the *Hávamál,* an Eddic poem understood to be (the real or metaphorical) words of Odin on behavioral ethics, open to a listener's interpretation.

Heathens generally believe that the NNVs were gleaned from the *Eddas* and the sagas as the foundations of a good life. The NNVs were either codified in the 1970s by John Yeowell and John Gibbs-Bailey of the Odinic Rite or, in other belief, compiled by author Edred Thorsson during his time with the AFA.[56] Either way, the NNVs are an invention of modern Heathenry and an important component of the argument about what it means to be accepted as authentically Heathen. Leif explains:

> If people are going to identify themselves as Heathen in Ásatrú, I think that kind of takes a certain amount of responsibility as far as at least learning and somewhat living by the cultural aspects that go along with that. So what I mean by that is, just anybody who decides "Oh, I want to pray to Freyja" you know, out of the blue, I don't think that that necessarily makes you a Heathen, but if they want to pray to Freyja and adopt say, some of the cultural aspects or even the uh, you know, the Nine Noble Virtues or something like that, then I think that they might qualify as a Heathen or Ásatrúar.[57]

Although there is no officially agreed-on list, the NNVs are generally listed as courage, honor, truth, fidelity, self-discipline, hospitality, industriousness, perseverance, and self-reliance.[58] Heathens have argued for the NNVs as a list of genuinely Heathen behavioral ethics and aspirations, but they are decidedly WASP. As Erik explains, " 'Virtue' would have been totally alien to the Old Norse, and 'truth' is only what Odin needs it to be at any given moment. Ditto for 'honor,' 'fidelity'—um. Mistresses? Slave-girl rape? Affairs? C'mon, now. Industriousness, perserverance and self-reliance? Thank you, Ayn Rand."[59] One of the original lists, published by the Odinist Committee, founded in 1972, was referred to as the "Nine Charges":

1. To maintain candour and fidelity in love and devotion to the tried friend: though he strike me I will do him no scathe.
2. Never to make wrongsome oath: for great and grim is the reward for the breaking of plighted troth.
3. To deal not hardly with the humble and the lowly.
4. To remember the respect that is due to great age.
5. To suffer no evil to go unremedied and to fight against the enemies of Faith, Folk and Family: my foes I will fight in the field, nor will I stay to be burnt in my house.
6. To succour the friendless but to put no faith in the pledged word of a stranger people.
7. If I hear the fool's word of a drunken man I will strive not: for many a grief and the very death groweth from out such things.
8. To give kind heed to dead men: straw dead, sea dead or sword dead.

9. To abide by the enactments of lawful authority and to bear with courage the decrees of the Norns.[60]

Not all Heathens subscribe to this list, however. It is not lost on all Heathens that Odin broke the first two charges, Thor the third, almost all gods and humans the fourth, and there are accounts in the sagas where people choose to be burned in their halls rather than continue fighting. Some skeptics have interpreted "stranger people" as racially coded language. Josh Heath recalls his growing interest in reconstructionism during which he came to view the Nine Noble Virtues as a "pile of crap written down in a vain attempt to collate all of the different cultural norms from the Lore." He recalls that "practically every assumption I had regarding Heathen religious belief was called into question. The concept of Valhalla was thrown out and replaced with a non-dualist concept of afterlife in the grave mound. Rituals were done for a reason: to create a gifting relationship with the gods based on the concepts of *luck* and action."[61] Many reconstructionists argue that these virtues are a modern invention, unsupported in the historical or archaeological record. They criticize them as a Heathen version of the Ten Commandments and assert that concepts of morality among the Old Norse and Germanic tribes were less about individual integrity and more about community obligation.

Many Heathens, however, find encouragement and motivation in the Nine Noble Virtues, viewing them as a helpful guideline for right action and even as divinely inspired. To Brand, the NNVs are a daily practice, involving "noble deeds, right action, and good intent." They function as a moral code, giving him comfort in "knowing that you're doing the right thing for whatever reason it is."[62] To recons, such sentiment is beside the point, and morality is a Christian invention; only what matters for the good of one's tribe defines right action.

The Loki Debate

Everyone agrees that there was never any cult of Loki. —JOHN LINDOW

There is no evidence of [Loki's] worship among men. —H. R. ELLIS DAVIDSON

[Loki] had no discernable place in pagan religion. —CHRISTOPHER ABRAM

There is nothing to suggest that Loki was ever worshipped.
—E.O.G. TURVILLE-PETRE

There was no cult of Loki, and place-names based on his name are equally unknown. —RUDOLF SIMEK

Snorri's effort to produce a list of thirteen Æsir, of whom one [Loki] was to prove a traitor, looks suspiciously like an attempt to align the Æsir with the disciples of Christ. —ANDY ORCHARD[63]

Before we were to enjoy the gifting, camaraderie, and public cementing of alliances among kindreds at *High Sumbel* into the wee hours of the morning, the chieftain outlined the rules of conduct. There were over two hundred of us from different kindreds and areas of origin, with unique *thew*. Cementing general expectations of conduct is a necessity at gatherings of such diverse groups because it lays down the law of the hall for those present to avoid awkwardness or inadvertent insults. As he stood at the front of the hall, our chatter drawing to a close, he explained that, as a rule, "there will be no hailing of Laufeyson or baleful *wights*" during our collective rituals. Laufeyson, a moniker of Loki, is reviled by many and worshipped by some. A son of giants, he plays a major role in surviving Norse myths from the *Prose Edda* and the *Poetic Edda*. Like all Old Norse literature, the stories involving Loki were written after conversion, when Christians and Heathens interacted. To scholars of Old Norse religion, the potential Christian origin of Loki as a devil figure inserted into Heathen lore muddies our contemporary understanding and sheds doubt on Loki's status as a god among ancient Heathens. In the lore, Loki's deeds often bring about the misery and devastation of the gods, and in the end, he leads the forces of evil into the final battle of Ragnarok. On *Tumblr*, Lokavinr, one of many Lokean bloggers, summarizes the debate, noting that the arguments against Loki worship generally involve the following statements: "Worshiping Loki is wrong because He defied the Gods and will fight against Them at Ragnarok. His children will be responsible for the deaths of Odin and Thor, and the chaotic energies He manifests are in direct opposition to the order established by the Gods. Besides, there is no historical precedence for worshiping Loki!!!"[64]

One of the most contentious debates among Heathens, the Loki worship quandary is another fault line along which Heathens construct and reinterpret legitimacy and authenticity throughout the United States. To some, it is a tired, pointless argument akin to the folkish versus universalist debate (explained further in Chapter 6) that involves historical arguments about the legitimacy or existence of a Loki cult, various images of Loki in the Heathen imagination, the problematic transformation of Loki into a pop cultural antihero thanks to Marvel's *Thor* films, and caricatured stereotypes of his contemporary followers. At Trothmoot in 2013, a group of attendees held an unofficial after-hours *faining* to Loki in partial protest of the restrictions against hailing him during public *blót* I had heard similar warnings announced as official rules at other gatherings; at some gatherings the rules had been unofficial but generally understood. After the event, the debate continued online and in *Idunna*, The Troth's main publication, enflaming feelings on both sides. To many, the idea of worshipping a "baleful *wight*" conjures up troublesome images laden with symbolic and political baggage of those for whom Loki is a sacred figure. The arguments against Loki worship and those who practice it are deeply rooted in a wider social context. Opponents construct Lokeans as miscreant youths, labeling them "emo" mall Goths and stereotyping them as effeminate if they are men and as needy attention whores if they are women. The feminization of Lokeans leads to a devaluation of their experiences and renders acceptable a discriminatory attitude toward anyone who self-identifies as a fan, follower, or, even worse, worshipper of Loki. Opponents associate Lokeans with perceived illegitimate Neopagan eclectic practices and liberal political views on sexuality, and therefore with loose morality and lack of character. The image of "the Lokean" constructed as a pastiche of unfavorable qualities and stereotypes contradicts the masculine conservative image of the historically minded upstanding Heathen, akin to the images of propriety and high morality among Evangelicals.

In addition to arguments about historical inaccuracy, stereotypes of Loki worshippers constructed by opponents contain both political and cultural messages about proper Heathen behavior that exist in a complex relationship with conservative ideas of proper decorum. Opponents characterize worshippers of Loki as morally ambiguous, self-centered, and sexually deviant, an image parallel with that of the teenage delinquent up to no good. Heathens often interpret Loki worship as Heathenry's Satanism—the worship of a deity whose actions are deemed by many to be selfish and destructive. The resulting stereotypes of Lokeans label them as attention-seeking, overdramatic, emo kids—a bunch of bondage-pants-wearing mall Goths whining about being outcasts to buck the establishment to impress their friends. In a days-long Facebook conversation regarding Loki worship, Evan referred to Lokeans as "attention seekers, claiming emo god 'chose' their lameass and demanding 'validation' from a community intent on reconstructing Heathen religion." Randall recalled that he had "unfortunately met too many Lokeans who act very much like Satanists and treat it as though they are powerful beings who can invoke their wills over others." To Tim, Lokeans worship the outcast deity because they themselves feel outcast from society. He argued, "If you seek community or belonging; find it, make your place in the world by great deeds," suggesting that Lokeans are derisive noncontributors. Richard summarized a general stereotype with sarcasm and mean-girl teasing, arguing that Lokeans are "like the Heathen version of Satanists," who are rebelling for show against "all the big, bad and uncomprehensive bearded grown-ups who cant understand how deep, dark, mod and twilight-esque Loki is."[65]

The slights about Lokeans' maturity with a reference to *Twilight,* a series of novels and films about teenage vampires, popular in 2011–2012 among women and tweens, feminize and infantilize Lokeans, discrediting them as childish and inauthentic. In the lore, Loki provides an avenue for gender-bending and sexual transgression, in one story shape-shifting into a mare to attract the attention of a stallion. To adherents of Loki whose own experiences with sexuality are flexible or contradictory to heterocentric cultural expectations, Loki provides an avenue for sexual self-expression and identity work, attractive to many Heathens who identify as lesbian, gay, bisexual, transgendered or queer/questioning (LGBTQ). To others, the sexual ambiguity and Loki's popularity among what some derisively refer to as "fangirls" indicates a transgression of masculinity, a feminization of a deity and his followers. Such feminization is a common technique used by conservatives since the 1970s to disparage people, beliefs, behaviors, or material culture, echoing a greater societal fear about waning male privilege (discussed further in Chapter 5).

Patron Deities and Spiritual Seekers

As part of the debate, arguments concerning the nature of the gods and the desire to form a personal relationship with one or more deities receive a fair amount of consideration. To some, developing a personal relationship with gods one feels called to worship is a powerful spiritual experience that provides connectedness and meaning. To Elizabeth, a Pagan blogger, communications with Loki are inspiring and provide a loving relationship that keeps her grounded:

> Early in my acquaintance with Him, Loki told me never to accept anybody else's opinions without question—not even His. Loki is all about being true to yourself despite what other people think or say. But that doesn't mean that you can't let anybody else know your point of view, if only to remind them that there are *always* several sides to every story, and that seldom does it simply boil down to good versus evil. I don't think I've been able to see things through Loki's eyes because He wants me to unquestioningly accept what He does or says, or to dislike the Aesir, or to swan around as if I were some kind of prophet. I think it's been in the interest of showing me another aspect to the tales so often told about Him, and to allow me to make up my own mind about things. And after all, gods want us to understand Their points of view, too, especially when They love us and we love Them.[66]

To others, the idea of a personal relationship sparks ire as the vestige of a Christian desire to develop a connection with Jesus, expressed in Elizabeth's claim that the gods "love us and we love Them." Some Heathens claim that the notion of a personal relationship was not of interest or use to ancient Germanic people, or, as David explains it, was "not a part of normative Heathenry."[67] According to Erik, the lawspeaker of Runatyr Kindred:

> Heathenry is a worldview that espouses the public cult of gods. It does not, nor has it advocated a personal relationship with a god. Men and women were expected to bring their offerings to the community leader/ *Gothi* to impart those gifts upon the god(s). This leader may have had a close relationship with the god(s), but only in the capacity that he fulfills a public office on behalf of the folk. If said leader had no folk who trusted in his/her abilities to ensure a favorable treatment by the gods, he would have no close contact with the gods. Or he would, but only due to his sacrifice by the folk. Modern Heathens may be aspiring to foster a close knit relationship with a holy power, this has been called *fulltrui*.[68]

The ubiquity of patron gods among practitioners of American Heathenry points to a parallel with patron saints or a reworking of a spiritual connection to deity encouraged by Abrahamic faiths. Many Heathens take on supposedly Heathen names drawn from Old Norse, Scandinavian, or German languages or the lore, often as indications of their patron loyalties. To many Heathens, identifying a member as a "Thorsman" or "Odinsman" (or woman, although *Thorswoman* is a less common term) signals particular behavioral and philosophic expectations. Early in the day at a summer gathering, Tom, a thirty-something father of two, shakes my hand and introduces himself. He is wearing two Irminsul necklaces and a patch with a Tiwaz rune. By doing so, he has marked himself as a Tyrsman dedicated to the god of justice, law, and war. According to the *Prose Edda* and the *Poetic Edda,* Tyr, known for his great wisdom and courage, was the sole god to agree to the demands of the wolf Fenris, an enemy of the gods and one of Loki's children. He stepped forward to place his hand in the wolf's mouth as the gods bound the animal in fetters, after which, struggling against his dwarf-forged bindings and failing to break free, Fenris bit off Tyr's hand. To Tom, there is a difference between being a devotee of a god and merely being an appreciator. When I inquire about the difference, he seems frustrated or impassioned, I find it difficult to distinguish which, as he remarks with a sharp tone that people who are "devotees" of a deity must aspire to emulate the god's most unique qualities. "Appreciators," by contrast, are religious bystandars. As a Tyrsman, he tells me, he aspires to uphold what is just for his interpretation of "the greater good." He practices martial arts and unwavering honesty and always aspires to do what he feels is "right." He confronts me, "Who is your patron?" Flustered, I stutter, "Um . . ." Until this moment, I had never been obligated to choose a patron. Among this community in the Deep South, and in many throughout the country, patron deities are the norm. I feel obligated to keep up. I tell him that I am drawn to Tyr as well, although my interpretation of the term *justice* seems less martial and more humanitarian. Tom seems unsatisfied with my answer and asks me if I practice a martial art, because any devotee of the god of war should be trained in combat. "I have done some archery, in the past," I say, lamely. Tom, bedecked in runes and Tyr symbolism, is not impressed. To him, my status as a devotee is doubtful.

To Heathens, the devotee role or taking on a patron requires not just a greater understanding of a deity but a close personal relationship, often involving regular offerings to and communication with a particular deity. Some reconstructionists are uncomfortable with this trend, however omnipresent it may be among their peers. To David, "The very idea of a personal relationship with a god was not a part of normative Heathenry." Nor is honoring Loki, because, like Shiva, he "brings balance," adding disorder to an ordered universe, a common defense among Lokeans who believe that Loki represents the yang to the gods' yin. "This is the issue I have with 'Lokeans,'" David argues. "It is not worshipping Loki. It is the misrepresentation of personal beliefs, largely grounded in neopaganism, as being Heathen. It is their demand to be included in the Heathen fold, while insisting that those Neopagan beliefs not be subjected to historical evidence."[69] To David and others, this is the crux of the matter—Loki worship represents to them the impure influence of New Age sensibilities about a personal spiritual journey and UPG adapted to modern times, yet divorced from historical accuracy. During the same trip to the southern United States in which I was introduced to Tom, I met a kindred of college-aged youths—locals who had regular interaction with other area kindreds. As an outsider, I noted with interest that one of the members, Daniel, a young man in his early twenties, seemed to delight in making mischief. As he tended the campfire, he razzed his kindred, joking back and forth about his love of fire, both creating it and controlling it—a boon in his job as a firefighter. As he continued his playful interaction from the fireside, his kinsmen offered perspective by referring to Daniel as a Lokean. To this particular community, uninvolved in ongoing online debates and identity politics, hanging out with a Lokean was no big deal. The association of Loki with fire is not uncommon in modern Heathenry. It is taken from a theory advanced by linguist and folklorist Jacob Grimm, who labeled Loki the god of fire, like Prometheus; his theory was later popularized by Richard Wagner's interpretation of Loki (Loge) in *The Ring Cycle*. Yet both lay scholars and academics alike have contested this theory, noting that his association with fire is a Christian intervention, a misunderstanding as Loki became conflated with Logi, a fire-giant, and Christianity imposed on Loki a trickster label, rendering him the equivalent of a demon. To Daniel, however, the textual details of Loki's many narrative appearances or their historical accuracy is irrelevant because his own identities and self-presentation as fire enthusiast, trickster, and (therefore) a Lokean achieve coherence. In her blog, Hyrokkin expresses the meaning of her relationship with Loki:

> I am a child of Loki's. He is father, lover, teacher, warrior, and friend. I have heard much said on Loki, the vast majority being extremely negative. How glad I am that I do not take Lore as the ultimate authority! To say that Loki is "merely misunderstood" is a trite cliche. Loki is the bridge to understanding, the missing key, so to speak. Loki is the Trickster. His actions cannot be viewed in the same context in which the human mind operates. Lore is paradigm, not literal. To take it out of context and interpret it in a literal fashion completely negates it's purpose.[70]

To Hyrokkin, the lore is not the "ultimate authority" but a "paradigm" that should not restrict freedom of creativity or innovation in spiritual endeavors. To Josh Rood and others, Lokeans are "personal spiritual journeyseekers" incompatible with historically minded reconstructionism. Rather, Rood believes, Lokeans "only care about what feels good at the moment."[71] To Liz, however, a relationship with a deity is something external to historical reconstructionism. It is deeply personal, meaningful, and life changing. She recalls:

Loki also once told me that truth, like love, is a many-splendored thing, and no one has exclusive rights to it. So whether or not the things I've seen and heard from Loki over the years are "true" or not doesn't matter to me—what matters is that, because of His guidance, I have been learning how to be fair and compassionate, in a world that generally encourages neither. And that, to me, is as valuable as the understanding that seeing through Loki's eyes has brought.[72]

Another Lokean blogger with the moniker Raven argues against the restrictions of reconstructionism, reminding her readers that the lore is Christian work and therefore unreliable, and that innovation is a driving force in keeping religion alive and growing. To reconstructionists, she asks:

In Heathenry, How can you find knowledge if you stop seeking it? How can you learn information if you spend your life shutting doors? One of the many reasons Loki is so profoundly rejected, misunderstood, and hated is because of his outright refusal to stop seeing all creatures, beings, and realms and resources and would not care about others' "value judgments" upon them. You never know who has useful information, you never learn the secrets of places you never visit, and having allies among every sort of person, although it may offend the sensibilities or prejudices of some, seems much more hospitable and wise than closing doors based on the thoughts/feelings/experiences of others that yourself have not witnessed.[73]

The struggle that Raven outlines, between perceived tradition and the threat of progress, is not new. It is the driving force of religious and political conflict worldwide. Reconstructionist Paganisms, however, are in a unique position to define, in real time, the beliefs and practices that fall into either category. As they do so, those that are agreed on as rooted in historical practice or the lore are lauded as pure and authentic, while other practices, including Raven's sentimentality and urge to seek knowledge through innovation, risk being labeled as what many call "MUS" (made-up shit).

Other debates regarding the authenticity and the legitimacy of Heathen belief crop up throughout the online blogosphere. Heathens continue to argue, for example, whether the use of runes for divination or mystical interpretation is supported by the archaeological record, or whether runes were simply a system of alphabet. Whatever the argument, it is clear that American Heathenry is becoming both more historically minded, less cohesive, and increasingly embattled as elements once taken for granted are criticized as inauthentic. The divisions between those for whom Heathenry is dynamic, fluid, and not afraid of New Age or foreign spiritual influence and those for whom these influences are anathema to the growing challenge of maintaining authenticity become increasingly bitter, and American Heathenry becomes more and more a battle-ground. Rather than fostering a growing sense of solidarity, such identity wars have led to battles, bullying, name-calling, and "dick wagging," as some Heathens have called it, primarily online, where our lives are increasingly rooted. From the ashes of such mayhem, however, rises the occasional tribe or regional effort that develops meaningful and cohesive relationships in the flesh.

4

Cyber *Hofs* and Armchair Vikings

Building Community through Social Networks
(but Not without Problems)

In the dark and cold, a group of Heathens leave a cramped government-subsidized apartment on the outskirts of a liberal metropolitan town. They cross the street to an undeveloped grassy lot with a large tree to ask the god Tyr to bless various personal items they have brought with them. They are following instructions given to them via a Yahoo! group organized by the acting *Gothi,* a large, soft-spoken man in his late thirties with a full beard and long hair. Some bring swords; others, necklaces and various trinkets from home. They stand quietly in a circle as the *Gothi* pours the mead, using ritual items carted to the site from his apartment in his six-year-old daughter's red wagon. Cars whiz by on the busy road fifty feet away. The participants in this ritual barely know one another; they are acquaintances at best, and their obligations to one another are only to maintain *grith,* a truce among strangers. Despite the awkward unfamiliarity with one another, they speak of "the community," of "having a community" and the warm fuzzy feelings of camaraderie, support, and likeness. Once the ritual is over and they go home, most of them will not speak to one another again except online or on the occasion of another get-together at the small apartment across the street, maybe in a month or two.

Elsewhere, in Colorado on a warm summer day, a group of Heathens meet with members of their kindred with whom they have shared years of holidays, inside jokes, meals, and personal hardships. The home, a small house in a working-class neighborhood, hosts the kindred in its spacious backyard. Behind the cracked pavement and the detached garage, they have decorated a grassy area with a *blót* circle marked with white stones, erecting rune staves at its four quarters. They gather to celebrate their families and children at a "kinder *blót*" announced via Facebook. The adults have prepared Heathen-themed activities for the kids: decorating glass jars for offerings to land spirits, an obstacle course with an apple-bobbing barrel, and a "mountain" with a troll in it, built from a stack of hay bales with a kindred member hidden inside. As the children climb the mountain, he bellows loudly and shakes the bales, inducing delighted shrieks and laughter. They have all known one another for years, have taken oaths of loyalty to one another, and maintain *frith* (a term used to denote diplomatic, amicable, nonaggressive interaction) and good spirits through camaraderie and obligation.

A day's drive away in the Midwest, over 200 Heathens gather to cement bonds of community, reinvigorate their Heathen identities, and join together in spiritual expression. The annual event, posted on a website and announced via Facebook, requires a registration fee on site or submitted via a PayPal link to the event's host. Heathen groups gather from around the country, from Texas to Tennessee, from Mississippi to Minnesota. These "tribes," as many call themselves, have, over the years, developed alliances—public announcements of formal responsibility to support and protect one another. Many of them visit one another regularly, attending to family milestones and holiday celebrations—naming ceremonies for newborns (see Figures 4.1 and 4.2). Ostara gatherings (to celebrate the spring equinox), and Yule celebrations. They foster one another's children for weeks at a time, assist one another when times are tough, and keep in touch via Facebook. Although those in attendance represent a variety of kindreds across the Midwest and beyond, they share their time and often meager wealth in the spirit of community and collective identity. They are aware of the events, scandals, personalities, and politics of other regional groups that they read about on Facebook, but such matters are of little consequence to the community that gathers at that campsite in September. In the United States, this event and these tribes represent the possibilities of strong regional community.

In each instance, Heathens share a variety of relationships and levels of intimacy and obligation to their fellows, building layer on layer a broader picture of American Heathenry on a national scale. In the mid-1990s, when I began to settle into my Heathen identity, information on my faith was difficult to find. I had never met another Heathen, and it did not occur to me that I might ever meet one. Before the digital revolution my access to information about Heathenry, like that of countless others, was limited to fliers, books, and talks given at metaphysical bookstores. In chain book stores the New Age shelf was, and still is, occupied by innumerable books instructing readers in the tactics, practices, and philosophies of witchcraft, Druidry, Satanism, and even UFOlogy. Until about 2005, however, books on Heathenry fell out of print almost as quickly as they were published. Only a handful of early works were available to Heathens—Freyja Asywnn's *Leaves of Yggdrasil* (1990), Edred Thorrson's *Book of Troth* (1992), and Kveldulf Gundarsson's *Teutonic Magic* (1995), to name a few—and they were scarce. Mostly, the idea of Heathenry and Heathens themselves existed in an ethereal, boundless place somewhere *out there*. Before smart phones, Facebook, or sites like Meetup.com, my first face-to-face encounters were

LEFT: **Figure 4.1.** A couple conducts a naming ceremony nine days after the birth of their son. The ceremony honors the infant, publicly announces the child's name to his tribe, and provides an occasion for gifting and celebration. (Photo by the author.)

RIGHT: **Figure 4.2.** At the naming ceremony, the parents erect a god pole, where guests can leave gifts for the family. (Photo by the author.)

arranged via e-mail from a contact I found on Irminsul.org's international contact map. In the early years of the twenty-first century—my initial time spent researching and communicating with other Heathens—most of the planning, organizing, keeping in touch, celebrating, schmoozing, politicking, arguing, and apologizing happened online in Yahoo! group forums set up for local, regional, and national Heathen organizations, which then evolved over a decade into daily interactions and keeping up-to-date on Facebook and Heathen blogs. I have come to know, and know about, people whom I have yet to meet; I receive notices about events that are real-life convergences of online friendships; and I watch groups dissolve and reassemble—all online. Other groups, formed in the flesh, use social networking to publicize and legitimize their groups, to share art and ideas, to debate and redraw community boundaries, and to plan events at which technology fades into the distance. I have been oathed into my own kindred by a Colorado *Gothi* at Lightning Across The Plains and have received the wisdom that the first way to legitimize and publicize my new kindred was to build a Facebook page and invite friends to like it. I have made brief acquaintanceships with people at live events that then blossomed into friendships online, and online relationships that graduated to face-to-face encounters over a horn of mead. The many effects that this communication technology has had on Heathenry as an NRM are varied, and other scholars have outlined the differences between "religion" that has gone online and "online religion," which exists mostly in its virtual form.[1]

Religion and Virtual Spaces

Communication technology has largely negated space and has created an environment for diffuse NRMs to proliferate in more than one location in a variety of forms. Over the past two decades, the scholarship on Internet studies has grown by leaps and bounds. The first wave of Internet studies in the 1990s "sought to describe the practices of life online and the blurring boundaries of online culture," asking questions related to the "who, what, where, and when" of online life.[2] These scholars struggled to define *community*, offering descriptive analysis of how online religion functions in particular religious traditions. Others have remarked that "discussions of the nature and impact of the new public space opened up by the internet . . . suggest that the emergence of the world wide web may be changing the conditions of new religious life in our societies in significant ways"[3] and have called for work that accounts for the impact of the Internet on the shape of NRMs. Second-wave Internet studies further considered how themes such as community and identity function online, exploring in depth concepts of involvement or attachment and the interconnectivity between online and offline realities. In the past decade, third-wave scholars have found that "Internet users conceptually and practically connect their online and offline social practices as part of their social lives, rather than these being separate or disconnected spheres." Vital to these analyses is investigating how online groups reveal the reshaping of traditional concepts of community, indicating more profound social shifts within society concerning the nature of community in general.[4]

In *Religion Online,* Lorne Dawson expresses skepticism about "romanticized notions of offline community" as well as the ability of the Internet to create authentic online community, labeling many online groups mere "pseudocommunities."[5] He questions whether pseudocommunities can create the sense of "we-ness" that flesh-and-blood offline groups are capable of constructing, and he calls for research that provides evidence that online experiences can indeed foster, as Brenda Brasher notes, a "shared interpretive context."[6] Earlier scholars, however, have argued that religion online might indeed come to dominate the religious landscape. In the 1990s there were relatively few websites with the capacity for dialogue and "community" interaction. Since then, user-generated media with expanded social capabilities have mushroomed on the Internet,[7] a development that demonstrates the prescience of earlier studies. The separation between online and offline has increasingly eroded as the Internet has become "seamlessly interwoven into the fabric of institutional and everyday life."[8] In studying Paganism on the Internet, a space he refers to as "Cyberhenge," Douglas E. Cowan concludes that modern Pagans are colonizing virtual spaces that "provide hitherto unavailable venues for the performance and instantiation of often marginalized religious identities," arguing that the very "architecture and philosophy" of the Internet supports Paganism.[9] He asserts, however, that the Internet has also become a venue for a "what feels right must be right" construction of religion by many Neopagan groups, which leads to the public perception that modern Paganism is nothing more than a caricature of itself.

Before the past decade, a search for information on Pagan religious groups would most likely have returned a variety of information on Wicca and other New Age spirituality groups and very little information on Ásatrú. Since then, the Internet has been central in organizing and disseminating information on the Heathen community to its own members and to new recruits searching for something else within the scope of Paganism. The Internet and other computer-mediated communication technologies are both products and producers of culture, intertwined in a reciprocal process of change and transformation. American Heathendom uses the Internet as its primary but spaceless location for meeting, organizing, politicking, and reinforcing norms and values. On the heels of message boards, social networking sites such as Twitter and Facebook have reorganized the way in which Pagandom proliferates, communicates, and advances. User-generated blogs and media sites such as YouTube and Wikipedia have fundamentally altered the way in which people share and gather information. Social networking has redefined *community,* a term some scholars have argued is a slippery slope, preferring the term *belonging* as more definitive and nuanced and better capturing the fluidity of online relations.[10] Communication technology is no longer an artifact bound by function but instead has become a symbolic venue for religious discourse. Like Denise Carter's participants from the virtual community she calls Cybertown,[11] my informants expressed the overlap between online and offline with mixtures of appreciation and dismay. Heathens form virtual relationships that they maintain much like offline friendships that become part of everyday life. Carter's participants used terms such as *online* and *offline* or *virtual* and *real* quite randomly. "Rather than suggesting a dichotomy between real and virtual, they were simply positional, differentiating between social places."[12] Online resources transform the community in face-to-face gatherings by providing members with a venue for informal introductions where relationships are formed on the basis of textual communication, unhindered by social and physical cues.[13]

In the three waves of Internet research, few scholars have offered an empirical account of the connection between how religious subjects experience and use the Internet in the context of spiritual belonging and how these experiences shape and influence the trajectory of the movements of which they are a part. How Heathens organized their activities took a dramatic turn from the early 1970s, when what is now the Ásatrú Folk Assembly began, to the 1990s and the first wave of Internet users. A blooming of organizations came and went as the power and increasing availability of the Internet rapidly changed the way in which Heathens coordinated their activities and kept in touch through virtual space, without the need for membership in a national organization.

The Influence of the Virtual on Modern Heathenry

Within the greater Pagan milieu, formal organizations provide bureaucratic structure and rationalization on an international scale. On a smaller and more personal level, Heathens form local tribes or kindreds—chosen or actual family groups that network together. Not all Heathens become members of a group or organization, however; many stay on the periphery of local tribes or maintain contact with, but lack commitment to, other Heathens nearby, forming diffuse groups. Those without access altogether, however, join others online, in forums and in the virtual *hofs* of social networking sites. According to the Pagan Census Revisited (2009–2010),[14] a majority of Pagans identify as solitary practitioners networking via the Internet, an increase in such numbers from the 1990s. Within American Heathenry and other Paganisms, formal organizations occupy the most highly structured and rationalized position, serving as a source of affiliation and allegiance and creating a sense of connectedness for Heathens across the globe. Until the popularity of social media, the dissemination of information through publications and the credentialing process through organizational membership or formal clergy training came solely under the purview of national organizations. These organizations have high visibility; the national and international community pays close attention to their affairs and scandals, and they assist in the creation and maintenance of organizational myths. Yet membership in these organizations constitutes a minority of overall participation in Heathenry. Less formal but more closely bound by oaths of kinship and allegiances, local groups (called *tribes, kindreds, garths,* or *hearths*) consist of intimate congregations with core group members sharing high levels of commitment to the group and to one another. Less formal and committed than local tribes, more diffuse groups offer members a place to worship or study. The members of these groups spend more time helping each other do the homework of Heathenry through workshops, study groups, or informal and intermittent rituals. Many work together to glean ethics and morals from the *Hávamál,* thumb through the *Eddas* to interpret and discuss Heathenry's theological underpinnings, and offer mentorship and support but have lower demands for commitment or kinship. Although blogs and social media influence each of these forms, they also provide a space for unaffiliated Heathens to find belonging, creating virtual *hofs* of Facebook groups and message boards. A *hof* can be a home, a freestanding building, or a courtyard in front of a home. Heathens use the term to refer to both tribal groups and physical temples dedicated to community and worship. These groups are the foundation of the movement, in which regional and local social networking introduces an arena for discussion, conflict, and the discursive construction and maintenance of Heathenry.

Formal Heathen Organizations: Politics and Bureaucracy

Formal Heathen organizations, like many nonprofit businesses, are stabilized by a structure that aims at efficiency, growth, and, increasingly, identity management. Their structures are emergent, their boundaries are shifting, and they are, to a certain extent, unstable, a fact illustrated by the tenuous nature of Heathen organizations in the United States and overseas. Although many Heathen organizations fail to last over time,[15] those that have done so remain essential to the distribution of resources and a sense of affiliation and unity for the national (and international) community. Organizations such as The Troth, the Ásatrú Folk Assembly, and the Ásatrú Alliance (AA) share similar aims: to manage Heathenry and make it more accessible through organizational means. They provide members with a sense of collective identity and acceptance, where members can share personal, spiritual experiences and political ideological ideals with like-minded others.

Like other religious groups, Heathen organizations use websites and Facebook profiles to provide outsiders an avenue through which to learn about Ásatrú.[16] Online, outsiders and prospective members have access to introductory pamphlets and contemporary essays, as well as reprints or reinterpretations of the lore. The Troth's website includes answers to basic questions for beginners, a list of bylaws, a calendar of events, and a list of online articles, in addition to links to its Amazon bookstore, where it sells books written by members for Troth publication. In addition to these resources, the AA's website includes a catalog of Heathen goods produced by its own World Tree Publications, as well as information on how to apply to the Internal Revenue Service for nonprofit status. The AFA's Stephen McNallen publishes a blog and a podcast in addition to regular Facebook posts that provide informative updates about the meaning behind rituals, snapshots of important history, the interpretation of rituals, and most often inspirational questions or comments designed to prompt discussion among members. Additionally, members communicate through publications such as The Troth's *Idunna* and the AA's *Vor Tru,* magazines sent to members and accessible to nonmembers for a fee. Members of the international Heathen community can submit their work to these magazines and exchange ideas with others via social networking sites or Yahoo! groups. These publications contain articles on history, lore, crafts, and herbalism; recipes; songs; and book and music reviews, as well as letters to the editor and regular columns about modern Heathen life.

Primarily, Heathen organizations provide an avenue for networking, the dissemination of political and spiritual ideas, and the expression of various types of expertise. To many, they offer an arena for building *gefrain,* or reputation, and the opportunity to attend annual events as a culmination of these efforts. Online and at organization-sponsored gatherings, Heathens regularly make ritual toasts to their organizations, indicating a high degree of organizational membership identity. The Troth, the AFA, and the AA are examples of a variety of national and international organizations. They have membership require-ments, bylaws, mission statements, organizational titles, duties, and a calendar of events of Heathen gatherings, holidays, or other social get-togethers. They are all-volunteer, and to a certain extent they operate to provide users with a central connectedness to the national community. They also provide users with profes-sional training. The most formal training available for Heathen clergy in the United States is offered by The Troth in the form of an online seminary available to all Troth members. As Heathens fight for acceptance in wider society through lobbying to include the hammer on military gravestones,[17] seeking tax-exempt status for their groups, and educating the often misinformed public, the clergy program provides a sense of internal legitimacy. Kell, a fifty-one-year-old machinist, explained to me that membership offers extra benefits.

> I feel like it gives a little bit—and this gets back into "what makes a reli-gion a valid religion" question—a little bit of validity, to say "okay, we're tied to a national group so it's not just a bunch of screwballs running around here holding up horns and hammers and playacting." You know, so people know we're a little bit more serious than that. People do look and say, "Well, what are your credentials?" You know, we're still at that level of society, so it's kind of nice to go "okay, I'm credentialed through—" or "our group is affiliated with—" so . . . is it necessary? No. Is it something that facilitates life? Sometimes.[18]

Most of the participants whom I have interviewed are, or have been, mem-bers of a national organization at one time or another. They mention their membership along with updates of official news, recollecting old scandals, and inquiring about upcoming events. Online and at gatherings they make ritual toasts to their organization, indicating an element of membership identity. When Heathen organizations hold internal meetings to discuss the future of the community, they do so with their own organization in mind. Troth business meetings, held at the annual Trothmoot, involve organizational discussions about Troth publications, funding, and the appointment of various officeholders and a real-time summary of quarterly business reports already submitted to members. There is also a period for new staff members to take their oaths of office on a large sterling silver oath ring held by the steersperson. The mood is at once that of professionalism and solemn ritualism. Yet despite the ritual performance that here and there disturbs the bureaucratic dust, the mechanism of organization grinds steadily and monopolizes a fair bit of the discourse of formal Heathen groups. Heathen organizations provide opportunities for networking, contrib-uting to organizational publications, and feeling integrated into a larger national community, but they are not attractive or available to all members. To nonmem-bers, the formality, the imposition of membership dues, and the size of national organizations can seem to have little impact on a local scale. More often, how-ever, the association of national Heathen organizations with a brand of political ideology is a turnoff. Organizational stereotyping contributes to an environment where members take on even stronger political identities in opposition to competitor organizations, exacerbating divisive relationships among groups, a trend seemingly made worse as the national political climate becomes increasingly enflamed.

The Troth is alleged, particularly by members of the AA and the AFA, to espouse liberal ideologies because of The Troth's mission of diversity and inclusivity and its admittance of dual-trad practitioners.[19] Although some members of The Troth hold dual membership in other organizations, many other members of The Troth perceive the AFA as a conservative, closed-minded cult of personality around AFA headman Stephen McNallen, notorious for denying or revoking the membership of people with whom he disagrees, a common topic of conversation at the gatherings that I have attended. Those who choose not to join an organization nonetheless know about organizational gossip, stereotypes, and affairs. The (mostly online) discourse that Heathens engage in surrounding the history of organizations functions to create and outline the community mythology and bind members to one another through a sense of belonging and collective identity that transcends the local. Many of my informants are, or have been, members of a national organization at one time or another, or if not, they are aware of these organizations, their activities, and the stereotypes that surround them and choose to join (or not) in part on the basis of the congruence of their personal political identifications and organizational values.

Both The Troth and the AFA offer members the opportunity to plug in through Facebook and e-mail lists where members communicate in real time and lay the groundwork for community identity and boundaries that get fleshed out more thoroughly via e-mail. The online discourse of these organizations provides ample evidence of their differing levels of engagement in political activism versus theological musings. The Troth maintains a private Facebook group where users can interact and post updates, a change from a public page in response to increased heckling and trolling of "outside instigators," presumed dissidents to The Troth's "liberal" label. Although most Troth updates are personal or theological questions or notes on upcoming events, the group forum offers members a space in which to establish covenantal rules and expectations. The AFA's Facebook page, set up as a public page with administrators and status updates written solely by the leadership, likewise engages members in discussions of belonging and membership values. The status updates provide ample data about the organization's ideological and bureaucratic functioning because they typically fall under a few primary themes: updates on the activities of the group's leadership or most active members, inspirational interpretations of Heathen lore or lessons from Old Norse history, motivational musings on Heathenry as an indigenous tradition and a birthright of those of European heritage, or critical analysis of modern life and politics. On many occasions the updates are politically fueled editorials by the AFA leadership, disgruntled with current affairs. After the political turmoil regarding gun-control versus gun-rights legislation following the 2012 elementary-school shootings in Newtown, Connecticut, the AFA's page (and other Heathens' private Facebook updates) were awash with pro-gun memes and antigovernment sentiment. McNallen's status updates expressed deep-seated fear and resentment of government "tyranny" and concerns over disarmament, arguing that "the right to own arms is a spiritual matter as much as it is a political one. The AFA's Declaration of Purpose does not mention gun ownership, but it does state clearly that one of our purposes is 'The fostering in our people of a deep love of freedom and a hatred of all forms of tyranny.'"[20]

Affiliation with national organizations fosters a sense of community by way of team affiliation and allegiance. At the same time at which national organizations provide a general connectedness and a top-down model, they are in many ways losing their importance as regional efforts in the Midwest render them redundant. John, the chieftain of a large western kindred, explained to me that national organizations have failed to prove their usefulness. He and others have said that they did not feel connected or supported, and national organizations were more of a hindrance to their growing communities and goals of localism and regionalism. The size of national organizations and the primarily electronic medium that they employ aids in the perpetuation of ongoing political conflicts. These sentiments are reflected on the Midwest Tribes website:

> Here in the Midwest, there will be no "Leaders for Life." No top-down effort to artificially unify our beliefs. No collection of money from our people, by far-away leaders that do very little for our region. No internet-based theological battles to split our Folk. We accept no "King." The decision-making and control of our regional efforts, rests with the strong Chieftains, Gothar, and Elders of our Midwest Tribes.[21]

In the AFA, McNallen is an unelected headman who leads by virtue of having started the group, in contrast with The Troth's elected steersperson. To tribes that focus on localism and regional efforts, autonomy is crucial, and national organizations are of little use.

Local Tribes

Each year, the Midwest tribes gather at Lightning Across The Plains' Midwest Thing, an administrative meeting of elders, chieftains, and *Gothar,* and titleless leadership representatives of each kindred in attendance. Seated around a square, kindred leaders share their successes and struggles over the past year and announce their plans while also settling rumors and disputes. There are no higher authorities, there are simply event organizers. Among the Midwest tribes, status is the reward, earned through renown for deeds and accomplishments, shared throughout the year via social media. On a local scale, Heathens assemble in these semifixed tribal groups known most commonly as *kindreds* or *hearths,* each of which is independent from the others and free from any central authority, although they may be affiliated with a larger organization. Some kindreds fashion websites or Facebook pages to publicize their groups, share resources, and keep members up-to-date. In contrast to formal organizations, for which online community is central to relationship maintenance and daily interaction, local tribes see one another quite frequently in real time and use the web for organizing or small talk between meetings. On many separate occasions, Heathens from local tribes have expressed their exasperation with the infighting, bickering, and flame wars that the Internet seems to encourage among people. To them, they are an impediment to their goals of building up local face-to-face communities that engage with one another regularly, as tribes used to do, and modern church communities already do. To scholars and many Heathens alike, virtual interactions will never replace traditional face-to-face communities. "We are, after all, embodied beings, emplaced in our physical shells. . . . We cannot be online without being offline, and we do not need the former to exist in the latter. Until the reverse is true, this distinction cannot be overemphasized."[22]

These local groups are less organized than formal Heathen organizations but still boast leadership structures and proactive members, although there is no internal consistency and structures are highly nuanced. Kindreds often refer to themselves as "family" or "tribes" that revolve around a handful of core group members who are highly committed to the group and to one another and to building and maintaining an intentional community. Within such communities, "this attitude of choice profoundly affects the nature of participation itself and the power of communities relative to that of individual."[23] The voluntary obligation of participation in a community may lead to attachments and a deeper sense of obligation to the group. When I spoke with Kell, the machinist, about his family group, he referred to it as a "war band," connoting the strong comradery that binds members together. He also noted, however, that it was just like any other "dysfunctional" family. When I asked him what he meant by that, he responded:

> I think part of it is because like any family you have differences of opinions. Good days, bad days, grumpy days, happy days, and you know, just like brothers and sisters will tend to fight each other tooth and toenail, but when an outsider come by they'll join forces against them. So I think it's dysfunctional just like any normal family would be. Everyone has their own issues, political strengths, weaknesses. . . . It's not a smooth well-orchestrated entity, but rather typical of a family. A very organic family, in that it grows, and shifts and changes.[24]

Local tribes are often egalitarian groups whether or not they choose to maintain a leadership position. In many kindreds leadership is simple; a *Gothi* or *Gythia* serves as the administrator, and other congregants volunteer to complete necessary tasks. In the past few years kindreds, particularly in the Midwest, have adopted new offices. Chieftains serve as leaders who arrange or organize the skeleton of events, partitioning the division of labor among members and assigning tasks, frequently undergirded by online networks. Some groups with a chieftain also reserve a separate position for a *Gothi* who serves as the group's religious and spiritual functionary. Either way, coordination and preparation are often the responsibility of volunteers or officers "dubbed" by members. Others avoid leadership entirely and instead approach group functions with a congregational attitude, a parallel to lay-led Christian congregations. Many of the Heathens I interviewed were very vague in their discussions of organization, hinting at the lax hierarchical structure of many groups. Anja, a thirty-year-old information technology professional from California, offered her insight into how leaders are chosen: "There are groups that are led by one person who has control over some essential resource: the most books, a very large living room, the most education. That's the model [we] operate under, because [the *Gythia*] has a whole lot of stuff and a living room large enough to waltz in."[25] Anja described the *Gythia* as a leader "by default," in large part because of her resources and her knowledge, which is measured informally. Likewise, Ivor explained the ambiguity surrounding Heathen leadership: "There's a—kind of a truism, almost a joke, in certain parts of Ásatrú, um, I think it was formalized by Lou Stead a while ago, and it basically runs—if you call yourself a *Gothi* and nobody laughs, then you're a *Gothi* [*laughs*]. So, in a more serious tone, if you are functioning in that respect and people treat you as, you know, a *Gothi*, a priest, then you are one.[26]"

In many cases the bar for leadership rests on demonstrating more knowledge than other members, as well as the ability and desire to lead and be accepted as a leader. Unlike other religious groups, Heathen leaders are usually not seen as superiors or end-all authorities but rather as the *first among equals*.[27] Increasingly, Heathens have sought formal religious training through a variety of avenues—The Troth's clergy program, advanced degrees in Old Norse religion, or, in one case, studying for ordination with the Icelandic Ásatrúarfélagið. According to Rod Landreth, a *Gothi* from the Midwest, the job of Heathen clergy is to articulate Heathen theology, to advise as well as to enhance and encourage relationship with deity. In an age of easily accessible information, knowledge about the lore is no longer sufficient for spiritual leadership in all cases.

> Yes, Gothar need to know the Lore, but they do not need to have a Bachelor's (or higher) in History to do the job. In fact to be a Gothar they need to know many soft skills (arbitration, spiritual/pastoral care, applied theology, interpersonal skills, etc.) that *just* knowing the Lore and History does little to inform. They need to be able to *apply* the Lore, along with other solid experience, and other knowledges.[28]

Members of local tribes choose their own *Gothi/Gythia* and judge for themselves the individual's competence. Groups expect high levels of involvement from their Gothi, and his/her willingness to subordinate other mundane responsibilities to the interests and health of the collective. Some local tribes refer to themselves as "closed" kindreds, refusing to accept new members, while many others remain open to new members. Some kindreds choose to develop detailed entry systems with a probationary period for prospective members. These processes sometimes involve extensive training and study and an eventual vote by the group to affirm the individual's membership. Others require full members to take an oath of loyalty and good conduct, and non-oathed or peripheral members make up the bulk of the membership. Although these nonoathed members are crucial to the success of many endeavors, they do not have voting rights in important kindred decisions.

In American Heathenry's younger years, paranoia about new associates' alleged Wiccanness outweighed groups' interest in growing. The length of participation in the wider Heathen community, breadth of experience, and knowledge of the lore, as well as contacts with others, determined whether newcomers would be accepted and taken seriously. As Heathenry distanced itself from other New Age spiritualities by developing sharper boundaries, curious onlookers were sometimes enthusiastically embraced and mentored. The trend, however, seems to have reversed with the popularity of social media, where newcomers are frequently humiliated and criticized for any questions deemed entry level. Eskel, a thirty-three-year-old with an M.A. in religious studies who has been involved with Heathenry since the early 1990s, remarked:

> I think that to kind of gain entrée into the community, at least for me, you have to know the right person or the right group. In my opinion it doesn't take long to figure out what the bandwagon message of a particular community is, whether it's folkish or nonfolkish. As long as you espouse the quote unquote "community-sanctioned views" and stay within the approved literature, and don't really stray from the community-approved authors, then you're fine.[29]

If a local tribe successfully manages incompatibility and political infighting, the payoffs are huge. Members can rely on one another for familial favors and friendship. One member of a local tribe explained that her group would "drop everything" to help her out, with no questions asked. The absolute certainty of this level of commitment by other group members is one of the defining characteristics of local tribes. Formal organizations may be composed of members with loyalty to one another, but member relationships are frequently professional and bureaucratic, based on function rather than intimacy. Although members do build meaningful friendships in national organizations, there remains a level of disconnectedness because of their wide geographic distribution and infrequent opportunities for personal contact.

On a national scale, the Heathen community is fragmented into individuals and groups scattered across the landscape. Yet many kindreds are empowered by the collective identity that kindred membership can award, both internally for the individual and externally for the Heathen public. In the Midwest, where kindreds have joined together in formal or informal tribal alliances and friendships, face-to-face Heathenry receives a fair amount of emphasis. A website created as an introduction to the tribal approach in the Midwest reads:

> We are autonomous Asatru or Heathen kindreds and tribes that understand the value of gathering with each other face-to-face and building strong bonds of friendship and cooperation between our groups. We believe that by knowing each other and working together, we can get more done for our individual tribes, our region, and our Folk. We support a grassroots and regional approach to Heathenry, and while we seek a unity of purpose we will always respect and defend the right of each tribe to have its own traditions and *thew*.[30]

While Trothmoot 2011 attracted around 40 attendees, Lightning Across the Plains, hosted annually in Kansas by Jotun's Bane Kindred, boasted 240. In other parts of the country, kindreds meet at regional events to renew friendships, weaving a network of relationships. The model of regional tribal relationships has been so successful that the AFA, which once focused on a national takeover, has recently voiced its desire to be instead a *community of communities*.[31] The success of this tribal model comes partly from the painstaking labor and dedication of a few charismatic leaders whose skills at organizing and revitalizing the community are crucial.

While formal organizations must engage in the discourse of a steady, grinding bureaucracy, interspersed with political or theological arguments, local tribes discuss personal and intimate matters to a degree often unmatched within other organizational forms. Contact occurs on a regular basis, from weekly to monthly, and members become involved in all aspects of one another's lives. Particularly in the Midwest, the tribal model challenges the top-down model of national organizations with a bottom-up emphasis. Multiple kindreds meet regularly, driving or flying to one another's regional events and building lasting friendships and alliances that, in members' views, forgo the use of membership in a national organization.

As in any group that fosters meaningful friendships and spiritual connection, intimacy among members often leads to very deep and traumatic personal rifts when local tribes experience turmoil. In one case, friction between a member and his group resulted in a highly diplomatic vacation from the kindred, announced publicly with a politic "personal matters" justification so as not to incite rumors. For others, breakups lead to lasting distrust of the entire structure. Many Heathens have admitted to me that their relationships with their former kindreds are strained and injured. The reluctance to join other groups at ritual arises from personal incompatibility with core group members or, as Erik (introduced in Chapter 3) confessed, the fear that white supremacists have invaded all Heathen spaces. Members are often scarred by damaging separations from their tribes, to the degree that they feel as though they have been separated from their families. Some of them form their own groups, as occurred in 2013 when a large kindred in the West splintered under strained circumstances into three smaller groups. Although people may express feelings of loyalty and concern for the members of their former tribes, relationships are frequently strained, and members may shy away from the prospect of further group interactions. Instead, they often shift to participation in less organized, less personal, diffuse groups.

Diffuse Groups

Many local tribes begin with only two or three members, but those that become large enough may generate a larger "lay" membership that is less willing to expend the energy to do the homework or pull its weight in leading ritual or organizing events. These members may develop into the fringe of tribal groups, what Mark Stinson refers to as "folk community,"[32] or disperse and become their own diffuse groups. It is perhaps because diffuse groups suffer from a distinct lack of traditional "organic" or even institutional community that they speak of it the most.[33] They differ from local tribes in that they are ephemeral, and more akin to Hewitt's idea of "collectivities" that have little guidance and open, shifting membership and leadership.[34] Ernst Troelsch referred to this kind of collective as "a parallelism of spontaneous religious personalities."[35] They demonstrate characteristics of the "Institution *Lite*," an institution that "articulates with the 'free agency' of its members."[36] Traditional institutions arose to meet the basic needs of groups or even societies, providing a context for one's identity and sense of self. However, numerous traditional institutions have failed or disillusioned those under their purview. Consequently, people have invented alternative institutions that meet their needs, including providing an anchor for the self. In lite institutions members determine their own level of involvement and can bend various rules or norms to suit their needs. Diffuse groups are institutions in that they exist across local, national, and international levels, provide basic needs to members, and help anchor identities. They are lite in that they consist of nonpermanent transient members who bounce from one group to another without creating any official ties or loyalties.

Like local tribes, these diffuse groups are locally based, but members are less committed to the group and one another. Groups may form around rune or lore study, meet for coffee hour, or hold *pub-moots* (meetings at pubs). Diffuse groups, unlike local tribes, seldom host or plan events. Many solitary practitioners will join in a ritual event of a group once in many months, with only online contact in the off months. Valda, a forty-year-old environmentalist from the Midwest, voices the ambiguous and unofficial hierarchy of the local group in her area:

I mean, you have the, um . . . what is it, the *Gothi*? Or whatever. The-Wise-People-Who-Know-What-They're-Doing will usually lead rituals or, if they're qualified to do so, provide counseling type services, um . . . even be teachers, but they're the ones from what I've seen, like with Brand, who, keep things rolling along and try to keep people involved and keep that sense of community there.[37]

Heathens sometimes become, as one respondent put it, "Heathen refugees" seeking shelter from the emotional wounds inflicted by caustic political infighting of local tribal groups. I have often heard Heathens express their ambivalence or apprehension about commitment because they are alarmed by racism they may have perceived or experienced. More often, however, members who have formed a kindred find few others willing to commit their time or loyalty to the group.

I asked a former *Gothi* and *Gythia* what had happened to dissolve their kindred some years earlier. They took turns answering, explaining to me that the former members of their kindred had failed to do their share; they all expected to "just show up and participate" but not take an active role in the construction of *blót*. The *Gothi* and *Gythia* had expected the commitment found in many local tribes but were sorely disappointed. Because they were taking on the primary responsibilities of constructing *blót*, writing the ritual script, and engaging other members in their efforts, they burned out. After this, the "personal problems" and conflicts surrounding some members of the group led to the *Gythia*'s decision to close membership, limiting entrée to those adults she considered "mentally healthy." Her reasoning for these complications was the oft-cited saying "We're a fringe religion and so we attract fringe people."[38] Yet why people fail to commit is complicated. To many Heathens, the financial and time commitments of attending events are often impracticable. Others with less access to vibrant Heathen communities seek the friendship of other nearby Pagan groups, staying on the periphery of whatever community they find. Still others, as the *Gythia* explained, are not ready for the commitment or responsibility that comes along with loyalty to a group.

The discourse during the gatherings of diffuse groups reflects mundane personal topics, similar to the conversations one might engage in with other members of a club or a hobby group. Participants often situate themselves around a room and discuss their jobs or careers, health, and family—small talk without revealing too much. As a side note, they may also discuss rune lore, history, or other religious topics. Most of this religiously charged talk, however, occurs after ritual or during specified workshops and remains specific to the topic at hand. Other talk may serve to reinforce Heathen norms and values. Most frequent and most significant, perhaps, is the elusive subject of community. This mundane talk is essential; whether participants are friends or merely acquaintances, casual talk makes it feel like friendship and creates the illusion of community. Participants may hail "community" or "folk" in a *Sumbel* and then retreat to their lives with little in the way of connection or sense of obligation to those whom they toasted. To those on the fringe, the community discussion is invaluable in that it is the only true expression for many diffuse groups that community exists. Scholars have argued that American community is largely a discursive construct, based on the desire to return to the organic community of the past in which all members relied on one another through a division of labor and collective conscience.[39] The word *community* is used to indicate local, national, and international groups. It goes beyond the tangible and is used repeatedly to indicate a shared connection to a wider network of Heathenry that transcends time and space. The creation of community through everyday conversation occurs everywhere from coffee talk to ritual functions. By simply using the word *community,* Heathens emphasize their claims to having or being community.

This organizational form is characterized by more than "community" talk; it involves attitudes toward ritual functions and other members reminiscent of loosely knit support groups. Members attend ritual occasionally and periodically interact with one another online, where they also announce events. They are connected by geography and mutual interest in Heathenry, but in general, they come and go as they please, and there are no sanctions for nonparticipation. Members are not held responsible for assisting with preparations or coordination and instead rely on invitations to functions with the posture of attending a party, which often results in the burnout of the leaders who bear the brunt of this form's vague organization. Although this group form is characterized by individuals who are very loosely associated, some members may develop a closer relationship and form their own local tribe, which may choose to register with a formal organization as an official kindred and develop an exclusive group e-mail list online. Other members who may be geographically challenged or disinclined to interact with any Heathens face-to-face may opt for a more anonymous organizational form, that of the virtual *hof.*

The Virtual Hof

Heathens are geographically dispersed, and participation varies from single individuals separated by vast distances to large local organizations with official member lists. The Internet ameliorates the plight of solitary practitioners by connecting every Heathen with access (which most have) and provides the framework for the bulk of the community discourse. Online resources transform the community in face-to-face gatherings by providing members with a venue for informal introductions where relationships are based on textual communication, unhindered by social and physical cues.[40] To a large degree— although one should be wary of focusing too heavily on the "mythology of placelessness"[41]—the Internet changes our experience of time and space, minimizing the need for face-to-face intimacy while allowing its users to manufacture their own fantastic selves. Members are able to meet one another in real space, in person, after having experienced one another's online personas. The preconceived bias formed online assists in the real presentation of self and the creation of friendship bonds which, once created virtually, may develop in real life more swiftly.

In the past two decades, the Internet has been the primary resource for new recruits and spiritual seekers searching for something else within the scope of Paganism, leading to a disproportionate number of ex-Wiccans within American Heathenry. Although websites, e-books, and printable pamphlets are essential in publicizing and maintaining Heathenry, they are not the primary means of communicating Heathenry as a dynamic and ongoing process. Instead, Heathens keep up on the latest topics, gossip, and identity criteria by joining a discussion group through Facebook or Yahoo!.

On Facebook, Heathens form groups to interact with local or national Heathenry, to mock "inauthentic" Heathens,[42] or to publicize events. These groups often splinter when members experience personal or political conflict with one another, creating new groups and inviting select friends. Most of these groups are either completely private or are closed groups that the public can access but to which only members can contribute. Although Facebook groups are geographically boundless except for a few local or regional groups, Yahoo! groups are overwhelmingly regional or topical. For example, there are a "Pacific" as well as a "central states" and a "Southlands" list, a list for Troth members, and lists for those who knit and spin wool, brew mead and beer, or wish to discuss politics. In both arenas, users refer to communications from other lists, illustrating that even digital groups have permeable and unclear boundaries. As Eskel, the religious studies M.A., puts it:

> There tend to be local groups of various degrees of organization, a lot of solitaries, people who live in areas that don't have contact with anybody else in a direct way. Most of the larger organization I'm familiar with is Internet groups. . . . Most of the groups I've seen since [the early organizations] that have tried to organize on a larger scale are largely Internet-based groups. Because it's an easy way to communicate and network over long distances, and with a very spread-out group of people, that's convenient.[43]

Heathen e-mail lists can be organized into locally and regionally based groups. Local groups have the smallest membership, while regional groups are perhaps the most popular—large enough to involve the most varied, and often most heated, discourse. Many Heathens subscribe to multiple lists and groups at any given time; when they are asked to join more, they are likely to offer a variation of Jim's comment: "Thanks for the invitation, but I'm already on 26 Yahoo e-mail lists, plus a bunch of stuff specific to The Troth."[44]

On any given online group, the moderators are usually the group's founders and are therefore endowed with the privileges of accepting or rejecting another's membership request, as well as censoring and filtering discussion posts. Moderators are as formal as the hierarchy gets. Otherwise, the very fuzzy nature of the space in which online discourse takes place and the resistance of Heathens online to any form of governance prohibit official hierarchical structure, although de facto hierarchies emerge as people with garrulous personalities capture the attention of core forum members. Because online communication is intangible and impersonal, the structures of leadership and status hierarchies are ambiguous and often only implied. The "more democratic, even anarchic, conditions of cyberspace"[45] are highly compatible with Heathenry's acute individualism. Some scholars have argued for the democratic potentials of online discourse, noting that computer-mediated communication facilitates "greater possibilities for interaction, and thus more direct forms of participation."[46] Unlike the hierarchy of the formal organization and the local tribe, the virtual *hof* has no *Gothi*, no leader, and no officials; it is an arena in which personality reigns, etiquette is optional, and—like a child who throws the most dramatic tantrum to win attention—people are rewarded for being the most boisterous, sensational actors. Although some members may post online with some authority, influence is granted to them on the basis of their positions in the local tangible community, but to strangers, all members are equal and equally fallible.

Because of the depth and breadth of conversation that occurs on these e-mail lists, members come to know one another intimately without the need to meet face-to-face. I discussed Internet use with Sally, a fifty-year-old telephone operator from the Midwest. I stood in her kitchen doorway as she washed dishes and inquired about her experiences with e-Heathenry. I asked her whether she had met various well-known members of the local Heathen community. Although she had spoken with many people for years, she said, she had never actually met them in person. Online relationships may "facilitate frequent, reciprocal, companionable and often supportive contact," the placelessness of which facilitates this long-term contact over time and space, without the loss of friendships often characteristic of residential mobility.[47] All of Sally's interactions were online, and despite the lack of face-to-face contact, she felt genuinely close to them, shared (virtually) in many of their intimate life experiences, and considered them friends. Many Heathens, like Sally, rely solely on the Internet as their connection with Heathenry and may remain solitary practitioners, never participating in Heathen events or engaging with local Heathen groups. Rather than fueling a decline in religious participation, however, the Internet has extended social networks and invitations that before would have been limited to smaller enclaves. I spoke to Einar, a thirty-three-year-old ex-teacher from New England, about his thoughts on the impact of the Internet on our community:

> I think there are a lot of cyber-Vikings or armchair Vikings, I think it's really easy for a lot of people to pretty much rely on the Internet and Heathen lip service is pretty much their full connection with any feeling of community at all. Aside from maybe going to an occasional Heathen

gathering, or they might belong to a local kindred, but I do think that for many people the Internet is a very big and major thing for connection and community and discussion.[48]

That some Heathens use the Internet as their only source of interaction with the community also argues "for the potential strengths of online relationships and networks."[49] The Internet connects Heathens coast to coast, urban and rural. Einar further expressed to me that "as a result of our community size on a national scale, the Internet has become even bigger for us as a means for finding out where we are and having community and getting together."[50] For some, being online with others is a powerful way of being together. Bonds created among groups online often lead people to meet face-to-face, resulting in local groups and friendships. Although many members of local groups have expressed to me their disenchantment with the online world, it remains their main source of current events and interaction with other Heathens. The Internet offers protection from face-to-face interaction for those who would otherwise find it uncomfortable, but it also offers them membership in a community of like-minded individuals, as well as exposure to individuals who may not share their politico-religious views. The Internet provides a forum for "moral deliberation."[51] On the Internet, democracy and dialogue are the key practices by which the Heathen community engages in cultural negotiation.

Virtual Battles and Community Politics

After Trothmoot 2012 a ruckus erupted involving a private *blót* held in honor of Loki, a subject of great contention. For weeks, members discussed at length, in hundreds of e-mail exchanges (which continued on Facebook), the pros and cons of The Troth's policy against the hailing of Loki at *High Sumbel*. Arguments that would not have occurred with such ferocity in person escalated into heated debates behind the buffer of the keyboard and the screen. People argued on both sides, ultimately recommending a revision of policy that either allows such expressions or eliminates them entirely. The Rede, The Troth's governing body, active in the conversation, took members' concerns to heart and promised to deliberate formally. Such scandals occur nearly annually because online communication lacks the nuances and concrete rules of etiquette that face-to-face deliberations demand.

In response to McNallen's support of gun ownership after Sandy Hook, members issued hails of support, with only one or two voicing disappointment in McNallen for his political ideological takeover of his 501(c)3 religious organization. More typical, however, were statements such as "The right to bear arms to defend oneself and one's family, to fight against oppressors and conquerors, to stand up against evil is a human right—a right given from the Gods to us; the US Constitution merely recognizes this right. Only thralls are denied weapons, otherwise known as slaves. Are we Thralls?"[52] Other comments from members highlighted the symbolic politics of identity, arguing that "Heathens are not hippies" or that "we are warriors by nature,"[53] framing gun ownership as not simply a spiritual right but a religious obligation in the sight of the gods. In this way, the AFA's Facebook page and Internet forum provide members with a sense of belonging where political ideals can be safely expressed and shared with sympathetic others, and where agreement on political issues is taken for granted. On The Troth page, discussions at this time were apolitical, focusing instead on members' theological reflections and updated Troth stationary, with no mention of gun rights.

These social media have had perhaps the greatest modern impact of all, leading to round-the-clock discussions among participants from around the globe, a perpetual working and reworking of tribal alliances, relationships, community norms, and values, and dramatically increased contact. The American Heathenry of 2015 is dramatically different from its beginnings in the 1970s, primarily because of the impact of online communication, and not all of the change is positive. The sociology of religion has typically understood religion "as a voluntary or chosen ground of meaning and identity that, by definition, provides protection from the corrosive, anomic aspects of late modern society."[54] This protection, however, has been eroded by the interactional nature of online communication. The wars being fought over identities and authenticity have taken a turn for the worse, degrading into bullying and name-calling. In many ways, the Internet has exacerbated alienation instead of ameliorating it. On Facebook, Mark Stinson asks his audience:

> Ever Get Tired of Nay-Sayers? There is a minority group of on-line Heathens that spend their time tearing down anyone that is actually doing anything real in the world. You host a gathering, and they spend their time spreading negative misinformation about your gathering. You start a kindred, and they spend their time trash-talking your efforts. You work on any sort of forward-looking Heathen effort, and they spend their time mocking your efforts. Nevermind that they have never attended your gathering, have never met your kindred, and know nothing about your efforts. And nevermind that they aren't really doing anything themselves except posting on-line, and mostly posting attacks and negativity. Again, I can't say for sure why they do this. But, it seems to me that if they can tear down everyone else's efforts, it makes it alright in their mind that they aren't really making any positive efforts of their own. If no one else succeeds, or they find a way to mock anyone else's successes, it makes their own lack of action or successes somehow more personally acceptable.[55]

Stinson's statement indicates that although online interaction is the most prevalent form of interaction in today's digital age, face-to-face interaction is privileged as "real." Among Heathens, cultural negotiation often comes in the form of highly sensitive discussions, which are routine and have frequently led to rifts and fissures among groups in the community when members feel slighted by one another, sometimes over stark political differences, sometimes over semantics. To find an example, I asked Ivor, a *Gothi* of a local group, what he remembered of a previous incident I had heard about at the South West Moot:

> There was a kerfluffle involving the Central States Moot a while back, where someone posted an old poem by Kipling to the list, which generated a lot of heat and noise about what constitutes racism, some things were said, some people got bent, and some folks left The Troth as a result. Is that the incident you're remembering? If so, I wasn't directly involved in any of it, though I can cite a lot of the arguments chapter and verse— we spend an inordinate amount of time in Heathenry spinning these particular wheels.[56]

Moreover, the spinning of the wheels happens primarily online. Ivor's story is another example of online politics, one that affected the entire community, causing rifts in real-life relationships and real-life membership in The Troth. Extreme political discussions are routine and have led to other rifts and fissures within and between groups. Meetings in person are ideally bound by *frith*. Many sign the ends of their e-mails and discussion-list posts with "In *Frith*" to indicate a lack of animosity. Yet the hostility is often unmistakable. On Facebook and e-mail lists, disagreements escalate into harassment, bullying, and flame wars.

Because of the anonymity of computer-mediated communication, members are more likely to engage in talk that they would avoid face-to-face. They can ignore the rejections they suffer online more easily than under less enigmatic physical conditions.[57] Online, "limited social presence may also encourage people to communicate more freely and creatively than they do in person, 'flaming' others by using extreme aggressive language."[58] The importance of this medium in the maintenance of the community, however, leaves members shaking their heads in awe when I ask them what the community would be like without the Internet. For example, Eskel is as avid an Internet user as any other Heathen, and he demonstrated this wonderment when we spoke. He studied his coffee in front of him for a moment as he considered his answer:

> Without the Internet? [*pause*] . . . That's hard to conceive [*pause*] . . . I suspect that there would be a bigger emphasis placed on the gatherings than there is currently. The impression I get, the Ásatrú Alliance Althings, used to be these massively important gatherings and the big political events. . . . Whereas now, people seem to get together and amiably chat and have, you know, eat together and drink together and have *blóts* and *Sumbels* and workshops, and all the politics goes on online. Even for The Troth, which is old enough to have an organizational structure not

based on that and still, the web groups that have sprung up in relation to it seems to be where all the political fighting goes on, which is good in the sense that I can go to a gathering and not have to be involved, but it's very interesting that that's where the real communication happens. I suspect that there are a whole lot of people who are very actively involved in the community and very known that wouldn't be so well known if it weren't for the Internet. Because the people who don't travel so much don't go to the gatherings but have a big voice online.[59]

Academics and the media alike have repeatedly commented on the alienating and hostile world of social media and Internet commentary. In the past few years teen suicides linked to Facebook bullying have periodically dominated the headlines. At the same time, racism, homophobia, sexism, and xenophobia are both perpetuated and illustrated by comments on YouTube and other social media sites to which online commenters contribute, free from accountability. Social media bullying and hostility are an Internet phenomenon, not a Heathen phenomenon, but they have had profound effects on American Heathenry. Heathenry's overwhelming whiteness, racial insecurity, lack of formal leadership and control, hypermasculinity, and increasingly salient political identities exacerbate the already alienating influence that the virtual can have on its users. This has led to a general sense of distrust of online communication, as well as its widespread critique. It has created an environment in which Heathens try to out-Heathen one another, where hypermasculine one-upmanship is the name of the game—this time, in insults challenging one another on every level about the lore, UPGs, and knowledgeability. In one instance, Vincent, a Facebook user, posted to a group about the recent death of his wife after her struggle with a terminal illness. In his grief, he shared that he was comforted by his belief that she was in Valhalla, where he hoped to see her again some day. To some Heathens, Valhalla, a place for warriors slain in battle, is the equivalent of heaven, although the lore is clear that it is only one possible location among many for the afterlife. On a separate message board used for policing Heathen belief and behavior, Vincent's post was copied, pasted, and mocked. After a weeks-long theme of criticism throughout Facebook regarding claims of entering Valhalla or queries about how to get there and what counts as death in battle (cancer? domestic abuse? psychological battles? overcoming severe hardships?), Vincent's post was among those ridiculed as a misinterpretation of the nature of Valhalla. Even in his grief at the loss of his partner, the Internet trolls sought to police Vincent's interpretation of the afterlife as ahistorical, unsupported by the lore, and ultimately a product of Christian influence.

In the 1990s meeting other Heathens was cause for excitement. National organizations and kindred groups expressed a general sense of oneness with like-minded Heathens. "E-Heathenry," as Erik put it, has led to the deconstruction of community and the erosion of solidarity. A few Heathens have spoken out recently, for example, about the use of the term *brother* as a term of camaraderie. The glut of online Heathens and the varying beliefs and divergent socio-political alignments of Heathens throughout the world have led to a general sense of caution, limiting the use of *brotherhood* and *sisterhood* to tribal enclaves—terms not to be used lightly by just anyone. Yet the impact that the Internet has on the Heathen community is paramount because the greater part of all communications occur there. The construction of any identity requires discussions and negotiation about what behaviors, beliefs, and practices are acceptable or undesirable. Whether one participates in the discussions or merely observes them, the impact of this distribution of information on community norms and values remains critical. Heathens who engage in discussions on regional lists are less likely to run into one another face-to-face and have the remoteness of being strangers separated by greater distances. As Einar aptly put it:

> I think because the Internet is so impersonal, it's a lot easier for Heathens to be a lot more abusive to people they disapprove of and be a lot more bossy about the lore. Certainly than more direct face-to-face human contact. . . . I've known a number of community Heathens who just type these messages after messages with text after text after text. . . . They just go on and on, getting into these very in-depth detailed reports about "no, you have a wrong slant on the lore, and I have the correct slant, and here's all my back-up evidence" quote, quotation, quotation, quotation.[60]

Many Heathens who engage in online discussions do so with the misleading certainty that they can assert their opinion with caustic self-confidence and remain unscathed. They do this on the way to the creation of authenticity, a challenge more likely to confront online groups who have only textual evidence to prove themselves. Many of those I interviewed voiced their distress at the tumultuous environment of the discussion lists while at the same time acknowledging their necessity for communication with the rest of Heathendom. Brandon, a musician from the West Coast, remarks:

> There's also the problem of trolls and online d-baggery. Online arguments are easy to escalate and there's no holding people back. I've seen it happen repeatedly, been the target of a few attacks, and I've seen it just ruin any chance for people to meet in person. The problem with the Internet is you make a statement, and there's no real chance for real interactive dialogue. People don't interact, they post at each other.[61]

Although the online Heathen community is fraught with name-calling, contests of wit and one-upmanship, and often scathing displays of misogyny and racism, the Internet is the site of the re-creation of Heathen identity through discussions of what being Heathen really means and looks like. Through discussions of lore and politics, Heathens reiterate publicly the norms and values that they should aspire to practice. The Internet is the primary means by which communication occurs and the space in which most Heathens spend a majority of their time with others. It is the arena in which Heathen novices find mentorship, guidance, and information about their chosen faith—if they can weather the onslaught of criticism that seems inseparable from the Heathen experience on social media.

I t seems contradictory that Heathens, who base their belief system on an oral culture from the Dark Ages, rely so heavily on texts and modern technology to support and cradle their movement. The reestablishment of an archaic belief system by geographically dispersed, rugged individualists who are suspicious of authority and longing for community has multiple outcomes. The worst outcome is that American Heathenry continues to degenerate into a bastion of hypermasculine posturing, name-calling, and online antagonism, following the rest of the Internet into the antisocial wasteland. "Don't feed the trolls"; in other words, don't play into the hands of Internet megalomaniacs and bullies by responding to their taunts with heated emotional reactions. Yet, as the virtual expands possibilities and seemingly dislocates people in time and space, Heathens are craving just the opposite. Heathens are increasingly vocal about the alienation fostered by social media. As the Internet undergirds and makes possible the success of formal organizations and the communication and planning of public events hosted by local tribes, Heathens are able to spend more time with one another face-to-face, in resistance to the hostile takeover of their communities by the virtual. The result is that American Heathenry continues to develop vibrant, close-knit, and dynamic regional and local communities that provide their members with personal and spiritual meaning, where the Internet functions as a tool to facilitate communication and community rather than a means to annihilate it.

5

Valkyries and Frithweavers

Women's Shifting Roles—from Warriors
to Domestic Caretakers

Þ á mæ lti Gangleri: "Mikit þótti mér þeir hafa þá snúit til leið ar, er jörð ok
himinn var gert ok sól ok himintungl váru sett ok skipt dægrum, ok hvaðan
kómu mennirnir þeir er heim byggja?" Þá svarar Hárr: "Þá er þeir gengu
með sævarströndu Borssynir, fundu þeir tré tvau ok tóku upp trén ok
sköpuðu af menn. Gaf inn fyrsti önd ok líf, annarr vit ok hræring, þriði
ásjónu, mál ok heyrn ok sjón, gáfu þeim klæði ok nöfn. Hét karlmaðrinn
Askr en konan Embla, ok ólst þaðan af mannkindin, sú er byggðin var gefinn
undir Miðgarði."

Then said Gangleri: "Much indeed they had accomplished then, methinks,
when earth and heaven were made, and the sun and the constellations of
heaven were fixed, arid division was made of days; now whence come the
men that people the world?" And Hárr answered: "When the sons of Borr
were walking along the sea-strand, they found two trees, and took up the
trees and shaped men of them: the first gave them spirit and life; the
second, wit and feeling; the third, form, speech, hearing, and sight. They
gave them clothing and names: the male was called Askr, and the female
Embla, and of them was mankind begotten, which received a dwelling-
place under Midgard." —THE PROSE EDDA

According to *The Prose Edda*, Odin, Vili, and Ve created the first man and
woman, Ask and Embla, simultaneously, as equals, from two lifeless
trees on a beach. Neither was created to serve the other; instead, both
were given spirit, life, wit, feeling, form, speech, hearing, and sight, and "of them
was mankind begotten." My earliest conversations with other Heathens involved
the discursive construction of Heathen women as bold and self-reliant equal
partners to their male comrades, with imagery that mingles bits of Wagnerian
Valkyrie with historical Old Norse farmer. The ancestral women whom Heathens envision are idealized in masculine terms as strong, forthright, cunning,
and free from the Victorian influence that so greatly colors our image of women
today. They are embodiments of Heathen virtue, industrious, perseverant, and
disciplined, and in the Heathen imagination they are magical, closer to the
sacred, wise, and formidable. Although there is no concrete set of traits expressed

by all contemporary Heathen women in lived experience, the existence of an imaginary one to aspire to lies ever in the making.

Hallgerd, a Goth turned Heathen, was a forty-something stay-at-home mom, overweight, overstressed, soft-spoken, and living in subsidized housing with her gentle, overworked husband and two young girls. Like many American families, they made too little money and had too little time for housekeeping, for therapy, or for entertainment. When I arrived at the house on one of my many visits, Hallgerd excused herself to change her clothes. I picked my way across the living room to the couch to take a seat, stepping over toys, piles of clothing, and a soggy, half-eaten playing card. Both of her children were there; the toddler was sticky and wet, with a large piece of cereal stuck to the hem of her dress. I picked a half-eaten gummy bear off the couch and took a seat as the toddler stared at me, making one-syllable noises and wringing her messy hands. The elder, a six-year-old, bustled around in the corner of the room, pulling clothes out of a plastic tub, including a pink leotard, a purple tutu, and one of her mom's black silk scarves, which she tied around her waist. The house had a suspicious smell, which I suspected came from the toddler. Hallgerd reappeared with a clean but wrinkled shirt and began to redress the toddler and wash her up in the bathroom sink. Next to me, the vacuum cleaner was leaning up against the couch, forgotten. Hallgerd, self-conscious about the mess, assured me that she had planned on cleaning that day but was not motivated, so she would clean tomorrow instead. While she bathed the kids' guinea pig in the kitchen sink, she turned on the television, assuring me as she did so, lest I think that she was an inattentive mother, that she did not like to use it as a babysitter.

By her manner, she seemed young and unsure of herself and her capabilities. I got the impression that she approached many endeavors, from motherhood to homemaking, as a neophyte anticipating getting it right eventually. Often during my visits to her home, Hallgerd would recall in conversation the beliefs and practices of the Old Norse woman as a frame for many of her actions and for the kind of woman that she found herself to be. She explained:

> I used to be a Frejya worshipper, and she's about sexuality and love and beauty. . . . But when I had children, I found Frigga calling to me, and Frigga is the mother. She's the mother of the gods, Odin's wife, and I just find such a draw . . . such a strong feeling to my children and I identify with that and I want to be the best mom to my children if I can. . . . I think it's about not bowing down to your gods, about believing that those gods are one and the same with you as well as believing they're separate, being self-sufficient and not asking the gods for things but they help you when you help yourself.[1]

Her circumstances were such that self-reliance, discipline, and many other Old Norse virtues came as luxuries only now and again. Ongoing mental health issues, mood swings, financial concerns, and reoccurring physical ailments stalled any drastic change in her life, but she nonetheless maintained as part of her identity the qualities of the strong, steadfast women of her ancestry.

The same snowy evening on which I met Hallgerd, I was introduced to Freydis. Self-reliant, disciplined, and rugged, she lived with her children and libertarian husband in a one-room house they had hand-built on their friends' small, isolated ranch. The family slept part of the time in a camp trailer and the rest bundled up in the uninsulated one-room home that was still under construction; her two young children were situated in an attic loft accessible only via a ladder. Hallgerd and I both agreed that Freydis was quite the model of industriousness, a noble Heathen virtue. Also a stay-at-home mom, Freydis had taught herself traditional skills practiced by Old Norse women: spinning, weaving, knitting, and dyeing cloth using local plant materials. Like many Heathens, she felt that these skills connected her to her ancestors, the gods, and *wyrd* at a metaphysical level. She spent much of her time engaged in these activities when she was not milking goats, shearing sheep, or tending to her family's large garden. She discussed with me, but rarely complained about, the financial strain on her family, although now and again, she did express concern about where her family's inadequate funds were going—most notably to increase her husband's arms cache instead of toys or clothing for her kids. Usually, however, she met circumstances with wise retorts and hope for the future. The stark differences between the lived experiences and expressions of Freydis and Hallgerd were remarkable, despite their shared beliefs in the image of the Old Norse woman. Freydis's disconnection from the outside world had earned her the ability to escape a great deal of the contemporary baggage imposed on women, while Hallgerd had remained, in large part, a compliant victim of pop psychology. While Hallgerd decried her life's impediments to the dull drone of Dr. Phil in the background, Freydis disengaged from popular culture and, to a large degree, the local Heathen community and instead immersed herself in diligent household production. That these two women lived so differently and yet expressed and held the same beliefs led to my inquiry into gender as part of Heathen collective identity.

Heathens and scholars alike puzzle over the constructions of gender and the relationship between men and women experienced by the Old Norse, whose account of creation diverges fundamentally from the dominant Judeo-Christian biblical worldview in which woman was created from and for the service of man. This chapter investigates how American Heathenry's conceptualizations of gender both resist and are informed by mainstream politics and culture. I explore concepts of women in Old Norse society and how images of the masculine woman as Valkyrie informs modern Heathen treatments of women in the faith, and I discuss whether the reframing of traditional oppression as empowerment creates social change and equality or reinforces existing inequalities. There is a paradox in Heathen women's identity as strong, rustic women in their appropriation of masculine power through gendered performances and their willing adoption (and conflicting definition) of hegemonic gender norms. To discover how gender is constructed and negotiated, we must explore both power and resistance and not only how dominant institutions and groups inflict and enforce certain meanings, but also how subordinate groups challenge these conceptions and formulate alternative meanings.[2] Although gender norms and expectations have changed over the past thirty years,[3] mainstream orthodox and conservative religious organizations regularly support dominant models of gender, particularly those in which gender norms are highly structured and the subordination of women is normalized in the home and the workplace. Scholars have therefore viewed women's participation in conservative religions as a form of oppression, false consciousness, or lack of agency. Yet women have always participated and continue to participate in conservative religions. Study of women's actual lived experience, however, illustrates that women are creative agents who are not blindly submitting to religious authority. Rather, women are adapting religious beliefs and practices to their daily experience in ways that sometimes subvert more oppressive religious teachings.[4]

In the mid-1990s American Heathenry was decidedly male dominated, with a ratio of 65 percent male to 35 percent female. Since then, the participation of women in all varieties of Paganism has increased. In Heathenry the ratio is nearly equally divided "between women and men, with 50.8% female and 47.8% male and the remainder defining themselves as transitioning between genders or as other."[5] This finding from Helen Berger's Pagan Census Revisited (2009–2010) mirrors my findings from exploratory survey research. Although Berger states that she is "unsure what effect the increased feminization of the religion will have, if any,"[6] my work illustrates a change intricately reliant on heavily politicized notions of masculinity, femininity, equality, and ownership.

Heathen women have created for themselves an arena in which they come to feel ownership and domination, traditional masculine notions, over the home and family. That is, they model their domestic lives and gendered division of labor after a pastiche of romanticized and historical archetypes from ancient Germanic cultures. I discuss this by outlining the relevant literature on gender resistance in subculture and religion. I follow this with an outline of the historical source for gendered behavior in American Heathenry, specifically women's place among the Old Norse, and an explanation of how modern Heathens construct gender. Particularly, I outline how Heathens incorporate elements of warrior masculinity into women's more traditional roles as domestic and spiritual caregivers, as well as how they challenge and construct their traditional roles as women within the community in terms of empowerment, control, and ownership. In addition, I look at the implications behind the politically charged masculinization of Heathenry and the feminization of other NRMs as central to the struggle over rights to the authentic Heathen identity.

Reframing Gender and Resistance

Sociologists who have studied the experiences of women in conservative religions have found that oppressive, patriarchal religious teachings do not always reflect women's lived realities. Evangelical women who cite a religious belief in male dominance and female submission still often work in careers outside the home and take part in domestic decision making, a distinction that scholars have termed "symbolic traditionalism and pragmatic egalitarianism."[7] Research that explores other traditional and anachronistic religions, such as Orthodox Judaism, reveals that although newly converted women generally support and perpetuate patriarchy, they still retain many of the values associated with mainstream feminism, particularly the celebration of the female.[8] Sociologist Lynn Davidman found that educated women turn to Judaism with full agency as a response to their alienation from and disenchantment with modern life.[9] Other scholars have documented that Orthodox Jewish women report feelings of empowerment in their newly adopted traditions but are altogether conscious of gender inequalities and their role in perpetuating them. Heathens share much in common with Orthodox Jewish converts, including a focus on traditional ethnic religion, a (willing or unwilling) perpetuation of patriarchy, and a belief that they are "theologically equal to men." Patriarchy is embedded in Heathenry but exhibits a softer quality, manifesting as an acceptance of male archetypes—men as fatherly, wise authorities and strong leaders emphasizing toughness. This is the implied breadwinner and man-of-the-house status of classical gendered divisions of labor. Both groups also share a tendency not to directly challenge the social structural foundations of gender inequality. "For the most part, they do not challenge male hegemony in the public. They do not acknowledge that the feminine virtues/capabilities that they separate also serve to maintain a gendered division of labor."[10] In other words, once the gendered division of labor is rendered sacred, it is depoliticized by both groups.

Reading History: Finding a Place for Heathen Women

Unlike the Jewish women whom Debra Kaufman observed,[11] Heathen women do not possess the advantage of an unbroken lived tradition on which to base their ethnicity. They are challenged by the ongoing (re)construction of modern treatments and performances of gender that are informed by their understanding of gender among historical Heathens. They focus on adapting to contemporary conditions what they believe ancient Heathen women did at home, their beliefs about men and masculinity, and their roles and positions in their farming communities. In a sense, Heathen women are constructing their socioreligious gendered selves from the ground up in ways that both challenge and support existing social arrangements.

Modern Heathen women cannot escape from contemporary definitions of gender differences or expectations of feminine bodies, performances, and selves. Even women who are completely immersed in Heathenry and its worldview cannot entirely avoid the influence of culture, whether mainstream, pop, or something else. Yet, as with any reconstructionist faith system, in order to understand what Heathens are doing right now, we must appreciate what they think their forebears were doing "back then" and why they think this. Over twelve hundred years ago, the Old Norse maintained a unique perspective on gender that led to the relative freedom of Old Norse women compared with the rest of European women during the same period, who were already subject to oppressive canonical law. A large sector of the Heathen community takes this history into account as it carves out a niche for women that allows them expression and belonging in their ethnoreligious community. The image of the ideal Heathen woman as a contemporary echo of her ancient women ancestors has become part of the community's collective identity. Many of my respondents view Heathen women as somehow unique and often describe them in traditional masculine terms as strong, forthright, independent, and confident, unlike what Heathens feel are the mainstream norms for women's performance of femininity. In other cases, women are described as divine, weavers of peace, matronly, or domestic. Like Hallgerd and Freydis, Heathens situate gender in the historical context of the Old Norse during the Viking age. In a blog entry titled "The Standing of Heathen Women," user "heathenblogr" illustrates this trope:

> In ancient times, women in Northern Europe enjoyed a position unheard of in other cultures of the times. They had the right to seek redress from anyone who had wronged them. They could be the head of a household, or demand wergild. They could own land, servants, or serve as advisors to a King or Queen. They were generally acknowledged as better at frithweaving. Taticus [sic] writes that the ancient Germans felt there was "something sacred and provident about women," they consulted them in all matters of life. This was true even in such "manly" duties as war and rulership. So where does that place modern Asatru women? This means that modern Asatru women are not limited in any way by history, tradition, or religious culture.[12]

Throughout the discursive construction of gender, Heathens rely in large part on romanticized and idealized images from the lore, often portraying Viking society as a sort of feminist wonderland. The image of Old Norse women in history, however, reveals them as domestic laborers, sexual objects, and political pawns. These discrepancies among the lore, historical sources, and modern interpretations remain largely unexamined in public Heathen discourse. Other infrequent and marginally supported evidence from the lore indicates instances when women were more like those fantastic figures from paintings and more recent Wagnerian stories: Valkyries, shield maidens, armor laden and fearless, active in the process of determining their own fates and equal in every respect to their male comrades. Soren, a thirty-six-year-old professor in the southern United States, explained to me that "some women are drawn to Heathenry because it does offer a lot of strong female role models. In the sagas you've got very assertive and independent minded figures like Aud the Deep Minded or Bergthora, the wife of Njal in Njal's Saga, and mythologically you've got figures like Freyja and legendary heroines like Brynhild and Gudrun."[13] This image of the strong, warrior-like Viking woman is popular within the Heathen community and leads its members to bypass the unpleasant realities of women in the past and to seek to re-create, instead, a modern ideal of gender equality as they believe it should have been back then. The contradictions are not lost on all Heathens, as Eskel, a graduate student, revealed when I asked him about his expression of ideal qualities among Heathen women:

> Of course the, you know, in stereotypical Heathen fashion, I would initially try to link it back to references in the sagas or something like that, because there definitely are examples of strong women there, but they're definitely a minority in the sagas, so frankly, a lot of that image probably does come in large part out of feminist movements, and even Wiccan influences into Heathenry. . . . It's easily supportable within Heathenry because of the presence within the Heathen pantheon of very strong goddesses.[14]

At the same time, Heathens actively engage in storytelling involving the few rights of Old Norse women that their contemporaries did not enjoy. Rather than discussing present realities or structural inequalities, this method of discursive sense making, of narrative construction and identity work, is among the most prevalent ones in discussions of gender. Brand, the young father and hypnotherapist introduced in Chapter 2, tells me:

> Women provoked their husbands into doing all sorts of things, they got them to vote—it's kind of an interesting role reversal, where, when women obtained suffrage in the US and were allowed to vote, men still told their wives how to vote, and in Iceland, when men would go to the Thing, the women would convince their men which way to vote, which sides to go with. Kind of an interesting role reversal, there were Icelandic women like Aud the Deep-Minded who owned property, freed slaves and gave out property and didn't need the authority of a man.[15]

Likewise, Ivor, an information technology professional and long-time member of the community, references the lore as a foundation for his explanation of contemporary gender equality:

> Marija Gimbutas in several of her books points out that women in Northern Europe, i.e., Celts, Teutons, Germanic tribes, kept a lot of their rights and so forth right up until Christianity came in. They were not kept as slaves in the house, à la the Romans and the Greeks, they were equal partners. Women could stand up and bring legal cases before the

assembly, they held the keys to the household, and there's a lot of that ethos going into the modern Heathen woman. They don't take a back seat, they're right in there with the guys, mixing it up. And I think that is one thing that even other Pagans don't necessarily get.[16]

In spite of the discrepancies between textual and historical sources and their modern interpretations, Heathens have created their own realities and realm of meaning, in which equality is taken as a matter of fact, and the prevailing image of the Heathen woman is modeled on the perceived best qualities of the Old Norse. Sources for beginners most often repeat these narratives, such as this encyclopedia blog entry on Ásatrú;

> Some of us, as past Christians, may not be new to the view that women are weak, and should be treated with contempt and loathing, due to giving in to the serpent's offer of the apple. It was a completely different story in Germania: women were viewed with respect and awe, and were somewhat feared by men. As wives, (the average age of marrying being 20—very late for those days!) Germanic Women were viewed as proud, independent and kept her own property and name. Germanic women whose husbands treated them badly were expected to take vengeance upon him—unlike the Roman women of the time, who were expected to endure any treatment by their husband, however horrible.[17]

Even if historical sources are not cited as a foundation for contemporary under-standings of gender equality, they are taken for granted. The narrative discourse surrounding perceptions of equality among the ancients and in contemporary life is pervasive enough that the argument itself has been absorbed to become a feeling of truth. It has become part of the collective Heathen imagination, with or without on-the-spot factual support. Vana, a forty-five-year-old woman and government programmer, explains:

> I can't even remember where I read it, but I read somewhere where, you know, men didn't just run off and fight in something, they actually con-sulted the women. Because, so I'm like—well then they played a part, there was a part there, you know, and I can't even remember where I read that at, you know, that they weren't just in some religions where they, their opinion doesn't matter, their opinion did matter.[18]

Members often base their ideas on statements that they hear repeated in community spaces on the Internet. Vana's unclear memory but nonetheless solid confidence illustrates the fuzziness of information sharing and that much of the information that Heathens gather from texts is distributed through discourse. They share information and various interpretations of the lore, reproduce narra-tives, and tap into the collective imagination of what Heathen women were like then and are like (or should be like) now. The focus on history and its role in the reconstruction of women's place within this movement has left women with very particular options, as Alice expressed in a blog entry on Heathen women:

> In these sources women either play the role of warrior, peace maker or magical shrew. . . . This has carried over into modern heathenry by way of expecting our women to be dedicated to the home by means of fiber crafts, children and folk magic. I cannot count the times I have been asked what I knit or it has been assumed that I practice seidth [seidr]. If we are not in the role of magic/holy worker or homesteader, we are expected to be a shield-maiden of epic proportions.[19]

Although some women are increasingly questioning the allowable expressions of womanness within the movement, more are not. Other scholars have documented the negotiations between religious selves and contemporary sociopolitical arrangements, arguing as I do that patriarchy and political mandates feel less oppressive once actors imbue particular roles and circumstances with the sacred.[20] Yet it is impossible to escape from the minefield of popular politics, bodies, and identities. More often than not, Heathen women take on these roles as magic/holy worker, homesteader, or shield maiden, navigating the system and finding meaning in ties to the past.

Navigating Gender: The Masculine Ethic

Research on drag kings highlights the performative aspects of resistance and the malleability of masculinity. Female masculinity offers an alternative mode of masculinity detached from misogyny that allows women to appropriate male power.[21] For Heathens, gendered behavioral expectations, particularly during the earlier years of the movement, were largely similar for both men and women. This is not to suggest that community norms have been constructed to engage everyone in both masculine and feminine performance; to imply that Heathens regularly challenge the polarization of gender would be misleading. Their expectations for both genders, like those of their forebears, lean heavily toward behaviors traditionally associated with masculinity, although they maintain de facto divisions of labor, with men as providers (despite the common two-income household) and women as workers, also responsible for the upkeep of children and the home.

From the 1970s into the early years of the twenty-first century, Heathen expressions of gender were highly patriarchal and masculine-centric and were modeled on an interpretation of historical arrangements. Among the Old Norse, the very idea of masculinity was an ethic of the time. It was considered the pinnacle of good character and therefore was highly prized and defended. Throughout the Icelandic sagas, both genders were praised for acts that today's society might consider masculine acts of violence or pride. Without transporting a surplus of

Oedipal baggage, we might say that Viking society was a very phallic culture. Women who exhibited pride or defended themselves and their families verbally or physically were greatly respected and honored throughout Old Norse society as superlative citizens. It is also evident that the Old Norse highly disfavored and reacted strongly to acts of femininity or effeminacy in men with strict social sanctions. Insults were a finely tuned art among the Old Norse, and many words were regarded as so vastly insulting that they were punished by a fine; they were fighting words that frequently led to the excused killing or hefty fine of the instigator. Dealings such as this, therefore, provide a unique perspective on the gender structure of Old Norse society. Insults that implied that a man had experienced the sexual role of a woman were actually illegal and gave men a reason to challenge each other in *holmgang,* or single combat. Men, as it stood, were under the constant threat of becoming weak or effeminate, which was thought to be inevitable with old age. Such feminization or emasculation resulted in a man experiencing *ergi,* a word denoting unmanliness or effeminate behavior.

> There are three words—should exchanges between people ever reach such dire limits—which all have full outlawry as the penalty: if a man calls another *ragr, stroð inn* or *sorðinn.* As they are to be prosecuted like other *fullréttisorð* and, what is more, a man has the right to kill in retaliation for these three words. He has the right to kill in retaliation on their account over the same period as he has the right to kill on account of women, in both cases up the next General Assembly. The man who utters these words falls with forfeit immunity at the hands of anyone who accompanies the man about whom they were uttered to the place of their encounter.[22]

Scenes from the sagas show women taunting old men, suggesting that in old age some men had grown out of their masculinity and were therefore not just like women but below them. Although women were believed to be naturally feminine, they were not incapable of stepping into the roles expected of men through warlike behavior, forthrightness, or financial independence. Those who were able to provide and produce were greatly valued, and women, in their domestic roles, were the producers of nearly every conceivable staple of Viking society.

Women's roles and deeds were recorded in the Icelandic sagas, which, although they are not accurate in a historical sense, offer us an idea of Old Norse attitudes and opinions on what qualified as a good society.[23] The sagas often portray women as formidable and seemingly masculine, particularly in their transgressive behaviors. The *Völsunga Saga's* chain-mail-clad Brynhilde, for example, was more formidable in battle than all but one of her male counterparts, and saga women such as Sigrun the Proud are remembered for their brazen resistance to attempts by men to subdue them through violence and oppression. Although some of what occurs in the sagas conflicts with what we know of ancient legal codes, these stories nonetheless "celebrated woman's normative undoing, making sex and gender mobile across bodies and identities."[24]

Ancient Heathen concepts of gender also involved the mobility of masculinity across both (and other) genders. Carol Clover contends that unlike the contemporary view of gender opposites—the "men are from Mars, women are from Venus" ideology—the Old Norse did not differ in their concept of womanhood but rather lacked one altogether.[25] There was one category of gender that held value, and it was male. There were strong men, extraordinary women, and the rest of society, which consisted of ordinary women, old men, effeminate men, children, and the disabled. Ordinary women were viewed as less perfect men, their internal genitalia being viewed as identical but inverted. Psychoanalytic theory might argue that they were perceived as less equipped and therefore somehow marginally inferior.[26] Although Freudian analysis of the body focuses more on symbolism and metaphor than on anatomy, the Old Norse believed in concrete biological distinctions that carried over into terms of perceived duties and capabilities, inside versus outside, and power versus powerlessness. Emphasizing such seemingly strict binary constructions of gender and power, Clover's model reveals how ancient Heathen concepts of gender compare with our own.[27]

No Fluffy Bunnies Allowed

Modern Heathens have in some ways revived this binary focus, constructing a masculinized (for lack of a better term) femininity that allows women to be tomboys and claim a share of male power while still engaging in and maintaining ownership over gendered domestic endeavors.[28] Religion is often an arena in which, through ritual and doctrine, "women and men are persuaded of the 'rightness' of male dominance."[29] Heathens, with their focus on the historical cultural meanings and practices of their forebears, risk re-creating a patriarchal system that parallels the one already in place. Although issues of patriarchy, oppression, and misogyny receive regular attention in online interactions, structural inequalities are too deeply embedded to receive more than cursory mention. Rather, the more superficial manifestations of inequality, particularly expectations placed on women to adopt qualities associated with femininity, receive the most critique. As Heathens remain steadfast in the discourse surrounding the ideal of Heathen women as strong, forthright, and independent, Heathen women contrast themselves with the Victorian influence on a femininity that compels women to be dependent and compliant. I spoke with Sulda, a writer with an interest in women's studies, about this legacy:

> There's a femininity, in my opinion, sociologically and culturally speaking, um, the Victorian era, with its emphasis on that sort of weak wallflower woman on a pedestal kind of thing, really sent us back. And I do think that that's something that should be thrown away. I think that it is outdated, I think it was probably wrong when it started but it is what

it is. I think that in many ways, American culture especially, fills—views women through a Victorian lens, you know what I'm saying?[30]

Reminiscent of the experiences of Lauraine Leblanc's punk girls,[31] a comfortable fit in Heathenry requires that women be assertive and often aggressive or at least appear to maintain the capability. Many women come to American Heathenry wary of its emphasis on maleness, often viewing it as a haven for chest-beating and mead-swigging manly men. They come to learn that these behaviors express a manliness not just reserved for men. For Heathens, both men and women ideally share this power, and many, like Alvis, believe that "a Heathen woman should be smart, a Heathen woman should be strong, she should be, you know, she should be all the things that a good Heathen man is."[32] Likewise, a running joke in some circles suggests that the Heathen motto should be "Heathenry: Where men are men, and women are men!" In effect, Heathen women engage in an attempt to avoid girly sissy stuff while maintaining ownership over traditionally held feminine domains. Partly, the treatment of femininity in Heathen discourse reminds us that the feminine has often "served as the negative counterpoint, the 'Other,' for the construction of positive masculine identity."[33] It is often approached similarly to the Old Norse idea of gender as power versus powerlessness, where hyperfemininity risks being labeled as weak, fluffy, or, worse, Wiccan.

This idea is echoed in Heathenry's gendered history, in which one branch of American Heathenry, Ásatrú, began in 1972 as the Viking Brotherhood, one of the first gasps in the emergent mythopoeic men's movement that grew out of men's collective attempts to "disengage themselves from feminism"[34] because feminist critique of male dominance was "experienced as indicting the morality of all men."[35] Men responded by attempting to recover a "lost" masculinity through retreats, rituals, male-empowerment workshops, a revival of the image of "the male warrior," and a belief in a "loose essentialism" in which mythopoeic men treat "gender, masculinity and the category 'men' as if they were primitive constituent elements of the universe" rather than social constructs while allowing themselves flexibility in their own masculinity.[36] Indeed, the discourse surrounding "real Heathen men" and a gendering of Heathenry continues. During Freyfaxi, an annual celebration of fertility and abundance, Stephen McNallen reflected on "manhood" in the following update to his AFA Facebook group:

> I'm an Odinsman, through and through; always have been. Odin shows us how to transcend; how to become a God—but Frey shows males how to become men, which is truly the first step toward Godhood. (Freya plays a comparable role for women.) And we need men, in this day and age! Far too many males in our society never grow up, never shoulder the duties that come with manhood. They live for nothing, and when they die, they die for nothing. . . . They are deservedly forgotten. Men are to be firm and upright . . . in every sense! They are to contribute to

their lineage by having children, or if that is not an option by otherwise adding to the family honor. They provide abundance for family and kin, they are sources of joy and pleasure, and when necessary they fight, even if the only weapon at hand is an antler. They are fighters AND lovers. Hail, Frey, and those in whom he lives![37]

This heavily politicized hypermasculine ethos concerns many Heathen women who are turned off by a masculine-centric Heathenry, where the spiritual is militarized and men yearn to be Vikings at the expense of the development of a mature religious community. To men who emphasize this focus, Heathenry is a masculine faith for tough guys, where attitudes toward women are patronizing and paternal and domineering misogynistic sentiments abound. Although this construction of Heathen masculinity was, for a time, on the wane, it seems to have become more popular as political attitudes in the United States shift ever rightward. After the school shootings in Newtown, Connecticut, in early 2013 McNallen released a Facebook status update equating gun rights with manhood, a common and powerful symbolic connection in the American imagination.

The attempt to disarm American citizens of effective weaponry is, among other things, the next logical step in the castration of the American male. Oh, I know there are many women who love guns and who are dead-eye shots; they are sisters of Freya, lovely and feminine but with a touch of the corpse-rending battle-demon; mothers and sisters and temptresses all, and I support them one hundred percent. But there is another tendency in America and throughout the Western world that seeks to remove the manliness from men, to make them soft (in every sense) and weak, and to tame them. This serves neither men nor women, but benefits only those who want a world that is controlled and manageable. I will fight this will all my might, regardless of the consequences.[38]

In response, members of the group applauded McNallen, with ninety-six likes and nineteen comments in agreement. Such vocal and repetitious pairings of manhood, masculinity, and virtue with conservative political ideology is nothing new. In the 1990s the leader of the Christian men's movement the Promise Keepers linked men's perceived loss of power and status to the "feminization of the American male . . . a misunderstanding of manhood that has produced a nation of 'sissified' men."[39] The fear of male feminization has held steady since the 1990s among Christian men and is a growing pattern within American Heathenry, a conservative Christian influence and tendency that create a troubling impression of Heathenry in the European Heathen and American Neopagan imagination. In further illustration of such gendering of political ideas, AFA members, primarily men, provided telling commentary through their growls of support, hailing guns and gun rights from every angle. Others followed traditional gendered scripts, celebrating hegemonic masculinity and denigrating the feminine with gendered remarks equating gun ownership with "real" manhood and mocking the perceived effeminacy of modern men with quips such as "Have you SEEN the Spring layout on Yahoo? Skirts and blouses and frills for the guys!" What little dissent there was came from a handful of women whose posts disclaimed support for gun control but questioned the need to own assault rifles, and from an English AFA member whose opposition was quickly ridiculed as fellow members called him a "liberal" and instructed him to "get on The Troth's page. I hear they are surrendering their guns and freedom." One commenter argued, "We must excuse [him], he's British. They gave up their right to protect themselves and their families a long time ago."[40]

Early in the movement, women attracted to Heathenry came to it largely from other Neopagan spiritualities, which most Heathens portray as flaky, girly, unfounded metaphysical hogwash. As Unni remarks, Neopagans are viewed as "flaky" people who cannot really make a commitment to anything.[41] In large part, this impression is rooted in the Neopagan tendency to do what "feels" good spiritually—whether it involves honoring multiple pantheons, borrowing cultural practices from around the world, or improvising. However, most members realize Heathenry's connections to Wicca at the same time at which they acknowledge the necessity of distancing from it in order to protect the movement's identity. When participants reference Wiccans or criticize challenges to the integrity of Heathen reconstruction, they do so in political and gender-coded language. Alfdis, the world traveler and ex-soldier, recalls:

> Ásatrú when it first came out, I think, because of the whole Viking mentality, was male-dominated. . . . A lot of guys came out to express themselves in a faithful or religious manner, but I also think in that same breath that this is an expression, I think that Ásatrú was probably a natural counterbalance to the Goddess-orientated and very top-heavy Wicca that was so predominant during that time, and started basically with huge numbers in the United States in the early '60s.[42]

To find acceptance in the "Viking" men's club, many Neopagan women had to avoid performances of "witchy" femininity in favor of more overt and dominating performances of Valkyrie masculinity, one of American Heathenry's main contrasts with the rest of the Neopagan world, despite the fact that the picture of Wiccan femininity is hardly so monolithic that it can be sharply distinguished from Heathenry. For example, Dianic Wiccans embrace a brand of masculinized separatist feminism and political lesbianism that is anything but the kind of girly witch that most Heathen women seem so opposed to. Yet the stereotypes of Wiccans as girly and liberal provide a powerful trope against which to define what it means to be Heathen or not Wiccan. These constructions of gendered selves include the not-self, the "other" that the new self has been constructed to oppose. The new self is viewed as somehow liberated and ultimately improved and empowered. In this way, Heathen women who have strong personalities are welcome in Heathenry, where they can escape religious and social censure for contradicting normative feminie behaviors. Over coffee in a snug artsy café, Eskel explains the expectations for Heathen women:

> Historically speaking, previous to my involvement in the community, Heathenry was predominantly a male thing. In my experience, there have been more substantial numbers of very outspoken, strong women involved. All of the groups that I've been involved with had at some point or another been led by women. . . . The ideal [Heathen woman] would be contrary to the stereotypes of larger society, is very outspoken, is artic-ulate, able to make their case independently without recourse to, to someone else having to support them in it.[43]

Men and women alike, particularly those who come to American Heathenry from Neopagan spiritualities, can adopt Heathen masculinity as one of the main ways that "we" are not like "them" but somehow better. The construction of the Wiccan "other" paints Wiccans as gynocentric. In earlier Wiccan traditions, like Gardnerian and Alexandrian Wicca, gender balance was the primary idea. The blending of Wicca and feminism that resulted in certain gynocentric vari-eties began in the 1960s and is still not representative of all—perhaps not even the majority—of Wiccan traditions. In his living room, sitting on the floor, I asked Brand to describe his concept of the "ideal" Heathen woman. He responded:

> Heathenry is one of those religions that encourages women to be stron-ger. Independent. In charge of things. Instead of the subservient "yes master" kind of role, it encourages women to step up and be just as big, strong and powerful as the men. That there is really no gender role, no gender gap, quite honestly in my opinion.[44]

Despite such emphasis on masculine performance, Heathen women are not exempt from social pressure to be superfeminine, ultrasexy, super moms while balancing high-powered and successful careers. Yet they have challenged this impossible and irrational expectation by reframing their economic and social gender norms as an aspect of their tradition, eschewing many of the performances that go along with so-called girlishness and thereby resisting the feeling of powerlessness, if not the daily grind of familiar routines. Femininities are con-structed differently than masculinities are. They do not "confer cultural power"; instead, they are "constructed as a variety of negations of the masculine."[45] And while "distancing oneself from hegemonic or hypermasculinity is about giving up power, symbolically if not in practice, distancing oneself from stereotypical femininity . . . is a claiming of power. . . . To oppose stereotypical or normalized feminine positioning is to reject the disempowerment that comes with it."[46]

Unlike other female performances of masculinity (e.g., drag kings) whose theatrics are subdued and "quietly macho,"[47] Heathenry often encourages forthright and unabashed in-your-face masculinities from both genders. Inga shared the contradictions of these expectations, of the cultural clash between community and wider social pressures:

> I was just talking the other day to one of the other female Heathens, that I really felt kind of out of place because I'm not a girly-girl, but I'm not butch either. And that's totally the wrong term, but I'm not, I'm not sad to be a girl, and occasionally I enjoy wearing dresses, and I do put on makeup, and I do like making pretty things, and I like cooking, and I like doing all this stuff, so it's like, part of me was going "Oh my gosh, I can't be Heathen and not be a hard-core ball-crusher." But you can. Because that's part of the culture too. So I think as Heathenry matures, we're going to start seeing a lot more women getting involved because it's okay to be a woman in Ásatrú.[48]

Inga's comment reflects a trend. As American Heathenry distances itself more and more from its concerns with "feminine" Neopagan associations (i.e., Wicca), women are able to embrace more conventional practices associated with the female domain. This has both positive and negative consequences. Women are able to distance themselves from performances of the Valkyrie battle maiden and become nurturing domestic divas, who, as Inga explains, sometimes like to look pretty. When "looking pretty" is no longer associated with "looking Wiccan," perhaps Heathen women will no longer feel pressure to resist performances of normative femininity. Yet the pressure is strong from all genders: to be feminine is to be Wiccan, to be "fluffy bunnies"[49] or "woo woo," gender-coded language quite strongly associated with being liberal, hippie, or absurd.

The limits and the acceptability of Heathen women's performances are still, to a certain extent, controlled by the boundaries imposed by Western culture. They are not exempt, for example, from the endemic focus on women's physical bodies. Thrain, a burgeoning author and professional website developer, admits that when he was a newcomer to the community, the most striking feature of the Heathen women he first saw was their physical appearance:

> If you land in the middle of the campground at one of [the] gatherings, the first thing that you notice is that most Heathen women are extremely overweight. . . . My own preferences—I'm a great admirer of classical femininity, um, there has to be a solid intellect and a good sense of common sense with that. I don't see a lot of classically feminine women in Heathenry.[50]

To him, many Heathen women defy classical or normative expectations of feminine beauty standards. When I asked whether obesity can be tied directly to

Heathenry, or whether it is a wider cultural problem, he assured me that the level of obesity among Heathen women was "astounding." The breach of normative beauty standards by Heathen women was his first and lasting impression, indicating that despite the discourse of Heathen women being strong, independent, and somehow unique, they are still held to account for violations of beauty norms. Some Heathen women turn toward the divine for means of resistance. In a Pagan-centered blog, Heathen author Cena Bussey asked other Heathens:

> Is there one among all of the Goddesses who bemoans her own ugliness? Compares themselves to another woman? Do any of them shed tears for the size of their breasts, or bewail the thickness of their waist? Is their [sic] one moment described when our Goddesses express malice, or outright hatred for another woman? I have never read or heard of such a thing.[51]

Heathen women, however, are not (for the most part) actively engaged in the resistance of both masculinity and femininity. Instead, many are claiming ownership over a masculine performance, adopted from a number of images of Viking women as warriors, such as Wagner's *Ring Cycle*. Wiccan author Lynda Welch, whose book on the Northern Goddess received venomous reviews from many Heathens, claims that "Norse women were known to march to battle and fight side by side with their fellow male warriors."[52] This claim, repeated throughout the literature written by lay scholars, irks many Heathen women who have increasingly problematized the entire concept of Heathenry as a warrior culture in general, and of Heathen women as warriors. Inga, the massage therapist, explains that this warrior emphasis can be quite off-putting to some women:

> I think the issue with attracting Heathen women specifically, if there even is anything to be considered an issue, is the fact that Ásatrú really, currently, focuses quite a bit on the warrior aspect, and I think that really does a disservice to Ásatrú, because, you know, the Heathens of the past and my family were hardly solely warriors.[53]

Likewise, Aud, a young woman instructor of mathematics, notes:

> People who think of Heathenry as a warrior culture are too hung up on the Vikings. Our gods and goddesses were worshipped long before people went a-viking, and our faith and holidays focus on seasons and agriculture much more than on war. Of course, in the harsh climate of northern Europe, raising crops and tending livestock could be just as much a battle as fighting with another people. To survive in those conditions, people had to be strong and capable (not necessarily warlike). That applied to men and women both, as it still does today when we are living as adherents to a minority faith.[54]

There are whispers in the sagas of women taking up arms, but the notion of "female warriors" remains both understudied and controversial among scholars, who lack conclusive material evidence to prove that women fought in battle.[55] One Icelandic saga describes Freydis, daughter of Erik Thorvaldson (aka the Red) as having held a sword against her bare breast to frighten off the Native Americans. Later in the saga she murders five women in a dispute over dwindling resources because the men she has charged with the task have refused.[56] Other sagas also speak of women taking up arms, although not in the capacity that we might imagine from Welch's illustration. This history is not lost on all women. Sulda explains:

> This is one of the problems I actually have with our emphasis on the warrior culture, you know, if you want to look back into the history, the Vikings weren't warriors all the time. They were mostly farmers, animal husbands. . . . Women were producers, and I think that, in my opinion, we should look at these examples because they lack the coloring, that, in my opinion, the Victorian Era and the rise of the Industrial Revolution gave women.[57]

The idea of the Valkyrie marching into battle with full armor and all the status of a man is a romantic Wagnerian myth. It has leached into modern literature and film, from comics to cartoons, staying in the minds of people for whom horned helmets and conical breastplates constitute the accepted default image of Viking men and women.

Politicizing Gender: Feminism Meets Antifeminism

As American Heathenry struggles to maintain a collective identity, grow as a spiritual system, and piece together a holistic worldview revived from the ashes of the ages, constructions of gender are constantly changing and adapting. Early notions of gender tilted heavily toward idealized images of heroic masculinity, but as the community has grown, and as Heathenry has developed multiple dimensions, gender expectations have begun to shift toward more traditional gender dynamics, with a focus on family and tribal groups. One of the most explicit expressions of women-as-domestics, and an example of the flammability of arguments that smack of mainstream conservatism, comes from a book by Heathen author Mark Puryear.[58] Puryear is somewhat marginalized and uninfluential in wider Heathenry, but his arguments are echoed in the Odinist communities, although less frequently among Ásatrúar. Yet his ideas, also expressed by other authors, such as Wyatt Kaldenberg, color the experiences of many Heathen women. His book, On the Nature of Ásatrú, is an explanatory guide to Heathenry from a (more conservative) self-labeled "tribalist" perspective. Despite the similarity of the sentiments presented by Puryear to those of many of the people I interviewed, his book has been harshly criticized by several members of the community—a polarization of ideas along political lines. Puryear begins his explanation of the gods by drawing attention to the "masculine paradigm of the ancient Teutons." He believes that this paradigm involved "manliness" as a combination of "heroism and benevolence," remarking that ancient Heathens did not "adopt feminine modes of behavior" but rather believed that "men should be proud of their gender, and women should value and respect them for this." Ultimately, Puryear believes that the reclamation of Heathen identity involves "living up to the ideal of manhood as displayed by our gods and heroes."[59] He writes that women are to be "strong, independent, and noble, without compromising their femininity" and argues that women can and should embrace "beauty, motherhood, sensuality, and nurturing." He echoes the popular but unverified statement that no other culture "in the world" honored women better than the Teutons and Celts. Heathen women, he claims, stood beside Heathen men "as equals." He notes that Heathen women, before Christianity, could "live their lives in any way they chose," leaving unquestioned the harsh reality of life and the rigid economic and social structure of the Old Norse.[60]

In Iceland and Norway, in contrast to Denmark and Sweden, "women enjoyed legal and economic independence and their rights were well protected by law."[61] According to Grethe Jacobsen, these discrepancies can be explained by the differing times at which the law codes were written; earlier laws allowed women more freedom. Icelandic and Norwegian laws were older and remained somewhat stable, but Danish and Swedish laws were rewritten to account for canonical laws that restricted the rights of women. As Christian influence gained sway, changes to the laws gradually resulted in the loss of rights that women and their female forebears had enjoyed for centuries. Even so, among the Old Norse, a woman was, by law, the property of her husband or father. She had very limited freedom to dispose of property belonging to her. She was prohibited from participating in most political or governmental activities. She could not be a *Gothi,* a judge, or a witness, nor could she speak at *thing*s (assemblies).

Despite this, Puryear argues that "there was nothing subservient about the position" of housewife, which today has been "devalued" by feminists, "essentially giving in to the patriarchal view that these roles are not as important as men's." Puryear avoids deconstructing the patriarchal system that he, in his way, is trying to critique or questioning men's place in it, but he is not alone. This is all too common a problem within Heathenry, but he is one of the milder conservative voices. In earlier years American Heathenry was polarized by participants' stance on racial exclusivity and by the "folkish" versus "universalist" divide (see Chapter 6). In 2015, as Republican hard-liners continue to change the political environment, American politics become progressively more divisive and polarized. The so-called culture war has an increasing influence on the Heathen social sphere. Thomas E. Mann of the Brookings Institution and Norman J. Ornstein of the American Enterprise Institute described the political polarization in their 2012 book *It's Even Worse Than It Looks* as "asymmetric polarization."[62] In Heathenry and American politics in general, the name of the game is the pitting of political ideologies against one another, dividing communities by political labels and identities. Within American Heathenry, these identities include those on the far right or right-leaning and those others on the small and difficult-to-locate left who, to the conservative imagination, represent a dangerous threat. Those few on the left who are politically engaged find support on Facebook and in groups such as Heathens United against Racism, with over 1,700 members, and Heathen Lefties and Heathen Anarchist's Hall, with around 100 each—small groups of people who talk among themselves. Accusations by conservative Heathens regarding those "liberal" others, as I have indicated throughout this book, takes place in a country in which politics in general are shifting rightward, and in which the Heathen "Left" consists of those who describe themselves as apolitical or independent, but who, through their silence, acquiesce in the dominance of stronger conservative voices. The task of this book is to focus on the apolitical majority. Those whom I have come to know over the years are much less right-wing than the loudest voices on Facebook and the Heathen blogosphere.

According to the dominant narrative among Heathens, to be conservative is to hate liberals, and with this political identity comes a parallel version of Heathenry, illustrated by Heathen commentator Juleigh Howard-Hobson, who argues that feminism "negates" Heathen folkways:

> The European-descended folk alive today are better served by a devout Christian woman in braids and long skirts who has 18 home-schooled European-descended children than by some Mjollner-wearing SCA "battle Valkyrie" feminist who has not provided a child for our folk future. . . . Our ancestors—female and male—were equal in all dealings from the moment they matured to womanhood and manhood. And their equal footing was not based on women behaving like ersatz men— which, when you look at it, is not equality at all but a pathetic mimicry.[63]

This argument, published in a Heathen journal, received passionate criticism, but it symbolizes a growing strain of far-right Heathen thought. Both Puryear and Howard-Hobson argue that feminism is to blame for problematizing patriarchal oppression and thereby tainting the concept of "traditional" motherhood or female roles. It is because of these modern feminist notions, they argue, that women are no longer accepting traditional roles. It is a convoluted mix of praise and rejection of equality and feminism for those who fear words too "liberal" and thereby Neopagan.

The growing strain of misogyny and antifeminist thought finds other footing in Heathens' engagement with the lore. The lore includes many incidents that conflict with the idea of gender equality among ancient Heathens, including multiple cases of rape, for which the offenders are never punished despite its illegality in Icelandic law codes, and the commodification of women in which they are portrayed as generally passive receivers of men's wills, although occasionally powerful and respected. There are contradictory messages throughout the literature in reference to the status of women. The law books indicate that women did indeed enjoy rights and a status that allowed them more freedom than their contemporaries in other regions of Europe. The sagas suggest that the Old Norse imagination allowed extraordinary women to be warriors, resisters, and gender benders. Other passages, however, reveal that the status of women was much less than ideal in many cases. In one such example, Saxo Grammaticus's account of the death of the god Baldur, Odin, the alfather of the gods, is compelled to seduce Rind, a woman who has previously rebuffed his advances, so that they might conceive a child to avenge his beloved son Baldur's death. Because of Rind's nonconsent, Odin's method of accomplishing this task is problematic. Dressing up as a nursemaid, he beguiles Rind into drinking a supposedly healing draught that renders her unconscious. Once she is immobilized, Odin rapes her, and she becomes pregnant, fulfilling his task. Her father finds the situation of little consequence, and Odin's ensuing exile from the kingdom of the Aesir does not occur because of the rape but because he was dressed as a woman and therefore experienced *ergi* (meaning effeminate, unmanly, sexually passive, and cowardly). Some Heathen women view this story as evidence that Odin was a misogynist. One participant in an online debate regarding whether Odin should be considered a misogynist or just a bastard describes this rape as divinely necessary. Sapphire Runesinger remarks:

> There is no reason for a woman to be a friend of Odin. . . . [He] is the original male chauvinist pig. He's unfaithful to His wife, Frigga. He treats His many mistresses and dalliances no better; He says outright in *Hávamál* that He lies when he flatters them. He also claims that women are fickle, deceitful and not to be trusted. Odin seduces and abandons Gunnlod to win the mead of poetry and boasts about it later. Rinda is raped outright. He forces the Völva to reveal her prophecy to Him. He has no feminine qualities; He is not a god I would call on lightly.[64]

Another perspective, "Rebuttal" from Arlea Æðelwyrd Hunt-Anschütz, states:

> I would argue that Oðin is a true egalitarian who is in touch with his feminine side. He sees women as worthy and equal opponents. He makes no special allowances for them. He can't afford to. The female gods and giants are just as intelligent, resourceful, and tough as their male counterparts. Oðin will use every resource at his disposal, including seduction, to accomplish his goals. In this way his behaviour is a lot like Freyja's. . . . When other methods fail, Oðin is willing to put women under spells, seduce them or even rape them in order to accomplish what he feels is an important goal. He clearly feels that the end justifies the means. Does this make him a misogynist? No, it just makes him a

bastard. He is equally ruthless with men. In his role as a god of war and death, he has to be.[65]

Additional accounts of rape and wife sharing occur throughout the sagas, conflicting with the law books of the period, which decry rape as an inexcusable and severely punishable crime in the interests of protecting male property, particularly if the victim is a virgin. Women throughout history have been subject (and the object of) to societal rules regarding their sexualities and freedoms. Viking women married when they were deemed competent in matters of "inside" labor; that is, they had learned the tricks of the trade from their female relatives in order that they might keep a successful household. In his *Germania*, written around 98 C.E., the Roman senator Cornelius Tacitus observed that women "are not hurried into marriage. As old and full-grown as the men, they match their mates in age and strength, and the children inherit the robustness of their parents."[66] Marriages were arranged by a woman's male relative, her "engager," who took the responsibility of arranging the transaction between the groom and the family of the bride with little strife. Women had little say in whom they chose to marry, although evidence hints that their opinions were taken seriously. Yet the male-dominated and frequently misogynistic episodes in the lore indicate that we cannot assume that ancient Heathens (particularly in Scandinavia) shared our contemporary ideals of gender equality. Saxo's accounts of the lore receive perhaps the least focus from the Heathen community; whether because of his ultrahistorical perspective and language use or the lack of hype for his work, the interaction that the average Heathen has with the lore is rather with a more generalized and ideal concept of how it should be or how it is perceived.[67] Saxo's lore, dry and lacking clearly defined boundaries between accounts, is not the lore of Wagner or modern prose renditions of Germanic myths and legends.

Resistance to Patriarchy

Despite such confusing back-to-the-kitchen arguments and violence against women in the lore, most Heathen women claim that Heathenry is empowering. It offers them central leadership roles in sacred performances, but they also believe that the lore supports their status as somehow close to and the embodiment of the sacred. In this way, men and women in Heathenry are understood, at least in discourse, as equals. Scholars can examine hegemonic masculinity by looking at what "Big Men" do in a social group "because what they do, by virtue of their dominance, constitutes masculinity in a community."[68] We cannot, however, study "Big Women" because they are mostly absent, and so it is impossible to discuss hegemonic femininity at all. "There can be no hegemonic femininity, because being in a hegemonic position is also about being in a position of power; it is about being able to construct the world for oneself and others so that one's power is unchallenged and taken (more or less) for granted as part of the order of things."[69]

Figure 5.1. Brad and Destiny of Bifrost Way Kindred (Oklahoma) stand before a newly erected and dedicated god pole in honor of Thor as Destiny (the *Gythia*) blesses the horn and its contents. (Photo by David L. Ballard, 2014.)

At the same time at which antifeminist political ideology is taking hold, Heathenry's leadership and popular personalities are increasingly female (see Figure 5.1). One of the West Coast's major kindreds is led by a *Gythia* and held together by strong support from its active female membership. The community also boasts many strong, outspoken female authors. In his blog, Swain Wodening, a leader in the Anglo-Saxon Ealdright, notes that

> within the Asatru community, Diana Paxson lead The Troth for many years as Steerswoman, while Yngona Desmond noted Heathen author leads Hodmimir Holt (a mystical guild) and Heimat Hof. Theodism has known such leaders as Winifred Hodge Rose who found Frigga's Web and co-founded the Angelseaxisce Ealdriht, Teresa Wodening who leads

the Miercinga Theod, and Jennifer Culver, leader of the mystical guild Widsith. Each of these women have had their hands in many areas of Heathenry.[70]

These leaders offer Heathen women strong role models that many claim were missing from previous religious experiences. Valda, the forty-something single mother cited earlier, was new to Heathenry when I met her. When she first began exploring it, she found it more empowering than her previous experiences:

> The women I grew up with were always in submission to their husbands. And especially my mother who I love dearly, but she had, I've just watched her allow herself to be walked all over and make bad decisions and, there's so many ways that I don't want to be like her, and the women I grew up with, yah, just—and just believing what you're spoon-fed, taught. . . . You know, I like having the power to question what people tell me and be able to find a true partner in life, and not be ashamed of anything, any aspect of who I am, whether it's knitting baby booties or dressing like a boy, you know. I feel much more freedom to be who I am than I ever did my first 24 years.[71]

As Valda demonstrates, Heathen womanness is often constructed in contrast to narratives of mainstream religious oppression and devaluation of women. When religious inequality is discussed, it is often mentioned in the context of other religious groups, as opposed to an internal focus on Heathenry's own particular dynamics. Brand's comment is a typical expression of this idea:

> Christianity came in and really did a lot to destroy the value of women, the power of women I should say, and Iceland has been known to be one of the few countries in the world where no matter what class or what gender you had the same level of education, the same basic responsibilities.[72]

Whether feminism or Christianity is to blame, the common understanding among Heathens is that the Old Norse enjoyed an (idealized) natural, functional, and generally better gender arrangement. Yet despite the patriarchy embedded within American Heathenry, part of the empowerment that Heathen women claim they feel comes from their opportunity to worship beings more like themselves than the patriarchal God of monotheism. This fact is often cited as a reason for Heathen women's initial attraction to the group. When I asked him whether Heathen women were "different," Egil, a friendly middle-aged man, explained that Heathen women are, first, "not sissies." He continued:

> I think that Ásatrú enables women to be as strong as they can be. I think it encourages the women to be strong and to play prominent roles in the

religion and not take a back seat to, or defer to men. And I think it's because of that, I think, that Ásatrú is one of the most liberating of all of the spiritual paths that's out there. . . . Any of the Abrahamic religions seem to want to keep women down.

Later, Egil continued to engage in gender comparisons while explaining what he perceived to be the shortcomings of mainstream religious practice:

We go to our women for council. I go to my wife and um we discuss anything . . . that's major—and I talk to her you know, she's my greatest counsel. And the women, the women are not subservient in Heathenry in any way, unlike Christian women are supposed to defer to their husbands. I find Heathen women to be outspoken, to give their opinions freely, and to be good strong dependable partners. . . . You know, they're—they're very strong, they know what their strengths are. Viking women are—I mean, they ruled the farm. I mean the whole deal about wearing keys on the belt, the more keys you had the more responsibilities you had, and it was great pride in having a large key ring. And so they ran things when the men were off. And so we respect our women, we hold them in great esteem.[73]

That Egil chose the words "our women" indicates the othering of women and the not-uncommon feelings of ownership over women by men. The pride in holding the key ring is being construed as a privilege and as presenting a positive perspective on domestic labor. Not only is this privilege interpreted as an honor for women, but also the more responsibilities women take on in the home, the more pride and honor they should presumably experience. In one way, this more domestic or passive ideal for Heathen women is empowering in that it allows for a reframing of domesticity that would otherwise maintain its mundane normativity and meaninglessness or perhaps oppressive experience.

Frith and Domesticity: The Sacred Mundane

Upon marriage in Old Norse society, a woman's husband gave her the keys to his house and the title of housekeeper.[74] Housekeeper was the highest status available to a woman and entailed considerable labor. Ancient Heathen women performed the tasks of gathering, drying, processing, and preparing food for their entire families and serving them, but they rarely ever took a seat themselves. A woman's authority over matters of the home and the pantry was absolute and rarely challenged.

This image of Heathen women as domestic in-the-kitchen types with a warrior zeal bleeds into even the simplest Heathen games, most notably a live-action game called "steal the wench," played at a large annual gathering during the "Viking games." It was midday, after the hammer toss, and I was standing by the open field under the hot sun, camera in hand, watching the last bout of kindred tug-of-war. At both ends of the rope were large bearded men, with only one woman among them. After a brief struggle, the kindred with the most guys won, to the sound of Heathen spectators cheering and shouting encouragement. I felt like a bystander at a competition between woodsmen and a biker-gang as the winners met their foes with cheerful backslaps and wrist-grab handshakes before taking their trophy, a giant wooden battle hammer, off to pose for pictures. Next, event organizers prepared the field by outlining with a rope the shape of a small square with an internal cubby, symbolizing a house with a kitchen. The premise is this: The woman player takes her place in the "kitchen" of the house, while her male challenger approaches from the outside. If he can remove her bodily from the house, to the sound of cheering, heckling, and applause, and drag her, fighting, to a marker placed about ten yards away, he wins and claims bragging rights, having "stolen the wench." If she wins by dragging him, bodily and disgraced, to the sounds of screaming celebration, into the kitchen of the house, he is her thrall and must do her bidding for the weekend. Although Heathen women are hardly laying down arms, the central premise is a tongue-in-check forceful taking of a woman from her rightful place in the kitchen, a task not unchallenging, involving, as it often does, a full-scale wrestling match. The women, I was told, never win, although some have come close, sustaining injuries in the process. The game involves stamina and determination, aggression for both sexes, and a clear symbolic message: the home is women's domain, and she has to fight. This narrative of women as domestic warriors undergirds Heathen expectations, particularly among groups who have taken on more tribalist structures. In the Midwest, where family is at the forefront of tribal philosophies, a notable chieftain toasted all the women present at *High Sumbel,* starting with his wife, who he explained kept him "in line" and was instrumental in the running of his kindred. He praised women at length as essential, powerful companions, organizers, mothers, and leaders. As a symbolic gesture of appreciation, he placed around the neck of each woman present a key pendant on a string. To modern Heathens, the key is a powerful symbol of ownership over the home because Old Norse women were awarded keys upon marriage and had sole control over food stores and other locked resources.

Religion has often been an avenue for women to navigate patriarchy and sacralizes their domestic lives. "Even within male-dominated religious contexts, women 'domesticate' religion by emphasizing rituals or symbols that give spiritual meaning to their everyday lives."[75] The increase in women in American Heathenry has softened the edges of patriarchy and has turned it toward domestic expressions of religiosity as an avenue toward constructing devout Heathen selves. To some, the chanting of runes over a pot of soup or doing housework as a devotional act to the goddess Frigga because, as one Heathen woman remarked, she is "not enamored with housework" and imbuing it with extra significance just "works" better.[76] Indeed, not all Heathen women adore housework. A dozen women devoted an entire thread in the Ásatrú Women Facebook group to a discussion of their lukewarm relationship with housework, primarily cooking and dishwashing. In the end, the women shared that they had to cook and clean to take care of their families and partners out of necessity. For Herdis, a forty-six-year-old information technology programmer, "the exercises of housework are an early learning step in devotions, discipline, and changing" herself.[77] To others, shrines and altars devoted to various Germanic goddesses serve as reminders of the divine feminine, places on which to leave offerings. Alda, a forty-something entrepreneur, artist, and mother of two, leads a kindred with her husband in the Deep South. Her home altar is divided into two parts, one side for her and the other for her husband. On her side are images of cats, sacred to Freyja, and statues of Freyja and Frigg, to whom she makes offerings. Frigga's statue, positioned in front of Alda's wedding photo, is positioned to guard Alda's marriage, protecting it from negativity. A Valkyrie Barbie stands atop an ornamental box in the center of the altar to remind Alda of her female ancestors, as well as to honor her family's military service, in particular, her oldest son, serving in Korea. Other items on Alda's side of the altar include crystals, flowers, a chalice for offerings, and a cross to remind her to persevere in the face of ridicule from Christians. The side of her husband, Sigi, is gendered toward the masculine, involving, among other things, a statue of Thor as protector and a money tree to symbolize financial success and security (see Figure 5.2).

Figure 5.2. Alda's altar is displayed. (Photo by the author.)

The development of ideas regarding what a Heathen woman should be like has changed over the years, in contrast to wider societal trends in which women relegated to the domestic realm fought for suffrage and acceptance into traditionally male domains. Heathen women, in contrast, transitioned from fighting for acceptance as "one of the guys," to current ideas that include more conventional roles. As the influence of women in Heathenry grows, the emphasis on warrior culture has begun to morph into an emphasis on a more traditional family structure that fits well with current mainstream religious ideals. Although women have regularly contributed to the economic production of their society, "they have rarely, if ever, had an equal role in the direction of the society."[78] Mani, a *Gothi* in an influential kindred, explains to me that this trend has grown a bit dry. To him, "Who runs/is the face of a Kindred is still pretty much a men's domain." He tells me:

> As I have heard many Heathens say, "They are usually too busy actually doing the work to care about such things . . ." Men posture and pose about honor, and politics, and such generally in the social sphere, but it is the women who make sure there is food through the winter, clothes on their back, that the house is clean, and the kids doing whatever they are supposed to be doing at the appropriate time. In other words all the stuff necessary so the men can go play their man games. The fact that so many women actually are the ones getting things done on a logistic and practical level that is just simply not acknowledged by men is wearing thin.[79]

In fact, "It seems that no matter what women have done, it has not been considered the valuable activity. They are still defined as the producers and care-takers of people—and doing that is less important" because it is defined as somehow separate from "real life."[80] Despite the increase in the number of women in the workplace and the discourse surrounding gender equality, larger changes in social expectations regarding the roles and positions of women within the home have been painstaking. To some Heathens, like Inga, this shift toward the domestic is a welcome one. She tells me:

> I think focusing on the family is a great thing because that gives women the freedom to be girls, to be women, you know, versus women who want to be men, which I think is unhealthy. So I think that we're starting to slowly turn away from Heathenry as a subset of the warrior culture and now Heathenry standing on its own, embracing the family and the family values, and I think that's really where it's coming from.[81]

Unni, a forty-three-year-old medical training coordinator, echoes Inga's desire to focus on a more traditional idea of womanhood:

I know that there have been several women who say you're supposed to be strong, you're supposed to be this, you're supposed to be that, and you're a warrior woman, and you're this—well, not all women are made that way. Some women aren't warriors. Some women are Frithweavers, you know, they're more at home—not in the corporate world, but they'd rather be home with their children.[82]

As American Heathenry has become more family focused, Heathen women have construed domesticity and the gendered division of labor as fulfilling a sacred calling, like Middle Eastern Jewish women, embedding the sacred fully within the profane.[83] Heathens frequently explain this by positing a natural difference (but equality) between the sexes, where discrimination is "simply the recognition of 'natural' difference,"(however culturally or historically produced), "which, [historically] and now, fits in nicely with cultural and political conservatism, an argument that "essentializes difference and naturalizes social inequity."[84]

"The political notion of equality . . . includes, indeed depends on an acknowledgement of the existence of difference. . . . Equality might well be defined as deliberate indifference to specified differences."[85] Within Heathenry, different assumptions and tactics are used to explain and justify differences between men and women. Women are construed as possessing a more passive nature that suits their roles as peacekeepers, mothers, healers, and caretakers who create and maintain bonds of community and family. Men possess a more active, outgoing, vibrant force. Ultimately, similar to other religious traditions, these conceptualizations of gender provide a spiritual essence or "calling" for preexisting gender norms, paving the way for the reproduction of dominant power structures. As Sulda points out, the ideas of difference and equality have consequences in practice:

It does lead to some sort of, what we would consider traditional gender roles and differentiation, but at the same time, it's not any better or worse, it's just different. So having experienced that and having had a lot of talks with people that deal with that, I personally feel that there is a difference between being a woman and being a man, that goes beyond the physicality to it. Now, does that mean that it's wrong? Absolutely not. Does that mean that one's better than the other? Absolutely not. Um, they're very equivalent, but they're different.

When I ask her whether this ideal leads to a sort of "separate but equal" scenario, she responds:

It is like saying separate but equal, but what they're saying is that it doesn't have to be that. You know, where I start drawing lines personally is that separate but equal makes a lot of sense, because let's face it—I don't have a penis. I don't, I will never know what it is like to have a penis because I don't have one. And just to get into brass tacks—we are different. But to me, if that difference is put into a rigid subordinate/dominant sort of hierarchical structure, that's a problem.[86]

The "difference" Sulda refers to as potentially "equal" has had its share of historical stage time. Despite her disclaimer, it very often does lead to a subordinate/dominant hierarchical structure, which Heathens of both genders claim to resist. "Difference" is also constructed in relation to mainstream femininities. Heathens have carved out a contemporary space in which women are allowed their own stories, which offer them feelings of control and veneration. Hilda, a thirty-year-old medical billing receptionist, notes:

> I have seen this kind of growth of using almost a separate-but-equal look at the lore mind-set to kind of enforce outdated stereotypes of women and gender roles. And I'm like, I don't know who you think you're kidding, but it's not me. You know. I see a lot of "only a woman who acts like this can be considered a strong woman." And I'm like "No, it doesn't work that way."[87]

Hilda evaluates what she feels are pressures to behave according to narrow definitions of femininity as Heathen women are given a "holy" or "sacred" reason for maintaining the status quo, for continuing their domestic labors and social responsibilities without critique. As we sat together in her dark, chaotic living room, dotted with children's toys, clothing, and broken crayons, Hallgerd, the woman I introduced at the start of this chapter, expressed her feelings on the issue of women's place in Heathenry;

> HALLGERD: I know that I'm expected to make sure that things in my family run smoothly. That in ancient times I would have been given complete power over everything, the property, the house, the children, the servants if I had any. We don't obviously have servants. [*laughs*] . . . As far as how the house goes, I'm in complete control, whatever I want to do I can do, Um I think that, I hope that that's the way for all women, hopefully some day it will be if it isn't.
> AUTHOR: So what do you think that says about equality?
> HALLGERD: I think I'm totally equal if not considered a little more, because I gave birth it makes me a little more sacred, maybe.[88]

Here, domesticity is reframed as empowerment and ownership, as under the feminine domain, while once again essentializing women as sacred or holy. Hallgerd would be at home with her children in her disheveled space regardless of whether she chose to buy into this definition. By sharing in it, however, she is able to retain a sense of control and power and to avoid the powerlessness packaged with the devalued role *housewife.* Brand believes that modern Heathen women share ownership over domestic space with their Old Norse forebears, among whom

> the women were in charge of the money, the finances, in charge of everything to do with the home, so it was like the man could do anything he wanted outside in the world, but when he came home the woman was in charge of everything, it was the woman's house. You know, even though technically it said that the man owned the property it was really the woman that ruled the house and the man wasn't subservient to her, nor was the woman subservient to the man, they were just—had their roles. No one was looked up higher or lower by gender.[89]

To Brand and most of the people I interviewed, men and women are different but ultimately, at least in the community discourse, equal. To many scholars of gender, it is essential that we understand that women are different. To lose sight of this risks "subsuming women into a general 'human' identity" in which we lose sight of female diversity; "we are back, in other words, to the days when 'Man's' story was supposed to be everyone's story."[90] Yet how the "meaning of difference is being constructed" is, to Joan Wallace Scott, essential to the understanding of equality.[91] Popular media, however, highlight the "difference" between men and women, perpetuating psychological arguments and the belief that the genders have "different values, different personality characteristics, different styles of communication, different problem-solving techniques, different perspectives on sexuality, and different expectations for relationships,"[92] and that this is unquestionably natural. Not all Heathens buy into this construction of gender, arguing from the sociological standpoint that gendered behavior is a product of socialization, and that it is a process, mutable and often arbitrary, and reinforces systems of inequality.

Wisewomen: Seidkonas and *Völvas*

The darkness is heavy outside, broken only by the unnatural glow of fluorescent lighting. I am sitting under a sheet-metal pavilion, surrounded by 150 Heathens, some in ritual garb, others in their Sunday best. The guy next to me is wearing chain mail and a sword. Across from me, four people are wearing biker cuts and smoking rolled cigarettes. Along the row of people at the table, I see Thor's hammers of every shape and size. At the front of the hall, a high table has been decorated with gifts given to the chieftain and his kindred, the hosts. From there, the end of each of six rows of tables stretch far toward the back of the hall. A smaller altar-like table separates them from the guests; on it sits a bowl, a huge drinking horn, bottles of mead, and other ritual items necessary for the night's *High Sumbel.* During *Sumbel,* the women of rank in the kindred—often the wives of the men of rank—take on the ritual role of Valkyrie and carry the mead horn from one guest to another through all three rounds of the ritual, emptying the horn into the offering bowls in between. On Facebook, I ask members of Ásatrú Women, a women-only Facebook group, whether they have experienced an expectation of gendered behavior or role performance. The women share that in their individual experiences, men tend to dominate conversation and ritual leadership, while women are relegated to support roles—cooking and cupbearing. For many, however, this ritual role serves a deeper purpose. In regard to cupbearing, Cat Heath notes:

> Those kind of roles I think are very much the domain of the woman. Not because we're serving (as I used to think and therefore hate them because I thought they were sexist), but because of the inherent power. We ladies are very liminal beings. Tacitus wrote about the inherent holiness extant in women and it's my UPG but I think it's the fact that we are very much "threshold" creatures. Our bodies are designed to bring new life into the world and we can come so close to death (and may even die) in doing so. I don't believe it's any coincidence that in traditional customs in a lot of places, it was women that were not only midwives but the ones that laid out the dead. My mother's aunt used to perform those roles in her village and that to me is deeply sacred. We see men into this world and we see them out. In the same way, when we offer or serve things during *Sumbel* or *blót,* it's almost like we're acting like the go-betweens between the sacred and the community.[93]

Observed in *Beowulf* and other early English and Icelandic poems, the serving of ceremonial drink to guests was a sacred task taken up by noble women of rank, whose job it was to cement alliances, preserve the position of their husbands or fathers, establish mutual obligations between ruler and subject, and maintain the social order.[94]

Not all Heathen groups observe this role; some pass the horn hand to hand. Some call the servers *cupbearer,* others *Byrele* (Anglo-Saxon, meaning "cupbearer"), and others *Ealu bora.* To those who observe this role, it is a critical position at *Sumbel.* In ritual, the horn represents the well of *wyrd* (*Urð arbrunnr,* the well of "that which was"), the great depths into which we speak our words, becoming a part of those who partake of the mead thereafter. Women who perform the part experience it as a great honor and deep responsibility, but it also ritualizes and sacralizes women's domestic role as servants and caretakers and sets women apart as mystical. To be a Valkyrie in ritual does not necessarily confer particular privileges, powers, or agency to shape the future of the kindred or change the facts of lived experience. Yet construction of the sacred is itself empowering and subjectively significant and is, in this case, reserved entirely for women.

Among the Old Norse, women oversaw the religious ceremonies of the household, acting as the family priestess or *Gythia.* In this role women participated in and oversaw religious holidays and the rites of passage of the members of the homestead. Women also had direct access to magical lore and what the Old Norse perceived as "womanly wisdom." Women who trained diligently to become magical specialists were highly respected and sought after in their communities.[95] Modern Heathens extrapolate the meanings and methods of *seidr* from historical accounts and the Icelandic sagas, interpreting it as "women's magic," appropriate only for women or gay men, despite the fact that there are straight male practitioners. Its modern understanding as a gendered practice is rooted in the use of *seidr*, historically, as a means of "community construction or protection," which, according to anthropologist Jenny Blain, was "acceptable when done by a woman, but . . . men were expected to seek other forms of redressing the social balance." Because of American Heathenry's strain of conservative spiritual and moral values, "Seidr practices exist in tension with dominant discourses of suspicion against men who do 'female' things, which permeate Heathen, as other, communities." Blain posits that the gendered order is interrupted by *seidr* when it is practiced by men because "a 'seeress' can be romanticised, but men who do 'women's work' are difficult to reconcile with the model of the independent 'Viking.'"[96]

One of my several experiences with women mystics took place during a balmy summer evening. There were thirty of us in a stone hall, arranged in rows of chairs on either side of an aisle. We were at a campsite, taking part in an oracular *seidr* ritual that women perform annually at this meeting. We onlookers sat in folding chairs, watching and waiting as the women *Seidkonas* arranged their chairs side by side at the front of the hall. The eldest among them, a matronly woman with an abundance of amber over her blue batik shift, sat in the center. Next to her, three other women, each in her own variation of an apron gown adorned with brooches and beads, moved to take up their seats. I noted the context of our ritual and its divorce from the practice of the Old Norse in their dim and smoky long halls. While they found themselves surrounded by pastures and the vast expanse of the country, we found ourselves muting our iPhones, surrounded by a gravel parking lot and prefab cabins. As we observed the ritual, our shoes made crunchy shuffles on the concrete, illuminated by bright fluorescent lighting. The elderly woman took her seat, and the other women aided her by leading the crowd in *Varðlokkur* (*seidr* song), a practice documented in *Eiríks saga rauða*. After some brief coaching in lyrics and melody, we all began to sing the *Völva* into a trance.[97] The woman to her right asked us if we had questions for the Norns, and people began to step forward to have the answers to their questions divined by the *Völva* with the aid of spirits. In a breathy voice, the *Völva* spoke, having traveled, in a metaphysical sense, to the root of the world-tree, to Hel, or wherever our answers or ancestors reside. In the crowd, during a silence broken by sniffles and fidgeting, I looked around at people's expressions and read a combination of rapt interest and obligatory attentiveness. Not everyone present bought into this "dog and pony show," as one participant called it, but the suspension of disbelief, for a moment, was collective.

Among the gendered expectations for women in Heathenry is that of magic user as either a *seidr* practitioner or a *spá-kona/Völva*. Among the ancient Germans and the Old Norse, women were venerated by the northern peoples as being holy, "imbued with magical power, and with a special ability to prophecy," a reverence that endured in Scandinavia until the advent of Christianity.[98] Tacitus, often cited by Heathens as providing "proof" of their ancestors' belief in female divinity (a tendency one woman called the "Tacitus reflex"), wrote of the importance of these women in the world of men:

> More than this, [men] believe that there resides in women an element of holiness and a gift of prophecy; and so they do not scorn to ask their advice or lightly disregard their replies. In the reign of the emperor Vespasian we saw Veleda long honored by many Germans as a divinity . . . a reverence untainted by servile flattery or any pretence of turning women into goddesses.[99]

Some Heathens express this link to the spiritual through Heathenry's more esoteric links to the past, through rune working, *galdr* (magical chanting), *seidhr* (sorcery), or *spae* (trance), documented by Jenny Blain in her work on *seidhr* practitioners. The last two are historically women's magic, although more men than formerly study these arts today. The concept of women as holy, sacred, or divinely connected to the gods is one that many modern Heathen women have revived. Heathen blogger Cena argues, "We as heathen women are the spinners of *Wyrd* itself."[100] The practice of *seidhr,* documented among the Old Norse, is a shamanistic practice that, loosely translated, alludes to witchcraft.[101] Another form of womanly magic is *spá,* the telling of prophecy, or as Heathens understand it, the reading of *Ørlög.* Throughout the Norse literature, female prophetesses and witches often bear staves, a practice modern staff bearer Kari Tauring has revived. Supported by grants from Scandinavian cultural centers in Minnesota, Tauring's practice involves "sharing her ethnic heritage through performances and workshops" through what she calls "Völva stav, an original system for teaching and practicing the staff carrying tradition." She argues that the goal of her practice is "to create alignment with the world tree, perceive and heal *Ørlög.* Healing patterns of Inherited Cultural Grief inherent in all cultures severed from their deep root traditions, is essential for creating a healed future for our children."[102] Like the *Völvas* of old, Kari is an independent entity, forgoing any allegiances to Heathen organizations or communities. Instead, she is welcomed by all and travels throughout the world to teach and engage others in her work.

Despite the difficult navigation between traditionalism and pragmatic egalitarianism sometimes experienced by Heathen women, Heathenry does allow for multifaceted gendered experiences because it shares many elements of youth subculture that allow girls and women alternative modes of gender expression. At the same time, it does maintain elements of traditional religious organizations; as women age or experience motherhood, their gendered performances and expectations merge with normative mainstream definitions. These varied expressions of gender resistance, masculinity, and traditional domesticity available to Heathen women are understood as different, more liberating, or at least less passive in nature than other feminine expressions. The shift from resistance to tradition echoes both the development of Heathenry historically in the United States and the experiences of women as they age in the community.

In her study of the Goth subculture, Amy Wilkins notes that subcultures have reproduced gender hierarchies as well as subverted or reworked them,[103] providing people a space in which to engage in what Mimi Schippers calls "gender maneuvering."[104] Girl punks are able to appropriate the "masculinist aesthetic of the punk scene" in order to "remake their gendered selves" and challenge normative femininity.[105] Yet both Ross Haenfler and Wilkins have found that this reworking offers subjective liberation simultaneously with structural pressures that serve to maintain a degree of inequality and stall radical change.[106] Heathens spiritualize, normalize, and take for granted gender norms that they define as essentially equal. Although they appreciate many elements of traditional family structure, they often criticize what they believe to be discriminatory beliefs regarding gender, domination, subordination, and patriarchal rule while doing little to enact radical change. Perhaps, like drag kings, Heathen women are engaging in "feminist reformulations of masculinity."[107] They may also be perpetuating a misogyny that decries femininity as they attempt to embody a masculinity that displaces them. Today, having to be both a successful domestic worker and a strong Valkyrie combines archetypes that may serve only to arouse our culture's fantasies of a comic-book heroine who does it all. Heathen women are, after all, still members of American culture and are therefore affected by the same social mechanisms as other American women. How members interpret these conceptualizations of gender and adapt them in their own systems of meaning and identity illuminates the detailed work involved in the greater construction of group culture. It also highlights the ongoing structure of that work, which occurs within the framework of the politics of difference.

6

Honoring the Ancestors

Dealing with Issues of Race, Ethnicity, and Whiteness
in Constructing an Ethnic Folkway

Late in my college career I enrolled in a sociology class on American Paganism. For my final project I chose to study Ásatrú. Excited as I was, I wanted to meet and interview a Heathen whose experience would lend insight to my assignment and perhaps even inform my new faith. In the 1990s Internet Relay Channel chat channels were the modus operandi for people wanting to network and socialize on the web. Facebook was yet to be born, so I scoured the list of chat rooms and came on a channel for Odinism. At the time, I assumed that the term *Odinism* was interchangeable with *Ásatrú*, so, I joined the chat. I entered the chat and politely introduced myself to the two members online. After an awkward pause, one of them asked me, "Where are you from?" I replied, "I grew up in Germany." Then he asked "What nationality are you?" I wondered why this was relevant. Why should anyone care? After some back and forth, I realized with a slow, painful sense of dread that his question was about race. He wanted to make sure that I was white. This was confusing and discomfiting, and I expressed as much, prompting the hostility of both members. "You're a nigger lover," they told me, and a "disgrace to your motherland." Then, without further ado, the chat channel blipped away—I had been booted, to sit in my chair, trembling, frustrated, and flushed with rage. This was my first and undeniably toxic experience with Heathenry and its ties to race and ethnicity. It was my first awakening that the relationship among whiteness, political identity, and religio-ethnic identity is complex, and that methods and reasons for inclusivity and exclusivity differ greatly. It took me five years to seek out another Heathen. After my entrée into the flesh-and-blood Heathen community, I experienced this kind of intolerance repeatedly and heard stories from other Heathens about their own similar encounters. I listened to Heathens discussing (and lamenting) Heathenry as an "ethnic" folkway in ways that made me uncomfortable and confused: Was Heathenry an ethnic folkway? How common is this particular frame? What does it really mean, anyway, and why does the idea make some of us so anxious?

With these questions in mind, this chapter is an endeavor to conceptualize ethnic identity as an important arena for the construction of whiteness and collective identity among American Heathens. It explores how members' whiteness provides an ethnicity that is negated by its invisibility in supposedly color-blind contemporary American society. In addition, it explores how members respond by the coconstruction of their own ethnic folkways, which are not without quandaries, disagreements, and complexities. Scholars have increasingly noted that ethnicity is both symbolic and mutable and can also be imagined.[1] Those who become Heathen do so by engaging in the reconstruction and adaptation of ancient Germanic culture and epic heroism to solidify ties with ancestors through dialogue with historical and fantasy narrative. Their choice to do so lends insight into the white privilege of shopping for ethnic identity.

Previous literature on the collective identity of ethnic groups has focused on the changing ethnic identities of people of color over time or on the deployment of so-called symbolic ethnicity by the offspring of immigrants, particularly European Americans. Much of this discussion highlights how people base their ethnicity on their recent ancestors within one or two previous generations,[2] with whom they have shared direct experience with their practiced ethnic culture. Much of the literature also assumes that white Americans engage in ethnic participation or adopt ethnicity on a piecemeal, occasional basis,[3] commemorating selected holidays and eating traditional foods but largely ignoring or overlooking entire aspects of cultures. The study of American Heathenry demonstrates how people can construct and render meaningful a holistic, though largely imagined, ethnicity without direct experience with the foundation on which their identity is based. To illustrate this, I divide the discussion into how Heathens maintain, construct, and negotiate group boundaries; how they coconstruct group culture; and how they create and maintain identity. In addition, I respond to previous illustrations of Heathenry as a platform for racism and white supremacy. Because the issues of ethnicity, race, and racism are inseparable, this chapter will address all three, highlighting the intricacy of invented or constructed white ethnicities unexamined in previous empirical representations of Heathenry.

Who Gets to Be Heathen? Race, Ethnicity, and Belonging

In developing one of the first white racial identity models,[4] Janet Helms argues that for whites, racial identity is about their perceptions, feelings, and behaviors toward other ethnic groups rather than their perceptions of their own ethnicity.[5] This presupposes an absence of actual ethnic identity among whites and presumes that whiteness is merely the by-product of perceived difference by those who, unlike white supremacists, are not active in conceptualizing race or ethnicity as a salient, conscious identity. The increasing numbers of Hispanics and Asians and the corresponding decrease in the comparative size of the white population have begun to highlight whites as a racial group and to call into question whiteness as an unmarked normative identity.[6] As whites have increasing contact with nonwhites, whiteness is becoming ever more visible. Consequently, at the same time at which Heathenry's very existence and construction are a demonstration of the privilege of ethnic adoption, its exclusivity and the (sometimes paranoid) attitude of ownership over it by its adherents can be interpreted as a reaction against the perceived threat and loss of entitlement brought on by this increasing awareness of cultural diversity and the concomitant palpability of whiteness. Even in this group of overwhelmingly white people, race is still operational.[7]

The first major American Heathen organization, the Ásatrú Free Assembly, was early on "bedeviled by the persistent efforts of white supremacists and Neo-Nazis, including members of the American Nazi Party, to infiltrate the organization and steer it in an overtly racist direction."[8] Jeffrey Kaplan outlines the historical growth and unraveling of American Heathen organizations, focusing on the split between Ásatrú and the more overtly racialist group Odinism over these same issues of racial exclusivity and white supremacy and arguing that at the time, the boundaries remained unclear.[9] In his later work Kaplan argues that Ásatrú suffers from the difficulty of separating racial pride from racial mysticism.[10] For many scholars, the course of American Heathenry is troubling. For Michael Strmiska, a fellow movement insider, who in 2005 had shared my sentiments that Heathenry is often misrepresented by the academy, has, over time, come to experience greater unease with "the right-wing views that are either present or quietly aided and abetted" by American Heathenry[11] and this has caused him to withdraw entirely from contact with them.

Mattias Gardell's *Gods of the Blood* has painted a grim portrait of racialist Heathens in the United States who use Heathenry as a platform to espouse nationalist ideology and racial separatism, about which most of my informants expressed ambivalence or unfamiliarity.[12] Many of the news stories on Heathenry focus heavily on white supremacy among American Ásatrú prisoners, many of whom have been *outlawed* by the Heathen community for their criminal misdeeds.[13] In her work on religion and white supremacist movements, Betty Dobratz conflates Odinism with Ásatrú, noting briefly the "debates about the role of race and politics" but ultimately labeling American Heathens "white racialists" and tying Heathenry to National Socialism, the Ku Klux Klan, and white supremacy in general.[14] The activities or public statements of the white supremacist fringe, a minority particularly vocal in the 1990s, do not speak to the direct experiences, beliefs, or diversities of individual members of the Heathen community, nor do they adequately capture the tensions among members regarding understandings and experiences of race and ethnic identity. This stereotyping has led the Southern Poverty Law Center to produce such headlines on its website as "A racist brand of neo-Paganism, related to Odinism, spreads among white supremacists," and, in reference to Gardell's work, "A Swedish Scholar Takes a Serious Look at Racist Neo-Paganism and Its Rise on The American Radical Right." Throughout these online articles, disclaimers are rarely, if ever, offered. Despite its rightward shift and the reasonable arguments to be made that American Heathenry is at least in part sympathetic to the racism of the Far Right, such singular portrayals of Heathenry's racist agenda mask the complexity of meanings in ethnic folkways or white ethno-religious identities and ignore the sizable contingent of outspoken antiracist Heathens.

Taking emergent racial meanings into account, I go beyond the upheavals of Heathenry's early years in the United States and previous scholarship that conflates Heathenry and white supremacy to examine firsthand the complexities of how practitioners incorporate racial considerations into a nuanced Heathen selfhood. I intend to show that American Heathens construct group boundaries by distinguishing between categories of folkish and universalist while mostly living between racial exclusivity and complete inclusivity in a historical and cultural context that demands that race be taken into account. Like other subcultural groups, Heathens engage in the construction of collective identity through boundary maintenance by self-consciously establishing symbolically meaningful categories to distinguish among practitioners' understandings of who gets to be Heathen. In this case, participants construct categories from racial/ethnic exclusivity and complete inclusivity in response to external cultural voices, namely, the legacy of racial inequality and ongoing racism in the United States, and to the troubling co-optation of Heathen symbolism by Nazis and neo-Nazis. Although a few Heathens find ancestry irrelevant, for most, it is significant to Heathen identity and belonging and the internal conversations that seek to define Heathenry as an exclusive indigenous tradition,[15] a system of faith separate from ethnic identity, or a complex folkway struggling to be ethnic while resisting racist labels. This book is significant because it signals that Euro-American Heathens exercise a great degree of agency as they fashion identities. It contributes to the academic conversation on how ethnicity is invented, constructed, negotiated, and contested in American society and culture.

"White" Ethnic Identity

American Heathenry is a cultural and religious system and identity that, like all identities, is constructed in a historical context. More specifically, the context in the United States is one in which being white and celebrating that whiteness are understandably problematic but increasingly significant in many people's lives. The civil rights movement of the 1960s redefined white identity and led to the creation of a multiplicity of potential whitenesses and, consequently, the elimination of any "normalized" form of whiteness.[16] In the following decades scholars turned toward an analysis of ethnicity as a category tied to culture and sought to uncover why white Americans had begun to cling to and pursue their ethnic roots with such vigor. Indeed, after the civil rights movement afforded black people greater entrée into the white world, many white Americans, a group whose ethnicities are often invisible, reacted by reconstructing and rediscovering their own ethnic identities.[17] This ethnic renewal was, in part, a defensive repackaging of racism in response to the increasing power and status of African Americans and other Americans of color. The concurrent perceived loss of white privilege, exacerbated by the decline of white working-class wages after 1970, served as an aggravating factor, prompting a focus on "white" identity as compensation for decreasing wealth and status.[18]

In addition to serving as a way for whites to repackage white privilege,[19] the growth of white ethnic identities is also a response to the forces of modernization. During the countercultural revolution of the 1960s and 1970s, people began to challenge their bureaucratized, hyperindustrialized reality by creating new symbolic boundaries. Ethnicity was seen as a "haven of authenticity that existed at a remove from the bloodless, homogenizing forces of mass production and consumption," spurring "a certain tribalism" as antimodernism's chosen manifestation.[20] New religious and ethnic revival movements are both testimonies to this change as people create community, identity, and meaning via reconstructed faiths and ethnicities. The Neopagan movement in particular spawned generations of amateur genealogists as Wiccans and other Pagans traced their family heritage hoping to find witches or Pagan practitioners. Celtic reconstructionists sought to revive the Pagan beliefs and practices of their ancestors, and Neo-Druids looked to uncover the mysteries of nature and the wisdom of their imagined forebears. Through the practice of Heathenry, some began to look closely at their pre-Christian Scandinavian, Anglo-Saxon, or Germanic heritage as a foundation for a spiritual practice sympathetic to antimodern sentiments. Others, less focused on heritage, nevertheless sought alternative faith systems whose intellectual practice and historical foundation felt authentic and meaningful. American Heathens, however, faced a daunting task: the reinvention of Germanic (i.e., white) ethnic and spiritual identities, as a subset of the larger category of whiteness, that would be clearly distinguished, if not totally divorced from, the legacy of white supremacy in a country in which racial politics and exclusion are woven into the culture's political and economic foundation.

Scholars discuss ethnicity as an identity and a feeling; those who have ethnic identity are "self-consciously ethnic" and view themselves as somehow distinct.[21] Ethnic groups make claims to kinship or ancestry, a common history, and symbols that capture the group's identity.[22] In establishing ethnic identity, it does not "matter whether or not an objective blood relationship exists," but rather that people perceive these things to be real.[23] The key is the "claim to primordiality that ethnicity typically makes."[24] In other words, it is the perception or attribution of blood ties that is important, not the actual existence of such ties.

Although ethnic groups tend to be self-referential, they are also affected by how they are viewed by outsiders whose attention leads not only to the group's self-consciousness but also to the construction and maintenance of boundaries delineating those "like us" from those "not like us." These symbolic meanings are not merely psychological constructs but creations of the social world and are influenced by their historical, cultural, and political context. How it feels or what it means to be German, for example, is less about lineage than it is about what external meanings a person is influenced by in regard to what Germanness should and should not look like. This definition suggests that ethnicity is, above all else, an elastic social creation and an identity different from, albeit connected with, concepts of race and power.

Negotiating Racism, Pride, and Faith

When they are pressed to talk about race and racism, most Heathens throw up their hands with a heavy sigh. American Heathens generally feel that race is a complex, nagging, and lingering problem that has created disquiet in the community since its inception in the 1970s. Although many organizations and kindreds have made it clear that racism and discrimination are intolerable and have pushed white supremacists to the extreme fringe, anxieties of the early years (as recounted by Strmiska, Kaplan, and Gardell) persist.[25] Accusations of racism horrify and exasperate most Heathens; the awareness of charges of racism shapes community dialogue and identity construction as participants negotiate being Heathen, being proud of their heritage, and being members of an exclusive social enclave.

American Heathenry as an Indigenous Tradition

Many Heathens argue that Heathenry should be counted among other indigenous faith traditions. Although many do not believe this to the extent that they exclude practitioners whose lineage is not visibly Germanic, Anglo-Saxon, or Scandinavian, some do. These Heathens speak of ancestry, bloodlines, and ethnicity as an indisputable fact, a focus they refer to as *folkish*, a term I discuss in more detail later. Because whites are unconstrained by the politics and visibility of race, they are free to choose from multicultural symbols and practices. Their whiteness allows them the privilege and "transparency" to view their appropriation of global cultures as an "extension of [their] own universal humanness."[26] Although it is still the privilege of Heathens to cross the cultural and religious boundaries of time and space, they are infinitely focused on "myths about common descent,"[27] specifically, their Germanic ancestries, pursuing the belief that "a person's own bloodline must be thought of as a meaningful guide to the path of her/his soul."[28] Heathen author Mark Puryear remarks likewise that "geographic distinctions are man-made and artificial, whereas our bloodline was given to us by nature, and for us Ásatrúar, by the gods and goddesses of our people!"[29] When this belief becomes exclusionary, it invites the label *racism*. When it occurs, racism among Heathens is represented through modern racist language that reflects a more subtle and symbolic racism than its more traditional manifestation of individual acts of meanness.[30] It is part of the white racial frame, a term Joe Feagin uses to refer to "a centuries-old worldview" that has involved "a racial construction of reality by white and other Americans, an emotion-laden construction process that shapes everyday relationships and institutions in fundamental and racialized ways."[31] This framing involves not only stereotyping but also "deep emotions and visceral images, even language accents and sounds."[32] A critical component of the white racial frame is the likening of whiteness to virtue, a tactic that renders white people incapable (in their own minds) of racist performances, stereotyping, or ideas. This is what enables practitioners who frame Heathenry as the inheritance of whites with northern European heritage to disclaim and dismiss racism as a reality while sharing racist sentiments, a tactic I explain later in this chapter.

As an integral part of ongoing community dialogue, Heathens discuss the perceived parallel between Heathenry and the idea of bloodlines and belonging among Native Americans, implying that blood (i.e., whiteness) is a fair measure of access. On one occasion I listened to a lengthy defense of the claim that Heathenry is a birthright, like Hinduism—born a Hindu, always a Hindu—but you cannot become one just because you want to, the argument went, despite the fact that people of all races adopt forms of Hindu religions. Native Americans and Hindus are not considered racist, so, according to the logic of these practitioners, Heathens should be afforded the same consideration, the privilege and legacy of whiteness aside. According to AFA headman Stephen McNallen in a public statement on the AFA's Facebook page, "If I was a Sioux religious leader, no one would question my championing the cause of the Sioux people or, for that matter, Indians in general. But, as a leader in a native European religion, I'm called a 'racist' if I try to promote the legitimate interests of European-descended people."[33] These conversations are not entirely unusual, because some Heathens view each racial group as somehow unique, a distinction threatened by the increasing homogenization brought on by globalization and the effects of rationalization on human life. A corollary of the argument that Heathenry is an indigenous pathway for Germanic-descended people is the view that all peoples should likewise aspire to their own unique ancestral traditions. In McNallen's *Ásatrú Update* blog, he writes:

> Ultimately, we European-descended folk are in the same boat as the Tibetans, the Karen, and the Amazonian tribes. We're all trying to preserve our peoples, cultures, and native religions in a world where transnational corporations and intrusive governments work to destroy all differences, to smooth out humanity into one featureless, deracinated "norm-man" fit only to produce, consume, and obey. Where will our vaunted Germanic freedom be then? What will happen to the Norse

spirit, the Faustian upward reach of the European soul, when we're all slaving on the global plantation for the bankers and the corporate elite? Let me tell you: These historic traits of ours will be dead. And the only way to prevent this "death by homogenization" is to be who we are, to honor that which makes us unique. We should do that for ourselves as Northfolk, and we should encourage other groups to do likewise.[34]

The genuine pride that many Heathens feel in their ancestry and the problematic baggage of white colonialism throughout history create a conundrum. Ignoring the different privileges and historical advantages of whiteness sets the stage for increasing frustration by Heathens who do not understand why they are labeled "racist" while Tibetans and Amazonian tribes are not. To many, the mere suggestion of white privilege as situated in historical circumstance invokes a defensive knee-jerk reaction of anger and resentment against "white guilt," a pattern made evident recently after a Heathen scholar published an article titled "Heathenry as a Postcolonial Movement" in which he held Heathens responsible for justifying "current social and racial inequalities by pushing the structures of colonialism off as a thing of the past."[35] Many Heathens bristled in response, decrying accusations of "racism" and painting all cultures in history as equally deserving of blame for slavery and the subjugation of other peoples. Others lamented their feelings of powerlessness to change existing arrangements, choosing instead to focus on their faith, without the weight of critical analysis.

One of my earliest experiences with modern racism and its relationship to disregarding the history of white privilege was my discussion with Torsten, a longtime Heathen. After he likened Native American folk tradition to Heathenry, I asked to what extent he believed that Heathens were searching for ethnic connection. I began to explain the difference between race and ethnicity, but before I could continue, Torsten interrupted, irritated:

> You can't say ethnic without including race. Of course it's race. White people are so afraid of saying that. We've been taught that. We're so afraid of being called racist, and that's *bullshit*. It's just *bullshit*. You know, we can be just as proud of our race, just as proud of our heritage as blacks, or Asians, or Latinos. Why is it okay for a black man to shout out "I'm black and I'm proud? It's a *black* thing," but if I say "I'm *white* and I'm proud," all of the sudden I'm *racist*? I don't buy into that. I don't buy that, I don't buy into that double standard. It's bullshit and I don't buy it. Multiculturalism seems to apply to every race except whites.[36]

Torsten's frustration illustrates the fatigue that he feels at white guilt and the double standard of racial expression, allowing people of color the freedom of pride but denying whites the same without sanction. This passage and Torsten's further frustrations also hint at a perceived threat to white privilege and a marked lack of insight into sociological factors surrounding race, ethnicity, and inequality—in particular, unequal racial arrangements as a legacy of white colonialism and how "white" and "black" pride have different implications. The unmarked status of whiteness has bestowed unearned and often savagely disparate institutional and systematic, historical, political, and economic privileges and advantages on white people. This lack of awareness authorizes whites to carry on with the belief that some inequalities are *natural*.[37] The belief in the naturalness of inequality manifests itself in countless everyday phenomena, such as the one reported by CNN in which a woman defended a local tradition of segregated proms by saying, "The white people have theirs, and the black people have theirs. It's nothing racial at all."[38]

Throughout my interviews, many Heathens employed rhetorical tactics of what sociologist Eduardo Bonilla-Silva refers to as *color-blind racism*, an ideological shift away from traditional, more overt "name-calling" Jim Crow–era racism. In his work on the changing landscape of racism in America, he writes that subscribing to an ideological frame is all-encompassing, ranging from "peculiar linguistic manners and rhetorical strategies (or race talk), to the technical tools that allow other users to articulate its frames and story lines."[39] As Bonilla-Silva suggests, white people feel the need to deflect the racist label while expressing racially charged feelings,[40] as Gunther did when he claimed during our conversation that he had "black friends" and had worked with "black people." Gunther, unemployed and in his fifties, also shared his family history, a story about his hungry European immigrant ancestors who, despite the racism they suffered, worked very hard and achieved the American Dream. His story was fraught with the symbolism of the "epic tale of plucky immigrants making their way in the New World through the sweat of their brow" that mobilized whites in the 1970s—a story that suggested "If we could do it, why can't they?" It is "one of the reigning ironies of the ethnic revival" with its "ethos of disquiet" and "even of outright protest against the homogenizing forces of modernity."[41] For Gunther, it was not simply a tale of pride and perseverance but of comparison with those (black) others who, through own shortcomings, had failed to achieve the same success.[42] Most white Americans are the descendants of Europeans, but few are actually children of immigrants.[43] Identification with European ethnicities by white Americans after the great European immigration that occurred in the late nineteenth and early twentieth centuries is all but symbolic generations later.[44] The tenacity with which people cling to ethnic identities is not without problems because the benefits of ethnic identifications are negligible for white people and potentially harmful for people of color, since ethnicity is something that white people adopt or neglect according to their whims.[45] Although this tale is not a product of Heathenry, it illustrates part of Gunther's connection to it. Despite his color-blindness, Heathenry is, as he explains it, a way for him to celebrate his perseverant and industrious ancestors while celebrating his own ethnic heritage. At the same time, his story is a modern racist judgment against those people of color who have failed to achieve success, presumably because of their own shortcomings rather than unfair economic, structural, and racial arrangements. Another example of ethnic pride turned racial resentment comes from an Amazon.com review of Puryear's book *The Nature of Asatru*[46] written (misspellings intact) by Spazmonkey:

> Though I agree with his condemnation of the "hate" ideology that is prevalent in some Ásatrúar, I think he goes a little too far in asking us to show automatic respect to all races and religions. We should not by default hate others, but on the other hand respect is earned. For example if a group of people consistently underperform or succumb to criminal behavior and such, I'm not going to ignore such for fear of "invalidating" them or "hurting their feelings," nor will I ignore scientific or social fact or any othe form of truth, because someone deems it politically incorrect. Anyway I'm glad to see someone taking a realistic, and honorable stance on the subject without being a psychotic exteremist or some liberal white hating femenist either.[47]

More recently, as the United States' political landscape has become increasingly tumultuous, the tenuous divide between Heathen religion and political ideology has further eroded. John Powell of *Media Matters* reports that at the 2011 annual conference of the white nationalist organization the National Policy Institute, "while listening to post-apocalyptic plans for a white 'ethnostate' and endorsements for recreating apartheid in American towns," he ran into a group of AFA members during lunch. The story, corroborated by AFA members with close ties to McNallen, further muddies the divide between folkish identification and nationalist leanings and adds further fuel to the already troubling stereotype of American Heathenry as populated by white supremacists. In his statement in response to the published report, McNallen argued that the AFA members present had attended as "private citizens," not representatives of the AFA. Yet Heathens with connections to McNallen and those in his inner circle have reported the opposite, citing the presence of the AFA attendees as a deliberate attempt at recruitment. The Pagan blogosphere was quick to tag the story, plastering it all over the web. In a blog entry titled "The Shadow of Racism in American Heathenry (or, Why American Heathens Can't Have Nice Things)," one Pagan author reports that the specter of racism is what alienates European Heathens from their American counterparts. Indeed, accusations and suspicions of racism continue, often aimed at the AFA or folkish Heathens, as McNallen continues to pen articles about the coming extinction of the white race, stating in his less-than-delicately titled piece "A Down and Dirty Look at the 'Browning of America'" that

> by the end of this century, European Americans will be between 10% and 30% of the American population. Apparently we are supposed to welcome this news, even though it means that our political and cultural clout will evaporate to a thin wisp of what it is today. European Americans

face minority status, then marginalization, and eventually extinction. White folks, shake hands with Ainu.[48]

In a more recent piece, "Wotan vs. Tezcatlipoca: The Spiritual War for California and the Southwest," McNallen continues to voice his anxieties about the changing status of white Americans, lamenting that "people of European descent will resign themselves to a subordinate role. In this case, our culture will be replaced by others, mainly Hispanic. Our percentage of the population will continue to drop toward numerical insignificance, and our political influence will shrink accordingly."[49] The portrayal of white people as victims is a deeply embedded part of white supremacist ideology. In an empirical analysis of hundreds of white supremacist publications, several hundred mainstream media reports, periodicals, newspapers, and transcripts of over three dozen appearances of white supremacists on television talk shows, all spanning two decades of discourse, sociologist Mitch Berbrier outlines the "victim claims" of white supremacists and breaks them down into the many tactics used by McNallen and others to decry the endangerment of whiteness through claims of (1) reverse discrimination, (2) rights abrogations, (3) stigmatization and the denial of white pride, (4) loss of self-esteem, and (5) racial elimination.[50] Through this ideology of victimhood, white supremacists present themselves (and indeed perceive themselves) as stigmatized persons and provide justifications and excuses for the attitudes and behaviors that others perceive as troubling. To combat the threat of white extinction and the impending loss of cultural and political power, McNallen calls on Heathens to engage in nonviolent resistance, furthering the "racial elimination" claim by envisioning a future in which Latinos undermine white dominance and the northern European cultural legacy once and for all:

> The spiritual descendants of the Aztecs are looking northward, coveting land which, they have convinced themselves, should be theirs—and, perhaps quite unconsciously, they are moving to conquer it by mass immigration, by language, by cultural influence. A dangerous few want to conquer by force of arms. But then, they haven't reckoned with Odin and Thor, and Frey and Freya, or the other Mighty Powers of Asgard and Vanaheim! Nor have they figured, in their calculus of conflict, on the spiritual will of those who follow them.[51]

Yet, despite a strong following from the racialist contingent of American Heathenry, many Heathens reacted in alarm and dismay to McNallen's writings, arguing against such a blatant blending of religion with politics, particularly from one of the United States' flagship Heathen organizations. McNallen's writings, troublesome in his coded (or overt) racist and xenophobic language, underscore a larger phenomenon beleaguering American Heathenry in the United States: the blurring of the boundaries between ethnic pride and white supremacy.

Yet it would be unfair to view Spazmonkey's or McNallen's willfull ignorance or outright denial of systematic, institutional social inequalities or other similar modern racist commentary as expressing a core element in American Heathenry. Instead, it reflects white American resentment of a perceived loss of status and privilege in modern, multicultural society in particularly divisive political times. These examples and others that I have come across illustrate most strikingly how members follow a reactionary politics carefully constructed by politicians and pundits to help whites feel like victims and thereby make them useful political tools.[52] When, for example, a Heathen elder dismisses the reality of white privilege in the Facebook comments contained in a shared link to the Un-Fair Campaign's public service announcement,[53] some Heathens react in kind, lambasting affirmative action as they lament their own underprivileged circumstances. In other words, it is not Heathenry that promotes racism, or Heathens in particular who are exceptionally racist; rather, most Heathens are not any different from the average person privileged with whiteness. When Heathenry facilitates racist social and political beliefs, often in the guise of "white man as victim," it does so particularly because it neither includes challenging or enlightening voices from people of color nor engages in discussions that even acknowledge the problems pursuant to white privilege. Specifically, it invites white people whose whiteness-as-ethnicity is not as invisible to them as whiteness is to so many white people. It is, rather, a central part of their constructed ethnic identity, with all its symbolic political baggage and racial meanings.

Honoring the Ancestors: Constructing Bloodlines

Where one stands in regard to the politically charged notion of racial and ethnic belonging has real consequences. In most cases members' racial ideology earns them a position in the *innangard* (within the community) or the *utgard* (outside the enclosure) of particular kindreds (tribes) or organizations, defining who will be accepted as legitimate or who is a troublemaker and poseur. Often, those who are in-group establish their feelings and claims of legitimacy through real or imagined blood ties to a northern Europe that is essentialized by a pronounced lack of descriptors of "which ancestors, in which land, speaking which language" but is nonetheless presumably white.[54] Scholars who have taken an interest in the ethnic identity of white Americans have documented the blurring of ethnic boundaries, pointing to ethnicity as increasingly symbolic.[55] Ethnic identities are no longer situated in ethnic social structures and have instead taken on symbolic forms, which are easily reshaped depending on the social context.[56] European immigrants' conversion to "European Americans," for example, provides them with a broader, more comfortable base as the nonwhite American population grows. This symbolic ethnicity lacks structural cohesion and is detached from the foundations of an ongoing ethnoreligious culture. To be symbolically ethnic is to treat ethnicity as leisure, where ethnic identity lacks salience. It is the feeling of Jewishness or Swedishness that many Americans emphasize rather than participation in ethnic organizations or cultural practices. In the words of Herbert Gans, symbolic ethnicity is "characterized by a nostalgic allegiance to the culture of the immigrant generation, or that of the old country; a love for and pride in a tradition that can be felt without having to be incorporated into everyday behavior."[57] Today, most white Americans have essentially become detached from a grounded, experiential connection with their European lineage.

American Heathens, however, look to ancient Germanic historical and cultural beliefs and practices with a sense of ownership; it is claims to the religio-cultural legacy of their real or imagined ancestors that undergird the argument of Heathenry-as-birthright, however socially constructed the actual nature of bloodlines may be. Indeed, to many practitioners, only geographic borders are social constructs; bloodlines, having more "concrete" biological and scientific significance, are experienced as "True" with a capital T. Alfdis, the world traveler introduced in Chapter 2, expresses the significance of ancestry to her identity:

> It means a great deal to me. It's been a part of my very upbringing. My grandparents were Gaelic. . . . Every time I visit my parents or my grandparents or my aunts or my uncles, it is simply who we are, it's not something that we do. I come from a long and noble Irish family line from the Earl of Dudland, I've been back to my ancestral land in Ireland, I've been back to my ancestral land in England, so as far as how important it is to me, I really can't put a quantifier on it because it simply defines who I am.[58]

The irony (not lost on some Heathens) is that much of what is believed to be authentically Germanic is borrowed from neighboring cultures or, in its modern reconstruction, influenced by other Neopagan practices. I asked Sulda, thirty-seven, a writer and active member of the community, whether she believes that ancestry is a prominent concern in the lives of her Heathen friends.

> Many of them, I even, you know, my mother's mother was Native American. So, I mean, don't even get me started. [laughs] I totally get the "listen, white man, stay out of my religion!" Stay out of my folkway. And, there's a point to that, in some ways. Where things are very delicate is that, the unfortunate reality is that there are people who use it to the wrong ends.[59]

The construction of Heathenry as a family faith or an ancestral folkway is ongoing and, as earlier illustrations have suggested, fraught with struggles over truth and meaning. A typical experience with issues of ethnicity and ancestry comes from Unni, the medical training coordinator. She argues that Heathenry and ancestry are inseparable:

I don't see how you could possibly be Heathen and not pay respect to your ancestors, because like I said, we trace ourselves back to the Frankish people, you know, their deeds are what we are today. They are who we are, if it weren't for them, I wouldn't be here, so absolutely.[60]

Unni is preoccupied not only with ties to ancestry but also to a very specific time and place, the "Frankish people." How much historians really know about the Franks, where they came from, the tribes they were composed of, or whether they shared a common cultural ethnicity is irrelevant to the feeling of connection that Unni has with the Franks and with her symbolic ethnicity. Later, Unni explains her perception of the connections between Heathenry and ethnicity:

UNNI: You can have Frankish ancestry and have any color. We would be considered folkish in the fact that we do believe that you have to have the ancestry, and what percentage of ancestry doesn't matter, you could be half black and half white, you still have the ancestry. Or three quarters and one quarter, whatever. You still have the ancestral connection.

AUTHOR: Okay, at the risk of being redundant, you believe that people have to have the ancestry, because otherwise it wouldn't make sense?

UNNI: Basically. All people, and this is an essentially folkish statement, but not a racist statement, there is a difference, all groups of people have their own gods. And to me it doesn't make a whole lot of sense—that would be like the Japanese gods calling to me. I don't have any Japanese blood at all, so for them to make a connection to me and the ancestors, that would make no sense whatsoever because they're not even of my people, you know what I mean? I want to make it clear that there is no skin-color connection to that one either.[61]

Unni expresses her desire to "make it clear" that Heathenry may be ethnic, but it is "not racist." To her, racism involves blatant exclusivity, not merely the exclusivity and reestablished privilege that occur as a by-product of the white racial frame and white in-group favoritism. She argues that neither she nor her kindred agree with exclusivist labels, regarding all ethnic groups and peoples as equally likely to possess sufficient ancestry for legitimate membership. Increasingly, as befits the American cultural tendency toward biological essentialism, Heathens have sought more concrete answers through the discussion about or the pursuit of DNA testing to pinpoint ethnic markers, fueling conversations about the significance of genetics for claims to authenticity. Others avoid stumbling through more recent genealogical charts and point to Bryan Sykes's controversial research that ties 90 to 99 percent of European descendants to the "seven daughters of Eve," seven specific women who are believed to have lived between 10,000 and 45,000 years ago.[62] This prompted one Heathen man to comment that if spirituality is genetic, "we should all be practicing some form of sub-Saharan animism." Wayland Skallagrimsson, a Heathen blogger, agrees, writing online that if religion is tied to ancestry, "we should all be trying to revive prehistoric religion," and that, because of interbreeding, "most people of northern European descent are not purely of ancient Heathen or Christian ancestry. Their ancestors likely include other European strains such as Celtic and Slavic, making the choice of Ásatrú nothing better than a random one."[63] The early pseudoscientific explanations of genetically coded ties to the gods, popularized in McNallen's publication "Metagenetics,"[64] has received a mixed reaction, with Heathens like Skallagrimsson explaining that

> the fact that proponents of the "genes determine our thoughts" (including religious ones) ideas have to ignore many empirical facts, have to twist their research to make things say something other than they really do, and have to rely on the research of pseudoscientists like parasychological [sic] researchers indicates what their real agenda is: an attempt to paint a veneer of respectability onto beliefs they are determined to have no matter what, onto their inherent prejudices.[65]

The focus of Skallagrimsson's remark is the argument that if we are of European stock, then we are all connected to the same, authentically European grandmothers, who lived before recorded history and thus certainly before our records of ancient Heathenry. This is all anthropologically dubious since it presupposes an "authentic" European ancestor who can be set apart from other human lineages. The rules of exclusivity that some kindreds employ, requiring ancestral connection to one of the so-called Heathen countries, toe the line at blatant racial exclusion. Do these ancestral rules apply to African Americans, many of whom have white ancestry? Or does the "European" heritage requirement really mean "visibly white"? When I ask these questions, the responses are often some variation of "it's complicated" and "Well, I don't care, but I know that some people do," indicating an inability to articulate the details. This illustrates the taken-for-granted nature of ancestry and that many Heathens have not even considered the scientific truths behind their genetic ideals.

Many choose their more recent ancestry as a tie to the past, although this too, is ambiguous. Joining Heathenry is more akin to joining a subculture than an ethnic group, and this makes exclusionary rules seem deliberate rather than rational or natural. Yet Skallagrimsson argues that "no Folkist actually believes the central tenet of Folkism: that the gods of one's ancestors are one's own gods, that religious predisposition is in the blood, determined by genetic predisposition." His position, which is shared by many Heathens, indicates a further blurring of the boundaries of *folkish*.[66] As the political climate in the United States becomes more sharply divisive and political identities more salient, being Heathen has begun to take on a more political meaning. In contrast to the emphasis on the centrality of ancestry is the not-uncommon ambivalence toward it. For the most part, my respondents are not concerned with or engaged in the kind of ideological discussions and "ethnonationalist" dreams of the future that Gardell argues preoccupy racist Heathens.[67] This is not to say that Heathens are entirely innocent of all charges of racism leveled against them by scholars and the media. My research has led me to believe, however, that although the vocal white supremacy that Gardell discusses is loudly present, it is not representative of the majority. A vast majority of the Heathens with whom I have spoken or whom I have observed online vehemently resent and oppose neo-Nazis and white supremacists. Yet they are infected to varying degrees, as are all Americans, by the racism and racial interpretations embedded in the white racial frame. Although their fascinations with ancestry, DNA testing, and genealogy certainly can (and often do) have racial implications regarding whiteness and privilege, to them, a focus on ancestry feels like a connection to an authentic, grounded past, irrespective of white supremacy or whiteness in general. Their roots are meaningful to them, providing an important avenue for feelings of shared belonging, collective identity, and connections to something untouched by modernity. The idea of bloodlines, however socially constructed, ambiguous, or contested it may be, is meaningful in that it is used in boundary work and is in some way fundamental to many members' sense of what it means to belong as Heathen. Labeling Heathens *racist* does little to help us understand or illuminate the way in which Heathens or other ethnic reconstructionists construct and understand race, whiteness, and the "other."

American Heathenry as a Spiritual System

For some practitioners, Heathenry is a spiritual path, and while the images and cultural legacy of Viking ancestors are epic and fantastic, the lineage itself is largely irrelevant. Signy, thirty-seven, a nurse practitioner, discovered Heathenry in the early 1990s, a time during which she says the community was much more "free spirited." In her opinion, there was a clear polarization between the racist and nonracist elements in Ásatrú, a line that blurred with the growth of Anglo-Saxon tribalism, particularly the subset of American Heathenry known as Theodism.

> See, when we were first involved in Ásatrú there was a lot of what was called "unverified personal gnosis" and I don't know what happened. It's now something that's regarded with a certain amount of skepticism basically and if you try to talk about it, you get a certain amount of flak. Some of the deeper spirituality seems to be lost in a search for trying to reconstruct a social structure that I don't think ever existed, that is not applicable in the modern age, and trying to go after pure scholarship rather than trying to go after the spiritual facts that underlie the scholarship. . . . I am almost to the point of not calling myself Ásatrú.[68]

To Signy, Heathenry is about spiritual exploration and experience—the very "mystical" experiences she claims drew her to the gods in the first place. She refers to having a spiritual connection to the gods for which ancestry is irrelevant. She worries, as do many Heathens, that the focus on ancestry creates the foundation for exclusivity and what she refers to as a more subtle "soft" racism, displaying rare insight into the nature of modern racism. Others, equally wary of a focus on ancestry, nonetheless give credit to its importance in people's lives. Valda was unsure how she felt about the relationship between Heathenry and ancestry, echoing a common local opinion, in the area in which Valda lived.

> I think to a very large number of people it is important to varying levels. . . . Then there are those who think it doesn't matter at all. I don't think you have to have the ancestry at all. But, I think it's possible that it's more common that people with that ancestry have natural inclination or are naturally drawn to it, by I don't know, genes, by some deep something inside of them and inner knowledge they're not aware of or just the whole ancestor connection maybe possible, but personally I don't think it's necessary.[69]

Valda's feeling that ancestry may provide an inclination toward Heathenry is part of the narrative that supports the importance of heritage, but her ambivalence demonstrates that not all Heathens believe that European ancestry is central to belonging. Sunna, a woman of color and *Gythia* of a midwestern kindred, explained to me her frustration about lingering feelings of alienation and her fear of being "othered" and rejected because of her dark complexion. The "soft racism" that Signy mentions is a common experience for Sunna and other Heathens of color. A daughter of an Arab Egyptian and a Sicilian, she identifies as multiracial but is frequently perceived as black. She tells me a story about a conflict with a racist Heathen woman whose confrontational attitude made Sunna feel unsafe:

> I felt that in a pinch the community would choose her and my kindred would suffer because of it. It harkens back to my general experience as a woman of color in the U.S. I have never fully had "permission" to express rage. Even when justified, any expression of anger is viewed as dangerous and inappropriate. Over a decade in this community, and building a strong kindred and I was suddenly confronted with just how precarious I felt my place in the community was.

On the other hand, she tells me, Heathens who identify as liberal are also guilty of objectifying her through excessive familiarity, unsolicited racial remarks, and overblown enthusiasm, a position she has come to label the "celebrated token." She explains that even among self-identified liberal Heathens, she is often perceived as the "other," albeit with good intentions. For her, the alienation is still palpable. She says that among these groups

> there was frequent talk of how nasty, wrong, and racist those of a "folkish" tact were, all without provocation. People felt the need to regale me with stories of how they had shut down racists, or how they would never be a member of the AFA. All while simultaneously complimenting me on how articulate and well versed I was.[70]

The word *articulate* is meant to convey that the person in question is well spoken—for a black person. It is a common compliment turned racial insult used by white people about people of color, as when Joe Biden called President Obama "the first mainstream African-American who is articulate and bright and clean and a nice-looking guy."[71] To Sunna, ancestry is not limited to "white" ancestors but rather includes all human ancestors whose deeds came before us. Heathenry is an ancestral religion in that it "ties back to pre-Christian worldviews and practices," but she does not view it as "ethnic." To her, the view of Heathenry as an ethnic folkway is a "misguided need to romanticize and own something." When I ask her what initially attracted her to Heathenry, she tells me that it was "the importance of deeds as a measure of self-worth and community worth. Also, the function of *Wyrd*." She explains, "It was a name for what I had come to believe for myself—that there is a foundation of things we are born to, and there is much that happens beyond our control, yet a person has the ability to steer the course of their lives (physically, emotionally, and spiritually)." Gunnthra, who does identify as black, has had similarly troubling experiences. She had corresponded with a local group in the South in reference to its upcoming event. She recalls,

> Within a week, I received an e-mail from the group's founder, wondering how it was I came to call myself Heathen, if anyone could vouch for me, and why I would choose a religion that was so obviously for "European Americans." I responded to her with civility and tact. Her last correspondence was to suggest that I start a group for black Heathens. I think I cried for a week.

Yet, she tells me, once she moved to another southern state, the social climate changed for the better. She felt accepted and welcomed and found a group to call her "tribe." She spent years in Germany as an army brat during her childhood and later during an army tour of her own, where she developed a close connection with German culture and folklore. She says:

> Let's be honest: I know next to nothing about Africa's many cultures, but because I spent part of my childhood in Germany, I know quite a bit about that country's culture. Plus, the U.S. is partially based on Germanic laws and values. Germanic culture is where I feel comfortable.[72]

Although she acknowledges that for others, Heathenry may have an ethnic allure, for her, it is tribal. "It is the tribe you make with others," she tells me, "the culture you feel most comfortable in." For Valda, Signy, Sunna, and others, viewing Heathenry as an ethnic folkway is potentially problematic; the Heathenry that they practice is a spiritual one. They acknowledge that the ancestral focus of their Heathen peers is a slippery slope, where ancestral reverence often translates into prowhite sentiment.

Tribalism: Depoliticizing American Heathenry

In 1976, when Garman Lord began Theodism, he did so simultaneously with—yet disconnected from—the Ásatrú of Stephen McNallen. McNallen observed the growth of Ásatrú on the coasts and in Iceland and Canada, and wrote "Metagenetics" in an attempt to explain through genetics what it was about Heathenry that attracted so many (white) people.[73] To Lord, Heathenry began with a decidedly academic focus—an obsession with reconstructing Anglo-Saxon language and culture through vigorous intellectual exercises. When the Ásatrú Alliance became embroiled in scandals after the infiltration of racist ideologies, Theodism remained decidedly apolitical. It defined itself as Anglo-Saxon tribalism and encouraged the construction of independent theods, or tribes, without any standardization and each with its own customs. For a while, Theodism's ideas lost popularity. In the past decade or so, Heathens have revived tribalism as an increasingly popular perspective and organizational philosophy. Tribes may not differ structurally from the more popular kindred model, because both may require oathing among members and maintain hierarchical leadership roles, but as an identity, tribalism implies much more. The tribalist's goal is to re-create a solid, familial socioreligious community based on fictive kinship, whose worship encompasses all facets of daily life and group interaction. Mark Stinson, whose arrival to American Heathenry in 2006 has reshaped its landscape in the Midwest, distinguishes between "social kindreds," which he likens to clubs, and "dedicated kindreds," which follow the tribal model. He encourages Heathens to develop tribes by including their families in building community:

> Spouses, children, men, and women . . . coming together as an extended family. Caring for each other, looking out for each other's interests, coming to each other's aid. . . . The children should see each other so often that they come to see each as brothers and sisters. When someone moves, everyone shows up and helps. If a deck needs building, everyone shows up and helps. When a parent is sick, another family should offer to take the kids for a bit. . . . A Kindred should have goals. They should be actively working to grow a Heathen community, both within the tribe, and around the tribe. They should be pooling money, with a goal to buy land and establish a *Hof.* They should be getting to know the

Heathens in neighboring communities, through modern communications . . . and by visiting them face to face. The Kindred should be working to leave their children with a more stable and developed Heathenry than we currently have.[74]

As tribalism revives community models of fellowship, Heathens must also decide how to negotiate members' political beliefs regarding legitimacy and authenticity. Some Heathens refer to tribalism as the "middle ground" between extreme folkishness and universalism, arguing that anyone accepted into a particular tribe is viewed, at least by his or her peers, as legitimately Heathen. To Skallagrimsson, people accepted by tribalists include "anyone who makes a sufficient effort to understand and adopt the culture of the ancient heathens." In his view,

> This gives Asatru rigorous enough standards to make sure our practice is like that of the ancients, and is well understood. . . . The gods first came to be known in the context of the ancient culture, so it stands to reason that they can only be truly understood in the terms of that culture. It also keeps us from the untenable argument that "other races" are somehow so intellectually inferior to the Norse and Germanic that they cannot attain this understanding.[75]

Although many tribalists identify as folkish and believe that Heathenry is based on ancestry, this emphasis is less salient as groups choose to focus on more practical concerns. The political divisions created by the folkish versus universalist divide, made increasingly harsh by the imperative of identity politics fueled by the so-called culture wars dominating the mainstream media, are not only less of a concern but also are made increasingly taboo. One may take on these identities, but tribalism is a covenantal agreement among kindreds to stay out of one another's business. Groups maintain solidarity internally and discourage political discussions in face-to-face interaction. Many tribalists, like Stinson, argue that the divisiveness surrounding the discourse regarding sexuality and race, in particular, is mostly what happens on the Internet. In the real world, where Heathen tribes are engaged in community interaction, canoe trips, family picnics, religious celebrations, and hanging out, political discourse simply is not an issue. In an Ásatrú 101 workshop, Stinson noted that many Heathens get preoccupied with the "myth" of ancestry, another distraction from what he feels are more productive real-world, practical concerns, such as growing the faith through cooperative local and regional relationships with other tribes. The differences among tribes, he argues, are reflections of historical Heathenry because Germanic tribes differed in beliefs, practices, and customs, and so do (and should) Heathens today.

As tribes grow and interact, many have come to accept the concept of *thew* and its sacredness, choosing to sidestep old conflicts over belonging and exclusivity and concentrate instead on spiritual and community growth. Tribalists focus, deliberately and with effort, on building and maintaining *frith*. *Frith* is a term central to Heathen community, and although its full meaning is complex, it essentially involves acting with peace and respect toward those in your *innangard* (inner yard); but it also involves a sense of kinship obligation, a bond that helps maintain order and stability. In its deeper sense, Mani tells me, *frith* involves the development of deep and meaningful bonds and comradery among individuals in a community.[76] Groups also understand that each tribe has its own *thew*, which is to be respected by members at interkindred events. In many ways, *thew* can be understood as the glue that maintains *frith* or *grith*, a concept less about comradery and more about maintaining diplomacy and the rule of law. On the micro level, groups interact with one another and build *frith*, establish *thew* as the rules that guide that interaction, and develop close relationships.

On the macro level, members may not challenge and are encouraged not to discuss the political affiliations, leanings, or ideologies of other tribes. In this way, the racist or homophobic leanings of one group are depoliticized because they may not be questioned or challenged by other groups, lest doing so lead to scandal or bad relations. Likewise, the presence of people of color in one tribe is off-limits for criticism by other tribes with divergent racial foci. Stinson acknowledges that race is a social construct and that ethnicity is, in large part, irrelevant to the spiritual purpose of Heathenry. To him, it is entirely possible to have a "very spiritual view of ancestry, and the connection back through the generations to our Folkway (a product of a certain family of cultural world-views and religious beliefs)," without expending time or energy obsessing about someone else's race or ethnicity. Like other Heathens whose vision of ancestry is firmly spiritual, he ties ancestry to *Ørlög*.[77] He explains:

> This *Ørlög* is passed from parent to child as part of their soul. What my father put in the well (his deeds, his successes, his failures) are passed on to me as part of my soul. We can follow this *Ørlög* back through our bloodline. What my grandfather did, who he was, is part of me. Same for my great-grand-father and on back. As a Folkish Heathen, I believe this portion of our soul ties us back through our bloodline to our ancestors, who once honored the Gods. In our very souls is the connection back to our Folkway. It is *not* about DNA. It is not about the color of our skin. It is about culture, tradition, and a very spiritual connection between a part of our soul and the souls of our ancestors.[78]

As such, he argues, Heathenry as a spiritual folkway renders a preoccupation with "other people's *Ørlögs*" or the authenticity or legitimacy of their Heathen identities irrelevant. To Stinson and an increasing number of Heathens, their individual and community value is found in their honor, trustworthiness, and deeds rather than their race, ethnicity, or personal connection to deity. In this way, the depoliticization of race makes problems of racism silent and unchanged, and Heathenry remains primarily religio-cultural.

American Heathenry as an Ethnic Folkway

Central in the construction of any ethnicity or collective identity is the creation and maintenance of boundaries.[79] Joane Nagel has discussed the controversy among Native Americans about who can rightly assume a Native American identity.[80] Similarly, Heathens, since the beginning, have quarreled over the question of who should be considered legitimately Heathen. These arguments generally demand that Heathens fall into one of two camps, folkish or universalist, a distinction also outlined by Strmiska and Sigurvinsson in 2005.[81] To the folkish, ethnicity is primordial and survives because it is basic to human life, tied to blood and ancestry. It is a matter of tribal belonging, an element of gemeinschaft.[82] To those who prefer a more inclusive or universalist approach, Heathenry is a faith to which members of all backgrounds can be called by the gods, whose choices are unquestionable. To universalists, ethnicity is an elastic construct based on circumstances and is ever shifting, changing, and relative. These polarities, meaningful in the process of creating group boundaries and placeholders for identity, do not fully express the fluidity of practitioners' national identities. Most Heathens live in the in-between, privileging ancestry while rejecting total exclusivity and overtly racist distinctions and accepting ideas from each camp without taking on an all-or-nothing mentality or geographically bounded and static ethnic groups with tribal, linguistic, or ancestral roots (e.g., who can be Swedish or not). Heathens often refer to their way as a "folkway," the ancestral and indigenous customs and religious beliefs of a given people. Members frequently reference "Native Americans, Hindus, and followers of Oriental Shinto religion" as examples of similar ethnic folkways.[83] American Heathenry lacks such foundations and relies instead on deliberate membership and chiefly imagined ancestries. Posting on the AFA Facebook page, McNallen complicates the folkish identity further, referencing an article from MSNBC's site that documents the return of some African Americans to Yoruba and other African folk traditions.[84] His argument, shared by others, is that all people—not just those of European descent—should return to their native folkways. He writes:

> I applaud African-Americans who are exploring their native religions. There is nothing racist in practicing and preferring the way of your forebears. Nor is it racist to know deep inside that the faith of your distant ancestors is intimately a part of who you are—something that is not and cannot ultimately be separated from you.
>
> As a man of Europe, Asatru was a natural for me. When we feel the ancestral pull in ourselves, we can that others might feel the same about their heritage, their essence, their lineage. This creates an attitude of tolerance, while still keeping our own identity at the core of our being.[85]

The argument that all people should return to their native faiths is the core of claims applauding diversity. Although, on the face of it, encouraging diversity seems to be a positive shift from the white supremacy embedded in other conceptualizations of the folkish ideology, its essentializion of peoplehood and lineage has also been used to argue against interracial relationships—a step further down the slippery slope.

To many, Heathenry is more than just a religion; it is a cultural system with modernized traditions reconstructed from those of the Old Norse, something participants often refer to as a folkway. Heathens honor the gods of their ancestors and express this through blacksmithing, spinning wool, brewing mead, writing religious poetry, or studying Old Norse or the *Eddas* and sagas. In this way Heathens search for an "authentic experience of traditional European folk cultures" that "no longer exist in their original form in their home countries."[86] This becomes a way for people to create "imagined communities" and salient cultural identities.

Navigating Race: The Folkish versus Universalist Dichotomy

The vast majority of Heathens are not as excitable about whiteness as Torsten and others who have expressed modern racist sentiments. Instead, their identities and efforts are bound by a complex dance of label avoidance and identity maintenance. On the one hand, they reflexively construct their Heathen identities and ethnic associations in a context in which they are hyperaware of the criticism focused both within their community and by the media on white supremacists. They spend an inordinate amount of time and energy avoiding these labels and bristle when the subject of race is injected into conversation. On the other, they are proud of their real or imagined ancestry and the cultural heritage they claim as part of being Heathen. In the discursive negotiation of this in-between identity, participants have relied heavily on the *folkish* label to delineate the boundaries of the unacceptable. The exact meanings of *folkish* are often the focus of debate, and given the label's ambiguity, Heathens use it to mean a variety of things. In an online Heathen blog, Bernulf attempts to clarify what it means to be folkish, a term and viewpoint that he agrees are divisive:

> By "divisive" I mean just that—at one point, in the 1980's, this issue splintered and polarized American Heathenry in ways that are still being felt. But what is meant by "folkish," why is it such a big deal? Folkish Heathenry, essentially (coming from someone who is not folkish), is Heathenry for the Folk—a central tenet to this path of Heathenry is that the Heathen religion is tribal in nature, and that it is the rightful heritage of people with Germanic/Teutonic heritage. It has as one of its missions the preservation and continued development of the Germanic/ Teutonic tribal descendants. Folkish Heathens do not (at least not in the main) consider themselves better than people from other races—they

simply consider that a religion based on Germanic gods and ancestors is best followed by people of Germanic heritage, and that people with no Germanic heritage would be better off seeking out the gods and ancestors of their own racial heritage.[87]

The disclaimer that folkishness is about cultural appreciation, not cultural superiority, has become part of a standard script recited by a variety of Heathens. The stigma tied to folkishness has arisen, in part, because white supremacists have frequently used the label *folkish,* often as *Volkish,* which some Heathens perceive as an allusion to Nazism despite the fact that the Völkisch movement began before Nazism as a "romantic revolt against the 'ills' of modern society."[88] At a back table in a dimly lit pub, I asked Alvis, the environmental protection specialist introduced in Chapter 2, about the polarizing issue. Alvis remarked:

> If you go and look at Heathen websites, you'll find two basic types of heathen groups out there. You'll find the Heathen groups who tend to, if not openly admit their racist leanings, will at least use language that makes it apparent that, you know, it's Ásatrú for Germans only, and then you'll find other groups who would spend, you know, the first three quarters of the page about their group explaining that they're not racist Ásatrúar, that they're not Folkish. That they would never ever do those terrible, terrible, terrible, things that the folkish Heathens are doing, and "Oh my gosh, it's so awful, we would never!"[89]

To Alvis and most of the Heathens I interviewed, the discussion is exhausting. When, over coffee, I questioned Valda, a novice member and friend of Alvis, about the definition of *folkish,* she became exasperated:

> The racist aspect of it. I would be horrified if anyone thought that I was somehow folkish in my beliefs. Thinking that it could only belong to people of Germanic or Nordic ancestry, or somehow *that* ancestry is better than other people's. There's that whole problem with it too, so . . . but then again, I was talking to someone about this. How—well maybe it's time to change people's perceptions and proudly declare, "Look at me, here's who I am, here's what I believe and I'm Ásatrú, I am the new face of Ásatrú." You know, so I still don't, I don't tell people sometimes. I'll say that I'm a Heathen or that I am a Pagan of Northern tradition.[90]

To her, the mere threat of being labeled racist was cause for anxiety. As Alvis and Valda both demonstrate, my research has uncovered Heathens who are fervently antiracist, as well as those who are as racist, conservative, indifferent, or ignorant of social injustice as any other white person might be, regardless of group affiliation. Outside another downtown café I interviewed Eskel, introduced in Chapter 2, whose combination of long hair, beard, and Thor's hammer pendant immediately marked him as Heathen. Inside, Eskel offered a clarification for a definition of *folkish* and its murky meaning;

> Folkish means to me that the emphasis is on biological descent, that—
> and I know not all people who define themselves as folkish will say that,
> but most of the people that I've interacted with and corresponded with
> who claim the term *folkish* feel that one of the primary emphases, one of
> the primary things of importance in the practice of Heathenry is that
> they are themselves of Germanic descent. A lot of them, not all of them,
> will say that you have to be of Germanic descent in order to legitimately,
> once again, practice the religion.[91]

Eskel does not identify as folkish, and the very idea makes him nervous and angry. His interpretation highlights the crux of the folkish worldview, which essentializes race and assumes that lineages are somehow distinct. His comment also highlights the ongoing complexity of establishing and maintaining boundaries defined by polarities. The folkish versus universalist spectrum is broad, and few members can clearly define their position on it, despite Eskel's cut-and-dried emphasis on the folkish notions of biological descent. Inga, introduced in Chapter 2, echoed a common perspective:

> I believe that my ancestors have called me to this path. And I don't care
> if anyone else believes that their ancestors have called them to this path.
> This is—it's a very personal faith. And so I believe that—for me—it is a
> family religion. It's a family faith. It's basically the honoring of the
> ancestors, and if someone else believes it, great, if someone else doesn't
> believe it, great. I don't believe in pressing my opinions on anyone else.

Although Inga is quick to tie her faith to a perceived family line and heritage, she is also careful to deflect assumptions of racism or exclusivity by claiming that "any different ethnicity can or cannot practice it." Despite this universalist statement, she tells me that she does define herself as "folkish." When I ask her to clarify, the discussion takes a more complicated turn:

> INGA: The general assumption for universalists is that they believe that
>   anyone can practice Ásatrú no matter what ethnicity or background
>   they have. There are those who put a negative connotation to it,
>   but that's their connotation. I'm not going to say that any one of any
>   different culture, any different ethnicity can or cannot practice it, it's
>   a personal journey. It's not up to me to decide.
> AUTHOR: But how's that different from what you were telling me earlier?
> INGA: It's not.
> AUTHOR: That definition would make you universalist, but you don't
>   identify as universalist.

INGA: Right, because for me personally, and this is just for my practice, my faith, myself, I follow the Folkish path because it is in my blood, whereas universalists believe it is more that the gods will call you.[92]

As Inga demonstrates, our ideas of our ancestors are often not based on fact or evidence but instead on imagined ties to a people we feel connected to, a heritage that we find meaningful. For her, the association with the term *universalism* has political connotations—liberalism, Neopaganism—unlike the hard-line and authentic feeling of identifying with "the folk." Blogger K. Henderson, a "lesbian feminist geek," responds to the ongoing conversation regarding folkism in an entry titled "I'll Never Understand Folkish Heathens." After criticizing the folkish requirement of Northern European ancestry and listing her German, Irish, First Nations, and Romanian heritage, she asks;

In the event that I don't meet the qualifications for the amazing privilege of being allowed to worship these deities. Which pantheon should I direct my attention to? Irish? Daceo-Thracian? Roman? Oh, my biomom thinks my dad has some Eurasian ancestry (though I can't tell you exactly where). Seriously, I could really use some guidance here! . . . You know, I'm kind of concerned for other Pagans out there. I've known Kemetic recons who aren't Egyptian, Hellenic recons who aren't Greek (or from areas the Greeks colonized), Roman recons who aren't from Italy (much less Rome), Vodouissants who aren't originally from Haiti (or even African-American, much less West African), Canaanite and Sumerian recons who aren't from the Middle East, Celtic recons who aren't from Ireland, Wales, Scotland, the Isle of Man, and other places most lump together under the name 'Celtic' (which is actually a misnomer), Mesoamerican recons (of various types) who aren't from Central America, and I'm kind of wondering why the Norse/Germanic/whatever-you-wish-to-call-it pantheon seems to be the only hardassed pantheon in the room? I can name a couple of traditions in that list who have equally strong traditions of ancestor reverence, and none of their deities really seem to give a fuck if their adherents don't have ties to them from the nth generation.[93]

In practice, the stigma tied to folkishness has arisen because racist Heathens, members of more political and supremacist factions, have frequently used the *folkish* label. What it means to be Heathen has become directly tied to the boundaries surrounding (and the acceptance or rejection of) racism, folkishness, and pride. Alvis states:

The first Ásatrú folk that I met, while not necessarily what you would call "Cross-burning racists," were almost what some people call the Folkish Heathens. Um, Ásatrú for German-descent people only. You've got to be pure white only. . . . I see a lot of division within the community about that. . . . It's a lot of wasted energy. And it's a sore point. It's a point that I have seen a lot of hard feeling within the Ásatrú community about.[94]

The debate is not a simple one. In an attempt to define boundaries within the community to differentiate between racist and nonracist ideologies, Heathens have created a label, *folkish,* that, because of its ambiguity, has been used to mean a variety of things. The tenacious stigma of racism that has been invited by the movement's historical associations with racist organizations, as well as by those in the community marginalized because of their overtly racist agendas, has prompted many Heathens to engage in resistance. One such attempt, an Internet campaign called "Heathens against Hate," begun in the early years of the twenty-first century, provided a banner label for Heathen websites to disassociate themselves from the stigma of racism. The site describes itself as an attempt to combat groups who "have appropriated and misused our sacred symbols and the names of our gods in order to promote their 'religio-political' views of hatred, racism, and fascism." Its home page reads, "The truth is that while Heathenism is a modern revival of the religion of our European ancestors, it has never, in any way, promoted nor encouraged hatred toward other ethnic or religious groups. Absolutely none of our sacred lore contains a mandate from our gods to promote hatred toward other cultures, ethnic groups, or religions."[95] More recently, a Face-book group called "Heathens United against Racism" has sprung up "as a response to the endless trolling by neo nazi racists trying to use online groups to try and recruit new heathens to their cause." The founders of the group feel that "by working together," they can "drive them out of Heathenry."[96]

Additional disclaimers include, but are not limited to, "We believe in the Gods and Goddesses' of our people, we do not shelter hate and racist agendas and politics" from Northwoods Kindred of Minnesota;[97] "We would like to make it clear that as a community, we identify as 'Heathens against hate,' meaning that we do not use, or tolerate the use of Asatru as an excuse to encourage racism" from Boarshead Kindred of Washington;[98] and "Our members and friends come from a variety of ancestral backgrounds, and like the vast majority of heathen organizations, we are opposed to racism and racial hatred" from Northwest Arkansas Kindred.[99] These disclaimers signal a deliberate and self-conscious attempt to neutralize the *racist* label and avoid further conflict, an effort that has substantially changed the landscape of the community since Kaplan's work on Heathenry in the 1990s. Those who are antiracist experience extreme tensions with those who are not, engaging in heated, persistent arguments and an enduring battle over maintaining the boundaries. The argument about whether Heathens are racist is ultimately consumed by the ongoing boundary negotiation that they themselves perpetuate by maintaining the *folkish* and *universalist* labels.

Many Heathens have argued that these labels are losing their relevance as the community matures and the racial and political landscapes undergo changes. Yet the disagreements and the omnipresence of race as a factor tied to Heathenry as a folkway attest to the labels' continuing symbolic significance. What the *folkish* and *universalist* labels help us understand is not simply that boundary maintenance is taking place but also how Heathens experience and conceptualize race and racism; they indicate that the discussion is perpetual and deliberate, that it defines what it means to identify as Heathen, and that these are the consequences of seeking to define a "white" ethnicity in a racialized world where issues of ethnic exclusiveness and ethnic-group affiliation are increasingly salient.

Identity: Textual Constructions of Antiracism and Belonging

> *Tha segir Harr: "Mikil skynsemi er at rifia that vandliga upp, en thó er thér that skjótast at segja, at flest heiti hafa verity gefin af peim atburdh, at svá margar sem eru greinir tungnanna í veröldinni, thá thykkjast allar Thjódhir thurfa at beryta nafni hans til sinnar tungu til ákalls ok baena fyrir sjálfum sér."*
>
> Then said High One: "It would take a vast amount of knowledge to cover them all, but it is swiftest to say, that most of these names have been given (to him) because, the many different nations speaking different tongues in the world, all wanted to change his name into their own tongue in order to address and pray (to him) for themselves." —SNORRA EDDA, Gylfaginning, XXXII

Early on, Heathen leaders like Kveldulf Gundarsson questioned the place of ethnicity, heritage, and race in the development of American Heathenry: "Having shown that an earthly blood-line reaching back to those who first worshipped the goddesses and gods of our folk is not needful for the practice of Asatru today, the question then arises: Is ancestry alone enough to make one true of soul?"[100] The answers, Gundarsson asserts, are to be found in the *Volsung saga, Egil saga Skallagrimson,* and *Hervara saga,* stories in which the players fall short of matching the magnificence of their ancestors. Heathens create (or re-create) ethnicity from such textual interpretation and historical evidence, circumventing the necessity of a "practiced culture" on which to base their own as they "borrow their symbols from extinct cultures that survive only in museums."[101] Through this process Heathenry "acquires a unique recontextualized cultural meaning," separate from the time and space of its originators.[102] As a construction of white ethnicity, Heathenry relies on a return to the epic past, the supposedly original Euro-white ethnicity of the idealized ancestors. M. M. Bakhtin's discussion of this "epic" or "absolute" past suggests that the epic as a genre is intertwined with cultural tradition and relies on it for survival. This past is separated from us, valorized, untouchable, and bound by time and space. It is only in the past that things are "good" and pure, and it is through tradition that we maintain our ties with this past. The epic and the past that it mirrors are sacred, and its distance "excludes any possibility of activity and change."[103] It is not the truth of such ideas about the past that Bakhtin is discussing, but rather how they are invented and employed in the reconstruction of the absolute past in contemporary discourse. Textual illustrations abound in the Icelandic sagas of intrepid and resolute sword-wielding heroes available for appropriation as role models for contemporary Heathens. Throughout the twentieth century, Germanic myth and legend, the stuff of Heathen establishment and reverence, was co-opted to strengthen nationalist agendas, such as Hitler's reframing of the German national epic *Das Nibelungenlied* as *evidence* of the German master race.[104]

Likewise, the Eddic poem *Rígsþula* is a cultural poem explaining the divine origin of the different castes of early society: the thralls, the peasants, and the warriors. Although scholars question its origin and whether it belongs among the Eddic poems, previous scholars have documented that it remains a favorite in supremacist discussions of why inequalities are necessary and natural. But Skallagrimsson and many others question these religious justifications. Heathens who paid attention, he argues, would realize that the "real motivation of these Folkists is not religious at all, but political."[105] All one need do is visit Stormfront.org, a white nationalist website, for a glimpse at the most vocal Heathen racists. Although Stormfront is not a Heathen site, a few on the supremacist fringe use it as an outlet for sharing their racist ideology. In one post, a member asks whether antiracist Ásatrúar are cowards, writing, "I swear every time I try to look up pictures relating to Norse symbolism, I run across dozens of web site [*sic*] that claim that 'bigots' and 'Neo-Nazi's' are mis-using the Norse pantheon to further their 'racist agenda.' What do these people think the Vikings were, a bunch of tree hugging homosexual hippies who spewed multicult dogma all day long????"[106] Others, in response to this line of thinking, cite evidence from lore and history to the contrary. For example, Skallagrimsson, in his attempt to outline the difference in perspectives among the folkish, universalists, and tribalists, tries to debunk the extreme folkish perspective. "There is no religious justification at all for excluding other races," he says. "The concept is not mentioned, even once, in any Edda or Saga. If it were such an important part of heathenry as Folkists . . . make it out to be, then it would have received at least a passing reference by the ancients. It's not like they were unaware of other races. They were great travelers, explorers, traders, conquerors, who ranged far into eastern Europe and even into northern Africa."[107]

Arguments against racism, however, also frequently make references to the lore. In the earlier years of the movement, Gundarsson was already asking Heathens to consider "whether our forbears had an over-arching 'racial' consciousness—whether 'race' meant anything to them or not."[108] Like others who respond to this question, he cites historical marriages between ancient Heathens and members of other races and offers divine examples of relationships between the gods and the giants. For example, he notes that "Odhinn himself is a 'halfbreed'—the son of the god Bor and the giantess Bestla. Freyr marries the giantess Gerdhr; his father Njordhr marries the giantess Skadhi."[109] Gamlinginn agrees, writing in his *Orthasafn* that "Ásatrú is a multi-ethnic religion." He challenges and preempts critique by conservative, folkish Heathens that this is a politically motivated argument, arguing that

> multi-ethnicity is fundamental to the theology of Ásatrú. Asgard, home of the Gods, is multi-ethnic. For example, Magni and Modhi, the sons of Thorr, are also the sons of their mother, Jarnsaxa, who is a Jotunn. Who will tell Thorr that his sons should not participate in something because they are not of "pure" descent? And what of the Vanir? Since the Gods of Asgard do not worry over these things, the Ásatrú people of Midgard certainly have no need to do so.[110]

Other Heathen writers have repeated this narrative, deflecting the racist interpretation of *Rígsþula* with other references that refute racial exclusivity. In his Internet publication Skallagrimsson offers a variety of historical examples that refute racialist interpretations:

> Ibn Fadhlan, the Arab, was allowed into religious rites. So was Tacitus' father. Irish slaves in Iceland, as well as Slavic, Finnish, and Sami slaves elsewhere are clearly shown, over and over again, as taking part in Norse culture, including Norse religion. Examples of this include the rites of Nerthus, in which slaves played a prominent part. . . . Indeed, such slaves often became integrated into the culture fully, as the Irish slaves did in Iceland. In fact, Icelandic law insisted that slaves take on Icelandic names immediately upon coming to Iceland. Norse slaves (again, who were most often foreigners, people of other races) were often freed after a time, and then took an equal place in society. Norsemen, when travelling afar, often took part in the religious rituals of the lands they travelled to, such as is found in the example of prime-signing, where travelling heathens took part in Christian ritual without renouncing their native gods. If the ancient heathens thought every bloodline had its own gods that should be stuck to exclusively, then why did they engage in this practice? Mythology too contains potent counterarguments to the Folkish viewpoint. Most notable is Odin. He seeks everywhere for wisdom and knowledge. He looks all over the world of humans. He looks amongst the Alfs, and the gods, and even the Jotuns. If true Ásatrú-ish wisdom is found only in certain bloodlines, then why does Odin do this?[111]

Heathens often look on the absolute past as the divine source of *truth*. It is the location of their real or imagined ancestors and their link to a new ethnicity and collective identity. As their source of folk wisdom, they approach the *Eddas* and sagas with awe, calling on them as tools for the construction or legitimation of ethnic identities and accounts, always in dialogue with current political realities.

Sitting in his living room, Brand expresses frustration at the "misuse" of Heathenry by the racist fringe. Like Skallagrimsson and others, Brand uses historical accounts to combat contemporary expressions of racism. After his friend was expelled from a Heathen gathering for fighting, he explains:

> [It] doesn't make sense because he was trying to stop people from being intolerant, and live up to the *Hávamál*; Truth and Honor, saying "hey this is not right that we're allowing these racists here, because racism has nothing to do with our religion, never has, never will be." There are Swedish—I mean . . . some findings were in Swedish graves with Buddhas in them, Turkish Gold, the Verengian Guard—Do you think the Verengian guard in charge of Constantinople and the Byzantine empire were racist? No, I don't think so.[112]

Heathens monitor and approach the lore as evolving textual how-to guides on behavior, relationship, and in essence "doing" Heathen ethnicity and whiteness, since one is not Heathen merely by virtue of social location, geography, or birth. Heathenry is not based on the practiced culture of grandparents or great-grandparents or on anything more tangible than evidence unearthed from archaeological digs and unreliable, biased narratives recorded by Christian monks from the ninth to twelfth centuries. Although Heathens selectively adopt theories, facts, and finer historical details as part of the "truths" they are engaged in constructing, they rely to a large extent on the interpretations of scholars and experts in the fields responsible for creating knowledge about ancient Heathen cultures. It is unlikely that mainstream churches would change their belief system if archaeologists unearthed solid, factual evidence that shook the foundations of their worldviews. Heathens, however, are largely beholden to the process of research and discovery, with a keen eye on changes and scholarly opinion that may lend more insight or clarification to how they might do Heathenry better by more closely emulating or honoring the ancestors. In Heathenry scientific discoveries are just as much religious discoveries that enrich the faith and bring practitioners closer to truth. Yet, as in all faith systems, their political, economic, and social locations and environments inevitably affect their interpretations.

Although there is nothing inherent in pre-Christian, premodern Heathen belief or doctrine that supports racist ideology, modern reconstructionist Heathenry has been complicated by racist elements born from nineteenth-century Germanic romanticism, creating an imagined sanctum for racist individuals. The majority of the community must self-consciously contend with potentially racist symbolic meanings, accusations, and labels. This has occurred primarily for three reasons: first, racists have indeed used Heathen symbols and identities to further their political and social agendas; second, American

Heathens are mostly white, and the reconstruction of their faith is influenced by the historical and social legacy of racism in the United States, just as other ethnic groups with tumultuous histories of genocide or apartheid must skirt accusations of harboring old feelings; third, Heathens must contend with racist symbolic meanings, accusations, and labels because their faith system and ideas about lineage are constructed differently from those of ethnic groups whose generational ties to a specific place and culture are ascribed. Heathen practitioners must construct new meanings out of outmoded cultural practices and attempt to synthesize the perceived fragments of modern life into a coherent whole, a peoplehood with the Heathen worldview as the foundation, contributing to the historical and ongoing "sharpening of the religious boundaries of ethnic association." Like other members of modern ethnic movements, because of a belief in "some combination of actual or supposed origin, language, or faith," Heathens "believe they constitute one people."[113]

Previous scholars, with few exceptions,[114] have approached American Heathenry as a bastion of white supremacy ideology, but I argue that the negotiations involved in navigating whiteness and racial politics in the construction of Heathen religio-ethnic identity are more complex. American Heathenry provides us with an example of a religion where primarily white people, whose ethnicities are not visibly marked, have invented their own ethnic associations. That this construction is complicated among Heathens from the United States demonstrates the geographically and historically grounded nature of racial meanings. In Iceland or other Germanic nations Heathens may take for granted Heathenry as lineage, bound by time and space since it is "rooted in the national cultural heritage in a very clear and direct way, which lends it influence, respect and resonance that extend far beyond its numbers."[115] American Heathens, however, reconstruct their traditions in a historical and cultural context that has been, and still is, quite heavily influenced by the legacy of racial discrimination. These racial meanings and the privilege of whiteness are inescapable; they infect the ongoing construction of Heathen ethnicity and make for contentious identity politics and intragroup struggles.

7

The Long Journey

I n the 1970s American Heathenry began amid the turmoil of changing political cal values and social arrangements. Stephen McNallen has said that his motivation to begin the Viking Brotherhood had more to do with his interest in Viking history and his military experience than with the countercultural revolution of the previous decade. Yet from the beginning of American Heathenry to the mid-1980s, it was shaped intimately by prevailing social and political paradigms. The post–World War II economic boom led to people's increased economic success and fostered a mounting belief in self-determination and individualism and an end to the age of communal values that had dominated the New Deal politics of prior generations. In the 1970s the social progressive values of the 1960s continued to affect people's growing political awareness. Women had fought for and won increasing political and economic freedom, contributing to a growing threat to traditional patriarchal arrangements and the feeling by many men that manhood was under siege. The environmental movement was rapidly growing, resulting in the declaration of the first Earth Day on April 22, 1970, and the subsequent creation of the Environmental Protection Agency. Shortly thereafter, the industrialized world faced an energy crisis as gas prices rose to an all-time high because of problems in the Middle East. This turmoil contributed to the revelation that reliance on petroleum products was an unsustainable environmental nightmare, fueling the ecological awareness that became the focus of Pagan groups worldwide. In response to this rapid social and political change, the industrialized world experienced a dramatic surge of NRMs attracting large numbers of disaffected youth.[1] In Eastern Europe, in the second half of the twentieth century, "empires disintegrated and nation-states became less significant as identity markers and as symbolic entities of emotional attachment and loyalty for their citizens."[2] Under these circumstances people began to turn to ethnicity and religion "as cementing forces of their diverse collectivities. Religion became, increasingly, the ground for redefining newly emerging polities, nation-states as well as ethnic groups in postcolonial and post-Soviet political formations."[3] In the past decade scholars have documented Native Faith movements in Bulgaria, the Czech Republic, Estonia, Hungary, Latvia, Lithuania, Poland, Russia, Siberia, Slovenia, and Ukraine,—each an attempt to hang the substance of indigenous identities on the scaffolding of religion. Although the context of Heathenry and that of the Native Faith revival in Eastern Europe differ in a variety of ways, reconstructionist Paganisms are all a response to the "uncertainty and volatility" of modern life and a return to what practitioners perceive to be true cultural roots.[4]

Scholars who have remarked on the relationship between religion and politics have often done so from the perspective that religion influences political belief, shaping our political system and party politics in foundational ways. There can be no arguing that Judeo-Christian values have shaped party lines in the past three decades and before, and that political systems in other countries are similarly affected by prevailing religious beliefs and customs. Yet the picture changes in considering the relationship between religion and politics when the religion in question is in its infancy, in flux, and therefore at the mercy of currents of political polemics. As scholars abandoned the term *cult* to popular culture and the shadowy nightmares of the anticult movement, defining NRMs took on even greater importance. One of the prevailing elements that defined NRMs was tension with the mainstream as NRMs maintained their peripheral, marginal position in opposition to dominant religious currents.[5] Yet despite such opposition, NRMs are informed and controlled by many of the prevailing cultural arrangements they position themselves to oppose. As a product of the significant social and economic upheavals of the 1960s and 1970s, NRMs are political constructs from the outset. The proliferation of Native Faith movements and other NRMs after the fall of communism, for example, reinforces the argument made by James Beckford and others that NRMs are formed during times of rapid social upheaval.[6] The relationship between religion and various social phenomena is therefore of primary interest to sociologists of religion, who view NRMs in particular as significant in "their potential status as windows into broader patterns of social change."[7]

All religions unfold as social constructions built by practitioners whose beliefs and values are externalized and contended as people vie for the right to define what is authentic and true about the world. Heathenry developed in a sociohistorical context fraught with social change and upheaval. In the 1980s, during the dawning of the Christian Right and Reaganomics, American Heathenry experienced organizational shifts, turmoil, and rearrangements. In the United States alternative religions were increasingly suspect as the Christian Right developed a stronger foothold in American society. The Satanic Panic was in full swing, and accusations of Satanism plagued all facets of American society.[8]

Popular culture, as popular culture does, shocked the morally righteous by pushing the boundaries of acceptability; gender-bending hair-metal bands and screeching metal music with satanic themes mocked the Parents Music Resource Center, led by Tipper Gore, leading to cries of alarm and public service announcements about the dangers of such music to our youth. Women were entering the workforce in greater numbers in response to the economic crunch; single-income families were no longer making ends meet; and divorce had begun to challenge the nuclear-family ideal. During this time Heathenry split because of conflicts over attitudes about race, racism, and ethnic identity into the Ásatrú Free Assembly and the Ring of Troth, with the Ásatrú Alliance as a confederation of independent kindreds. This was yet another step in the further politicization of American Heathenry, as represented in differing organizational ethoses, goals, and alignments.[9]

The Conundrum of American Reconstructionist Faith

Since the second half of the 1990s, scholarship on American Heathenry has focused on its relationship to Far Right political and racial ideologies.[10] The voices of moderate Heathenry have received little attention, as has the nuanced dialogue between the political concerns and beliefs of average Heathen practitioners and their construction of their faith. Religions and the people who make them are necessarily influenced by civil society's prevailing political and economic arrangements, norms, and values. The dominant political polemics of any generation shape not only people's identities but also how they do their faith. It is unlikely that the average Heathen experiences Heathenry as a product of political dialogue or even as politically influenced. Many Heathens are disengaged from politics, experiencing their often conservative political beliefs about society and social life as common sense. Although the focus on political polemics within American Heathenry seems to overshadow people's daily lived experiences, a person's political beliefs are a direct determinant of how they do Heathenry, with whom they interact, what rituals they perform, what games they play, what communities they join, and their very understanding of Heathen cosmology and the gods. In fact, although politics may not dominate conversation or face-to-face interactions (in contrast with its perpetual hashing out on social media), people's lives are intimately affected by their social and economic position, which influences their political beliefs. In this regard, there is little within American Heathenry that is not politically informed and determined. In every way, political considerations undergird people's choices, from the food they eat (or choose not to eat) to the brands they buy (or boycott) and the way they dress. These considerations filter through to people's religious perspectives, the kind of Heathenry they envision—to how Heathens reconstruct their faith and what kinds of innovations and outside influences they allow. In many ways, these very nuanced considerations are at the heart of the accusation of "Neo-Heathenry" and the identities of self-labeled reconstructionists. In creating something authentic and historically minded, however, Heathens are necessarily forced to tackle politically laden considerations. Is American Heathenry, for example, accepting of all people, or is it exclusive to northern Europeans? Is American Heathenry a militaristic religion with a warrior ethos that obligates its practitioner to be pro-gun? Does the traditionalism of Heathenry obligate its practitioners to hunt? Does it allow for, or require, animal sacrifice, and if so, what animal rights considerations must be taken into account? Or does its premodern foundation require that Heathens engage in voluntary simplicity? Does a practitioner's understanding of communal versus individual values within the greater society translate into how he or she approaches Heathen community (or vice versa)? As a religious movement in flux, Heathenry becomes defined by the political polemics of each generation.

Heathenry in the United States is a uniquely American Heathenry, different from its Norwegian, Icelandic, and German cousins. In his work on the relationship among religion, politics, and locality that documents Heathens in Norway, Egil Asprem reminds us that

> differences in the political and cultural climate of nations favour differences in religious ecologies. What this means is that studies of the dynamics of, for instance, revivalist Ásatrú in the United States do not necessarily provide the full picture of Ásatrú generally. Even when much of the ideological production of modern Ásatrú stems from an American context, its export to other countries is not to be viewed as a homogenising process, but will always involve adaptation to local cultural and political circumstances.[11]

In Norway and Germany, Heathens are beset by struggles for the heart of the movement, torn between right-wing organizations that blend "racist, anti-Semitic, conspiracy theorist and millenarian neo-Nazi political" agendas with an Odinist religious outlook[12] and those organizations forced to position themselves as antiracist, pushed to the left by the politics of their rivals. The obsessive and persistent racial and ethnic focus of many American Heathens is not present among their Icelandic peers, for whom the slavery of Africans and anti-immigrant sentiment are not prevailing legacies.[13] To Michael Strmiska and other scholars who have studied American Heathenry, American conservative politics and American Heathenry are intimately intertwined, creating what some have sarcastically referred to as "Ameritrú"—a uniquely American form of Ásatrú that privileges individual liberty and a militarism that is far removed from its European cousins, for whom the sacredness of nature is at the core of spirituality. Indeed, as this book has shown, American Heathenry has developed apart from its Icelandic and European cousins into a cultural system that is wholly and uniquely American, inseparable from its sociohistorical, economic, and political context.

Collective Identity and Belonging

How Heathens interpret and adopt their conceptualizations of gender and ethnicity into their systems of meaning and identity illuminates the detailed work involved in the greater construction of group culture. Their struggle also highlights the ongoing structure of that work, which occurs within the framework of the politics of difference. According to those I interviewed, Heathen women are somehow different from other women, just as folkish Heathens are different from universalists. This negotiation of authenticity and identity, however, is incomplete without an examination of the group's situated context between the cross and the pentacle. This examination of Heathens' affiliation with and disaffiliation from mainstream and alternative religious tradition lends insight into how identity complicates the very process of entering and exiting religion. It also highlights the importance of both identification and difference as processes of identity making, both individual and collective. The way in which Heathens create and negotiate identity and boundaries is similar to the findings of previous work on subcultural resistance and collective identity.[14]

The development of collective identity is a continual process involving both internal and external definition.[15] Members must be able to differentiate themselves from others by drawing on community-sanctioned norms and identity markers, a process that is "fundamentally about issues of belonging, expression, performance, identification and communication with others."[16] Kevin Hetherington characterizes this process in small groups as "neo-tribalism."[17] To him, cults and sect-like religious groups are case models for the study of "elective tribes" or "communities of feeling"—chosen communities based on "emotional, empathetic identification with like-minded others."[18] In other words, in a society built on organic solidarity—itself a product of differences among individuals—mechanical solidarity prevails where these differences are minimized and the members of society are alike in their dedication to a common goal or ideology. As Émile Durkheim notes, "Solidarity which comes from likeness is at its maximum when the collective conscience completely envelops our whole conscience and coincides in all points with it."[19] Members of elective tribes express identity through "ongoing performative repertoires"[20] that are essentially embodied theatrics, the only way in which we can engage with one another in the "politics of difference."[21] This performative process is ongoing and not without contradictions because "the bricolage of identity politics does not always produce a simple homology." It is complicated by differences in personal experience, political ideology, and biography and often leads to "an essentialism that wants to have clearly demarcated centres and margins in which friends and enemies, resisters and oppressors can easily be located."[22]

In Heathenry, differentiation both from Christianity and the mainstream religious world and from other Neopagan NRMs, primarily Wicca, allows Heathens to formulate a collective identity by creating boundaries and differences recognizable by outsiders. We must consider that they are created not only as alternatives to or in opposition to mainstream faith systems but also in relationship to other NRMs, all of which exist as part of the cultic milieu. Although the wider structural impacts and causes of NRM emergence are important, we must also account for the overlap and impact of NRMs on one another in terms of shared and conflicting norms, values, and boundaries as we further study the process of collective group identity.

When Heathens Go Virtual

The many discursive constructions of gender, ethnicity, and difference among Heathens occur primarily in contexts that are still relatively new to social research. Early NRM studies predated technological influences on how movements were shaped and on the diffusion of information. Cultural studies often assume that culture is both embodied and bound by physical location. The same can be said of NRM studies, which, until recently, have analyzed NRMs on the basis of members' physical bodies and spaces. By examining the setting of Heathen discourse, I have offered insight into the structural dynamics and variations an NRM may take when it is overlapped by (but not overcome by) the virtual world. The organizational forms of Heathenry interact and influence one another in a movable, permeable, and fluid relationship that is bound together through cyberspace. The influence of virtual space and communication on Heathenry's growth and real-life structure is evident in its forms, which also influence members' experiences and relationships.

Because these virtual *hof*s lack the face-to-face intimacy of other group structures, and because the Heathen community is burdened by disagreements over varied political and religious views, the Internet is the forum for much of the antagonistic infighting that, while assisting in the boundary maintenance of the community, often leads to bad blood between members. However, because the virtual boundaries of Heathenry are indistinct, the Internet also offers members the choice of either participation or nonparticipation without obligations. Turmoil causes rifts, but it can also be ignored as members bounce from list to list without embodied consequences or direct physical exile. If presentations of self fail online, members can try again, experimenting with cultural boundaries by testing taboos and definitions of authenticity.[23] Yet despite all the mayhem, Heathens manage to maintain their sanity, and their community continues to grow. Although it seems as though Heathenry could exist online without the need to organize offline meetings or community functions, the fact that offline Heathen events are highly populated and frequent supports Douglas Cowan's underlying assessment: offline community cannot be replaced by the virtual.[24]

Local tribes are the culmination of all the labor and passionate religious identities and interactions facilitated by the virtual. We need venues in which to test our physicality and share our expression with others. As Durkheim explained, religion is fundamentally a social phenomenon from which people derive feelings of "collective effervescence." He believed that "religious representations are collective representations that express collective realities; rites are ways of acting that are born only in the midst of assembled groups."[25] Although social media provide connectivity and feelings of involvement or belonging to the community, the groups Durkheim was referring to were made of flesh, not ones and zeros. The feeling of standing in a sacred space as the sun sets and watching a *Gothi*, his face and drum painted with runes in ashes, cannot be replicated by endless Facebook memes. The endless banter of social media or the hum of a hard drive cannot compete with the sound of drumming and gutteral *galdering* (rune chanting) around a bonfire, nor can virtual community on social media replicate the visceral and resounding "Hail!" of thirty people at a *faining*. Religious expression and participation in the sacred are fundamentally tied to embodied group experience. Even so, "out There," in that fuzzy boundless place, Heathens do create (and deconstruct) something meaningful: bonds of friendship, allegiances, and that longed-for sense of community.

Challenging Notions of Gender

These embodied experiences are inseparable from our gendered selves. In the sciences, when scholars discuss *gender,* they habitually do so in the dichotomous (though problematic) terms that they have constructed for it, namely, masculinity and femininity. They also attempt to identify performances that are neither or both to develop an alternative way of speaking about gender, expanding the literature on such things as women's resistance to gender norms. Some of this research concentrates on the microprocesses of gender play in religious or subcultural contexts, particularly male-dominated subcultures and patriarchal religions, and highlights women who carve out a distinctive niche in their setting by acting in opposition to mainstream gendered expectations.[26] As the Heathen community grows and new forms of technologies influence discourse and blur time and space, Heathens have become increasingly aware of gender as a political issue. On Facebook, on e-mail lists, and on Yahoo! groups, Heathens discuss the place of women in their communities, the artificiality of constructed roles, and the cliché of "Viking" hypermasculinity and argue for equal treatment and equal respect of Heathen women or quite the opposite, all the while maintaining traditional divisions of labor and largely conventional interests (in gendered terms, for certainly no one would call an interest in blacksmithing or yarn spinning conventional).

Scholarship regarding the gendered experience of religious participants finds that women typically focus on the *voice of relationship* or interpersonal relationships with other community members.[27] The roles made most available to Heathen women, as *frithweaver* or *spá-kona*, are social practices intended to build community. Heathens have embraced the idea, at least, of the sexes being equal but different, and in the subjective experience of many Heathen women, they are. Men are active leaders and warriors; women, for the most part, are peacekeepers and domestic laborers, an essentialization of gender norms that reflects traditional assumptions. Yet Heathen women resist the oppressive effects of patriarchy on themselves by adopting a "soft" patriarchal system, becoming in many cases "one of the boys" without having to be a "boy." Instead, they can participate in patriarchy and in sharing "power" without having to experience the powerlessness of normative femininity. They are happily fulfilling their traditional economic and social gender norms, which they have reframed in terms of ownership and empowerment. Heathen women are the keepers of keys, signifying symbolic (if not actual) ownership over the home and control of its contents.

During my research, the people I interviewed frequently referred to gender equality as a hallmark of Heathenry. They made this argument unfailingly in comparison to gender inequality within Abrahamic religious communities, and to the perceived lopsidedness of gendered perspectives in more Goddess-centered earth spiritualities. Heathenry, they claim, offers women true equality, the possibility to be partners without subordination. Notwithstanding such claims, in their endeavor to reconstruct elements of the social systems of ancient Germanic peoples (while paying lip-service to mainstream feminist notions of egalitarianism), Heathen women have also depoliticized gender norms. The influence of hegemonic masculinity and the patriarchal ideology of femininity sheds doubt on whether Heathens are truly engaged in gender resistance, or whether they have merely reframed, rather than resisted or changed, a traditionally oppressive and unequal division of labor.

Despite this dubious relationship of resistance and reframing, Heathen women do claim that they feel both powerful and empowered. Although Heathenry is undoubtedly not the sole vehicle by which women come to share in the power of masculinity, it offers sanctuary for women who may already embody masculinity too much to receive acceptance from or comfort in other more mainstream communities—those whose tomboy self-presentations did not disappear after adolescence, who would be labeled "pushy" in mainstream media instead of being valued as leaders, and who would be framed as "loud" instead of outspoken or "stubborn" instead of resolute. Heathenry offers women the impression that they may step outside femininity without sanctions, although the limits and the acceptability of their performances are still, to a certain extent, controlled by the boundaries imposed by Western culture. By embracing Heathen community norms, some women are able to renegotiate personal identity and reevaluate the negative qualities that defy conventional standards of femininity as strong, positive traits encouraged by their fellows. Although along with this, women are still engaged in much of what sociologists would consider gendered labor and behaviors, women are allowed these contradictory performances in connection to a past and a people that Heathens have marked as worthy of praise and emulation. In this way, being both a strong, femininity-defying shield maiden and a nurturing, albeit powerful, domestic caretaker is framed not just as compatible but also as desirable.

Missing from the gender analysis explored in this book is an examination of Heathen treatments of sexuality. New Age and Neopagan NRMs are typically more accepting of alternative and unabashed forms of sexuality. Because Heathens often identify with what some may interpret as conservative values, openness about the body and sexuality is, at times, less acceptable. In regard to homosexuality, in particular, Heathens have done what they always do—relate it, like many religious groups, to textual accounts or lessons. Although very many Heathens are tolerant or even supportive of so-called alternative sexualities, the discussion nonetheless exists. I leave the task of this analysis to subsequent works.

Examining Whiteness and the "Folk"

American society is no longer considered the melting pot of assimilation and homogeneity but instead has become the proverbial salad bowl: an amalgamation of multiple ethnicities that carry with them ethnic identities, ancestral cultural practices, and occasional folk religions. Early concepts of whiteness were tied intimately to class consciousness, when impoverished and struggling white workers "responded to a fear of dependency on wage labor and to the necessities of capitalist work discipline" by constructing whiteness in opposition to black workers, who were framed as "other."[28] We are left, decades later, with the legacy of this class struggle and its lasting images of race and racial stereotypes. Today, the meaning of whiteness has been consumed by its own invisibility, which has allowed whites to portray themselves as the default or normative American ethnicity, the axis of U.S. civilization. Whiteness these days is a silent heir of its early predecessor, allowing its bearers the experience of an ethnicity that is often unconscious because "societal norms have been constructed around their racial, ethnic, and cultural frameworks, values and priorities and then referred to as 'standard American culture.'"[29] It is possible to identify different cultures precisely because they are the unwhite, "excluded from the normative." Whiteness is constructed in relation to the "other" but is itself "boundless" and therefore "involves drawing boundaries . . . around the substantively empty category 'white.'"[30]

Despite the growing awareness of *white* as a racial category or *whiteness* as an object, the creation of a white ethnic identity retains a substantial element of boundlessness if it continues to be defined by what it is not rather than by what it is. It opens possibilities for many white Americans who lack clear, tangible lineages to their past to define their own white ethnicity and reconstruct, re-create, or invent a "shared culture, religion, geography, and language."[31] Yet whiteness is frequently equated with racism and discrimination but is otherwise viewed as largely lacking in content, and deservedly so; the conflation of whiteness and racism makes it difficult to view whiteness or white ethnic pride through a lens separate from this negativity. To categorize the cultural practices or behaviors involved in being white, rather than highlight whiteness, as a system of (often specific) privileges and advantages is rare and instead is reserved for narratives of people of color.[32] The racialized or ethnic experiences of white Americans likewise deserve consideration, if for no other reason than to illustrate the complexities and indissoluble predicaments of constructing and enacting whiteness. This focus is not without problems. The connection between pride in whiteness (even if this whiteness is conceptualized as, say, Swedishness or Germanness) and the exclusion of or prejudice against other, nonwhite ethnicities is complex.

Indeed, central to Heathen identity in such a context is whether the construction of white ethnicity is necessarily racist (as reflected in the language of exclusion or pride). Contemporary racism has changed from blatant and exclusionary to leaning toward in-group favoritism, a central component of the white racial frame that situates whiteness as normative and virtuous. Ideas that suggest that racism is merely intolerance of difference may be somewhat outdated because prowhite rather than antiblack sentiments are expressed.[33] John Dovidio and Samuel Gaertner refer to this as *aversive racism* and argue that although it is often unintentional, it is still perilous.[34] Even white liberals who claim to be resolutely antiracist have demonstrated in-group favoritism toward white subjects during experimental research. The negotiation of Heathen identity is intimately connected to racial and ethnic politics and privilege because unlike other Neopagan belief systems whose histories and hereditary ties are ambiguous and eclectic, American Heathenry is tied to a specific European cultural identity that has been co-opted to further racist and nationalist agendas by some of modern history's most notorious figures.

Examinations of American Heathenry are inseparable from examinations of whiteness as the benefactor of ethnic invention because ethnicity is also a "struggle between groups over new strategic positions of power."[35] Much of the ongoing discourse within the community itself reflects wider issues of white power, guilt, racial resentment, and ignorance. It is important to note that white people who choose to become Heathen have the ability to do so because, as members of the default ethnicity, they have the freedom to construct the symbolic ethnic and religious identity that is uniquely theirs, to empower themselves by re-creating an otherness that transcends time and space without compromising their power and status as white.[36]

Herbert Gans argued that this symbolic ethnicity is characterized by the *feeling* of cultural identification that many Americans emphasize rather than participation in ethnic organizations or cultural practices.[37] To be symbolically ethnic is to treat ethnicity as leisure, where ethnic identity lacks salience.

Because the construction of Heathenry is a continuously self-conscious endeavor, it is salient indeed. Although Heathens use just as many symbols of ethnicity as Americans who highlight their Irish American, Italian American, or German American (white) ethnicities during festivals and holidays, the Heathen folkway is much more complex than previous scholarship has expressed. It is a personal and collective identity expressed through lifestyle choices at the same time at which it is an anachronism whose cultural foundation is firmly rooted in conceptualizations of Viking-age Scandinavia and tribal Germania. In such a case, the belief in blood ties or common ancestry rather than factual links becomes all the more relevant.

In the negotiation of this identity, Heathen practitioners construct new meanings out of outmoded cultural practices and attempt to synthesize the perceived fragments of modern life into a coherent whole, a peoplehood with the Heathen worldview as the foundation. As Timothy Smith writes of members of modern ethnic movements, "For reasons of some combination of actual or supposed origin, language, or faith," Heathens "believe they constitute one people."[38] Perhaps this is what they mean when they employ the term *The Folk* during ritual, as in "Hail The Folk!" But the meaning is ambiguous. Which folk? Heathen folk? White folk? The struggle over claims of ownership of this peoplehood involves the division between members' perceived folkish and universalist leanings and reflects an ongoing battle over dominant political ideology and rules of inclusivity and exclusivity.

The contentious nature of this boundary maintenance seems to have become part of what it means to claim the Heathen folkway—to struggle for ownership over the identity while deconstructing (or avoiding) the label *racist*. Heathens are not alone in this; when "Irish pride" or "German pride" is translated into "white pride," it is rendered problematic. During annual Columbus Day parades, many Native American groups protest Italian "pride," arguing that taking pride in one's Italian heritage cannot be divorced from the historical conquest, plunder, and devastation of indigenous peoples. Celtic reconstructionist groups face similar accusations of racism, racial exclusivity, and attempts by hate groups to co-opt Celtic symbolism or infiltrate their organizations and have responded with a backlash and the development of Celtics against Oppression, Racism, and Neo-Nazism (CAORANN).[39] Heathens, likewise, are justifiably challenged to divorce the construction of white ethnicity from the baggage of history, ever negotiating the boundaries of we-ness and whiteness. Among studies of ethnic identity, American Heathenry is a dramatic case example. Its examination puts into macrofocus the fluid, symbolic, and constructed nature of ethnic affiliation and the delicate relationship between white ethnicity and racism. This book suggests, as others have argued, that despite such complications, ethnic identity is growing more—not less—important in the face of postmodernism. It is a response to, and perhaps an inoculation from, the increasingly McDonaldized and hyperrationalized world that we inhabit, where ethnic and religious identity are reenchanted and far more salient, even among whites, than many had anticipated.

When I ventured out into the field to begin my research, my knowledge of the Heathen community was limited; my experience was overshadowed by the ambiguity imposed on me by the member-researcher duality. I was, to a certain degree, still gun-shy from my expulsion from the online forum by juvenile racists. I also felt like a novice and, quite often, a poseur. As I proceeded through the field, I came to learn that there were many well-known, respected, and knowledgeable Heathens from whom to learn. There were those who had been active in the community for over a decade, whose names had appeared in Heathen publications, and those who had independently published handbooks on Heathenry or on various esoteric concepts related to it. There were members who were well known in their ordinary lives as stage comedians, fantasy authors, or other public personalities. The researchers were not strange to the community, either. Mattias Gardell and Jenny Blain had both left lasting impressions, for good or ill, and their legacies would both help and hinder my research and inform my ongoing ethnographic conundrums. Ethnographers are, among many things, secret keepers and obligatory mutes. Regardless of the backbiting, insulting, gossiping, strangeness, or blatantly unempirical political fearmongering that others shared with me, my position required that I remain silent so as not to damage rapport. And so I did, mostly, often with great difficulty.

My inquiries into Heathenry as an ethnic folkway have forced me painfully through the muck of reality that illustrates that racism in American Heathenry is indeed a fact. The more I review scholarly work that refers to Ásatrú as "racist" or "racialist" (noting the lack of scholarly work to the contrary) and each painful transcription of an interview with a Heathen expressing racist sentiments who, by his or her own account, is "not racist," the more cynical, distant, and disconcerted I have become toward my subject area and my religious affiliation. My ability to argue truthfully that "heathens are not this way" in response to accusations of nationalism, white supremacy, or overt racism has become more difficult to maneuver. Certainly, fieldwork of all kinds is beset by a myriad of anxieties. Ethnographers "worry over fulfilling their obligations to their subjects, over balancing personal debts to individuals against universal debts to the discipline of sociology, and over discharging obligations to subjects that extend beyond the life of any particular piece of research."[40] No doubt this book will provoke defensiveness from some Heathens who may feel that they have once again been cast as ignorant racists. They may argue that I did not represent their particular niche of Heathenry, or that my personal politics painted how I interpreted their beliefs. Nevertheless, the patterns of belief and behavior that I and other Heathens have identified indicate to me that the scholars whom I set out to challenge may have been onto something, even if the reality that I uncovered was less sinister and much more complex. It has not been difficult for me to find other American Heathens with whom I share a political worldview, and to whom I can express my abiding faith in the need for social justice, compassion, and social and economic equality. It has also not been difficult, however, to find those who express right-wing sentiments, who are anti-immigration, antigovernment, and pro-gun. Yet most of those whom I came to know and observe live in the in-between. They champion the cause of LGBTQ equality, but they also love their guns. They fight for women's reproductive rights but are ambivalent about social welfare programs. How these complexities inform their spiritual practice is what I set out to articulate. I understand that for many Heathens, and Americans in general, political ideological considerations are often not the fuel that drives them. The ideas that I find alarming are less salient for them than the concerns of daily living, of friends and family and simply being together. It is only in that space, in the mundane being together, that I found my place.

Who I am as a Heathen now has little to do with the group itself, the other members, the ongoing dialogue among various Heathen factions or even those many who I know are progressive, politically sensitive, fervently antiracist persons. Just like those who have disaffiliated from American Heathenry to become Buddhist, to become something else more peaceful, unburdened by the baggage of hatred or ambiguous political leanings, I find that my reasons for clinging to my Heathen identity rest solely in my love of history and the romantic and in a sense of continuity. My identity is only part of a collective insofar as it is connected to the collective memories created and recounted from the epic past and its textual echoes, and to those few Heathens with whom I have developed deep, meaningful relationships.

Throughout the years I discovered that behind the larger picture of Heathenry are small, intimate, kind communities of individuals who appreciate one another, whose passionate loyalty to one another is beyond anything else I have experienced. Somehow, these individuals cooperated and fashioned a larger identity, an entity greater than themselves that carried across states and nations and became something international, but most important, something meaningful and salient in people's lives. However disorganized the collective felt at the diffuse level, something had coalesced out of the ether of Heathen discourse. It was a collective identity, what Heathens were referring to when they said "How Heathen of you" to me. Although it was not necessarily agreed on by all, it was something understood as having qualities of Heathenness—a collection of traits, beliefs, values, and shared experiences. As a woman, I felt empowered. I felt as though the capability for strength, independence, and emotional ferocity that my mom had allowed me to take for granted was nurtured by Heathenry as a worldview as well as a community. As a person who grew up overseas as the child of a German mother, I felt a sense of ownership over those childhood bedtime tales about Thor and his great adventures. To me, those stories and images of gods and heroes are intertwined with my deepest sense of self and connect me to the place that I call home, more significant to me now that the U.S. Department of Defense neighborhoods, schools, and military bases of my childhood have all but disappeared—ghost towns now gone to seed. To be Heathen is, to me, a connection to the epic past, to Tolkien's Middle Earth, which itself is a product of his love for Germanic mythology. It is what I imagine the lore would look like on the big screen and has forever captured my heart.

Notes

1. BECOMING HEATHEN

1. Devyne Gilette and Lewis Stead, "The Pentagram and the Hammer" (Paper presented at the workshop "Wicca and Modern Heathenism" at the 1994 FreeSpirit festival in Darlington, Maryland), available at http://www.webcom.com/~lstead/wicatru.html, accessed October 15, 2002.

2. Margot Adler, *Drawing Down the Moon: Witches, Druids, Goddess-Worshippers, and Other Pagans in America Today* (New York: Penguin Books, 1979), 308.

3. Chas Clifton, "In the Mists of Avalon: How Contemporary Paganism Dodges the 'Crisis of History'" (Paper presented at the 2009 CESNUR Conference, Salt Lake City, UT, June 11–13, 2009); Erin F. Johnston, "'I Was Always This Way . . .': Rhetoric of Continuity in Narratives of Conversion," *Sociological Forum* 28, no. 3 (2013): 549–573.

4. See Ross Haenfler, *Subcultures: The Basics* (New York: Routledge, 2014).

5. Chas Clifton, *Her Hidden Children: The Rise of Wicca and Paganism in America* (Lanham, MD: AltaMira Press, 2006), xii.

6. Steve Bruce, *Choice and Religion: A Critique of Rational Choice Theory* (New York: Oxford University Press, 1999); Wendy Cadge, Peggy Levitt, and David Smilde, "De-centering and Re-centering: Rethinking Concepts and Methods in the Sociological Study of Religion," *Journal for the Scientific Study of Religion* 50 (2011): 437–444.

7. Mary Jo Neitz, Kevin McElmurry, and Daniel Winchester, "New Sociological Narratives of Morality under Modernity: From Subtraction to Multiplicity," in *Handbook of Cultural Sociology,* ed. John Hall, Laura Grindstaff, and Ming-Cheng Lo (New York: Routledge, 2010), 181–190.

8. Lorne Dawson, "The Sociocultural Significance of New Religious Movements," in *The Oxford Handbook of New Religious Movements,* ed. James Lewis (New York: Oxford University Press, 2004), 78.

9. Penny Edgell, "A Cultural Sociology of Religion: New Directions," *Annual Review of Sociology* 38 (2012): 258.

10. Marie Griffith and Melani McAlister, eds., *Religion and Politics in the Contemporary United States* (Baltimore: Johns Hopkins University Press, 2008).

11. Carol Hanisch, "The Personal Is Political," in *Notes From The Second Year: Women's Liberation* (New York: 1970), 76–77. This essay defends consciousness-raising against the charge that it is "therapy." Hanisch states, "One of the first things we discover in these groups is that personal problems are political problems. There are no personal solutions at this time."

12. C. Wright Mills, *The Sociological Imagination* (London: Oxford University Press, 1959), 8.

13. Jaimie Wood, *The Teen Spellbook: Magick for Young Witches* (Berkeley, CA: Celestial Arts, 2001); Francesca DeGrandis, *Be a Teen Goddess: Magical Charms, Spells and Wiccan Wisdom for the Wild* (Berkeley, CA: Citadel, 2005); Silver RavenWolf, *Teen Witch: Wicca for a New Generation* (St. Paul, MN: Llewellyn Publications, 1998); Silver RavenWolf, *Teen Witch Kit: Everything You Need to Make Magick!* (St. Paul, MN: Llewellyn Publications, 1998).

14. Jen McConnel, *Goddess Spells for Busy Girls: Get Rich, Get Happy, Get Lucky* (San Francisco, CA: Weiser Books, 2014).

15. D. J. Conway, *A Little Book of Candle Magic* (Freedom, CA: Crossing Press, 2000); Patricia Telesco, *Mastering Candle Magick: Advanced Spells and Charms for Every Rite* (Franklin Lakes, CA: New Page Books, 2003); Richard Webster, *Candle Magic for Beginners: The Simplest Magic You Can Do* (St. Paul, MN: Llewellyn Publications, 2004); Raven Willow, *Candle Magic: Simple Spells for Beginners to Witchcraft* (ePub: CreateSpace Independent Publishing Platform, 2014); Milla Walsh, *Wicca Candle Spells: Simple Magic Spells That Work Fast* (ePub: Amazon Digital Services, 2013).

16. Bruce A. Greer and Wade Clark Roof, "Desperately Seeking Sheila: Locating Religious Privatism in American Society," *Journal for the Scientific Study of Religion* 31, no. 3 (1992): 342–352.

17. Max Weber, *From Max Weber: Essays in Sociology,* trans. and ed. H. H. Gerth and C. Wright Mills (New York: Oxford University Press, 1946), 139.

18. Ibid., 148.

19. See Christopher H. Partridge, *The Re-enchantment of the West: Alternative Spiritualities, Sacralization, Popular Culture, and Occulture* (London: T&T Clark, 2005), 16.

20. Don Culpitt, "Post-Christianity," in *Religion, Modernity, and Post-modernity,* ed. Paul Heelas, David Martin, Paul Morris, (Oxford: Blackwell, 1998).

21. Wade Clark Roof, "Modernity, the Religious, and the Spiritual: Redrawing the Boundaries," *Annals of the American Academy of Political and Social Science* 558 (1998): 211–224.

22. Greer and Roof, "Desperately Seeking Sheila."

23. Rodney Stark and William Sims Bainbridge, "Of Churches, Sects, and Cults: Preliminary Concepts for a Theory of Religious Movements," *Journal for the Scientific Study of Religion* 18, no. 2 (1979): 117–133.

24. Dawson, "Sociocultural Significance of New Religious Movements."

25. Danny L. Jorgensen and Scott E. Russell, "American Neo-Paganism: The Participants' Social Identities," *Journal for the Scientific Study of Religion* 38, no. 3 (1999): 325–339.

26. Colin Campbell, "The Cult, the Cultic Milieu and Secularization," *Sociological Yearbook of Religion in Britain* 5 (1972): 119–136.

27. Jorgensen and Russell, "American Neo-Paganism."

28. Reka Szilardi, "Ancient Gods—New Ages: Lessons from Hungarian Paganism," *Pomegranate: The International Journal of Pagan Studies* 11, no. 1 (2009): 35, 36, 44–57.

29. Egil Asprem, "Heathens Up North: Politics, Polemics, and Contemporary Norse Paganism in Norway," *Pomegranate: The International Journal of Pagan Studies* 10, no. 1 (2008): 41–69.

30. Steven M. Tipton, *Getting Saved from the Sixties: Moral Meaning in Conversion and Cultural Change* (Berkeley: University of California Press, 1982).

31. Mattias Gardell, *Gods of the Blood: The Pagan Revival and White Separatism* (Durham, NC: Duke University Press, 2003).

32. Bil Linzie lists the Runic Society, the Viking Brotherhood, Ásatrú Free Church, the Nation of Odin, and the Odinist Committee as defunct groups. See Bil Linzie, *Germanic Spirituality* (Unpublished paper: July 2003), 6. Available at http://heathengods.com /library/bil_linzie/germanic_spirituality.pdf, accessed December 17, 2014.

33. Sara Pike, *Earthly Bodies, Magical Selves: Contemporary Pagans and the Search for Community* (Berkeley: University of California Press, 2001), 134.

34. "Twelve Lakes Kindred" is a pseudonym for this group.

35. Bindrunes are made by combining individual rune staves together into one, often chosen from the initials of a kindred's name. Bindrunes have a complex magical and historical significance to Heathens.

36. Seamus Heaney, trans., *Beowulf*, in *The Norton Anthology of Western Literature*, 8th ed., ed. Sarah Lawall (New York: Norton, 2000), lines 607–641.

37. "Three Oaks Kindred" is a pseudonym.

38. Émile Durkheim, *The Elementary Forms of Religious Life*, trans. Joseph Swain (New York: Free Press, 1965), 218.

39. Clifford Geertz, "Religion as a Cultural System," in *The Interpretation of Cultures: Selected Essays*, Clifford Geertz (New York: Basic Books, 1973), 87–125, 90.

40. Neil Price, "Between Sorcerers and Priests: The Social Construction of Viking-Age Scandinavian 'Religion'" (Paper presented at the HESP Symposium, IRMACS Centre, Burnaby, BC: Canada, February 15, 2013).

41. Linda Greenhouse, "Supreme Court Rules in Ohio Prison Case," *New York Times*, June 1, 2005. Available at http://www.nytimes.com/2005/06/01/politics/01scotus.html? _r=0, accessed on December 17, 2014.

42. In the late 1990s the AFA got involved in the lengthy quarrel over the remains of the Kennewick man, a prehistoric man found on a bank of the Columbia River in Kennewick, Washington, on July 28, 1996. It claimed that these were the remains of a European ancestor. In the brief, McNallen writes "While plaintiffs are not opposed to scientific research if done in a considerate and reverent way, they further feel that the ethnic and religious "next of kin" should have ultimate control over the bodies of the dead. And that is the key to this whole problem—there is very convincing evidence that Richland Man is a kinsman to plaintiffs rather than kinsman to the Umatilla tribes, and that the Umatilla tribes therefore have no moral, religious, or legal right to his remains." United States District Court for the District of Oregon, CV No. CV-96-1516 JE by the Ásatrú Folk Assembly, Stephen A. McNallen, and William Fox versus the United States of America, Section 9, page 7.

43. The most relevant studies include Jeffrey Kaplan, "The Reconstruction of the Ásatrú and Odinist Traditions," in *Magical Religion and Modern Witchcraft*, ed. James R. Lewis (Albany: State University of New York Press, 1996), 193–236; Jeffrey Kaplan and Tore Bjørgo, eds., *Nation and Race: The Developing Euro-American Racist Subculture* (Boston: Northeastern University Press, 1998); Jeffrey Kaplan, *Radical Religions in America:*

Millenarian Movements from the Far Right to the Children of Noah (Syracuse, NY: Syracuse University Press, 1997); Jeffrey Kaplan and Leonard Weinberg, *The Emergence of a Euro-American Radical Right* (New Brunswick, NJ: Rutgers University Press, 1998); Nicholas Goodrick-Clarke, *Black Sun: Aryan Cults, Esoteric Nazism, and the Politics of Identity* (New York: New York University Press, 2002); and Gardell, *Gods of the Blood.* The exception to this focus is the work of Michael Strmiska and Baldur A. Sigurvinsson, "Ásatrú in Iceland: The Rebirth of Nordic Paganism?" *Nova Religio: The Journal of Alternative and Emergent Religious Movements* (2000): 127–179.

44. Jenny Blain, *Nine Worlds of Seid-magic : Ecstasy and Neo-shamanism in Northern European Paganism* (London: Routledge, 2001).

45. Brian M. Rafferty, "Pagan 'King' Has Council GOP Nod," *Queens Tribune,* available at http://www.queenstribune.com/news/1253209214.html, accessed September 4, 2013.

46. Jennifer Lee, "Candidate's Religion is Point of Contention in Queens Race," *New York Times,* November 2, 2009, available at http://cityroom.blogs.nytimes.com/2009/11/02/candidates-religion-is-point-of-contention-in-queens-race/?_r=0, accessed September 4, 2013.

47. Steven Thrasher, "Grand Ol' Pagan: What Does the Republican 'Heathen' Running for New York's City Council Actually Believe?" *Village Voice,* October 26, 2009, available at http://blogs.villagevoice.com/runninscared/2009/10/grand_ol_pagan.php, accessed September 4, 2013.

48. Abby Eden, "More Details Surface About Cop Charged With Stealing From Mom" Fox 4 News, July 3, 2012, available at http://fox4kc.com/2012/07/03/more-details-emerge-about-cop-charged-with-stealing-from-mom/, accessed December 17, 2014.

49. Ásatrú Folk Assembly's "Declaration of Purpose," at http://runestone.org/index.php?option=com_content&view=article&id=69&Itemid=475.

50. Doug Stanglin, "Neo-Nazi Seeking All-White Town Charged in North Dakota," *USA Today,* November 19, 2013, available at http://www.usatoday.com/story/news/nation/2013/11/19/north-dakota-neo-nazi-all-white-town-arrested-charged/3640039/, accessed December 17, 2014.

51. Jason Pitzl-Waters, "The Ásatrú Folk Assembly and White Nationalism," *The Wild Hunt: A Modern Pagan Perspective at Patheos,* September 19, 2011, available at http://www.patheos.com/blogs/wildhunt/2011/09/the-asatru-folk-assembly-and-white-nationalism.html, accessed September 22, 2011.

52. The author constructed a survey using Google Surveys, with demographic questions written for a Heathen sample. The survey was deployed on Facebook groups, through e-mail lists, and by word of mouth to 678 Heathens within a couple of weeks in 2012.

53. Michael Strmiska, "On Becoming a Pariah (Personal Reflections on My Ásatrú Research)," unpublished paper presented in August 2012 at CPASE conference in Stockholm, Sweden, available at http://www.academia.edu/2339326/On_Becoming_A_Pariah_Personal_Reflections_on_my_Asatru_Research, accessed December 17, 2014.

54. Kaplan, "Reconstruction of the Ásatrú and Odinist Traditions," 194.

55. Karl Seigfried, "Worldwide Heathen Census 2013 Results and Analysis," available at http://www.norsemyth.org/2014/01/worldwide-heathen-census-2013-results.html, accessed March 7, 2014.

56. Anselm L. Strauss and Juliet Corbin, *Grounded Theory in Practice* (Thousand Oaks, CA: Sage, 1997).

57. Ruth Behar, "Ethnography: Cherishing Our Second-Fiddle Genre," *Journal of Contemporary Ethnography* 28, no. 5 (1999): 476.

58. Amanda Coffey, *The Ethnographic Self: Fieldwork and the Representation of Identity* (London: Sage, 1999).

59. Angela Coco and Ian Woodward, "Discourses of Authenticity within a Pagan Community: The Emergence of the 'Fluffy Bunny' Sanction" *Journal of Contemporary Ethnography* 36, no. 5 (2007): 479. Those Heathens who behave in a manner that other Heathens perceive as too New-Agey or too Wiccan, (discussed further in Chapters 4 and 5) are often labeled as "Fluffy," among other terms.

2. FLEEING THE CROSS AND THE PENTACLE

1. Stephen J. Hunt, *Alternative Religions: A Sociological Introduction* (London: Ashgate, 2003), 8.

2. Wade Clark Roof and William McKinney, *American Mainline Religion: Its Changing Shape and Future* (New Brunswick, NJ: Rutgers University Press, 1987).

3. Leslie Irvine, *Codependent Forevermore: The Invention of Self in a Twelve-Step Group* (Chicago: University of Chicago Press, 2003), 99–101.

4. David Bromley, "Leaving the Fold: Disaffiliation with New Religious Movements," in *The Oxford Handbook of New Religious Movements*, ed. James Lewis (New York: Oxford University Press, 2004).

5. Michele Lamont and Virag Molnar, "The Study of Boundaries in the Social Sciences," *Annual Review of Sociology* 28 (2002): 167–195; Musafa Emirbayer, "Manifesto for a Relational Sociology," *American Journal of Sociology* 103, no. 2 (1997): 281–317; Margaret R. Somers, "The Narrative Constitution of Identity: A Relational and Network Approach," *Theory and Society* 23 (1994): 605–649.

6. Lamont and Molnár, "Study of Boundaries," 168.

7. Steven Epstein, "Gay Politics, Ethnic Identity: The Limits of Social Constructionism," in *Forms of Desire*, ed. Edward Stein (New York: Routledge, 1992), 239–293.

8. David Snow, "The Sociology of Conversion," *Annual Review of Sociology* 10 (1984): 169.

9. Paul Heelas, *The New Age Movement* (Oxford: Blackwell, 1996).

10. Roy Wallis, *The Elementary Forms of New Religious Life* (London: Routledge, 1984).

11. Morris Rosenberg and Howard B. Kaplan, eds., *Social Psychology of the Self-Concept* (Arlington Heights, IL: Harlan Davidson, 1982); Richard Jenkins, *Social Identity* (London: Routledge, 1996); Patrick J. Williams and Heith Copes, " 'How Edge Are You?': Constructing Authentic Identities and Subcultural Boundaries in a Straightedge Internet Forum," *Symbolic Interaction* 28, no. 1 (2005): 67–89.

12. Snow, "Sociology of Conversion," 177.

13. Janet Jacobs, "Deconversion from Religious Movements: An Analysis of Charismatic Bonding and Spiritual Commitment," *Journal for the Scientific Study of Religion* 26, no. 3 (1987): 294.

14. Hilda (pseud.), telephone interview by the author, June 30, 2006.

15. Freya Aswynn, *Northern Mysteries and Magick* (revised edition of *Leaves of Yggdrasil*) (St. Paul, MN: Llewellyn Publications, 2002).

16. Daniel Sarabia and Thomas E. Shriver, "Maintaining Collective Identity in a Hostile Environment: Confronting Negative Public Perception and Factional Divisions within the Skinhead Subculture," *Sociological Spectrum* 24, no. 3 (2004): 267–294; Verta Taylor and Nancy Whittier, "Collective Identity in Social Movement Communities: Lesbian Feminist Mobilization," in *Frontiers in Social Movement Theory,* ed. Aldon D. Morris and Carol McClurg Mueller (New Haven, CT: Yale University Press, 1992), 104–129.

17. Cyntha Pelak Fabrizio, "Women's Collective Identity Formation in Sports: A Case Study from Women's Ice Hockey," *Gender and Society* 16, no. 1 (2002): 93–114.

18. Timothy B. Gongaward, "Collective Memories and Collective Identities: Maintaining Unity in Native American Educational Social Movements," *Journal of Contemporary Ethnography* 32, no. 5 (2003): 384–520; James Jasper, *The Art of Moral Protest: Culture, Biography, and Creativity in Social Movements* (Chicago: University of Chicago Press, 1997); Enrique Larana, Hank Johnson, and Joseph R. Gusfield, eds., *New Social Movements: From Ideology to Identity* (Philadelphia: Temple University Press, 1994); Taylor and Whittier, "Collective Identity."

19. Gongaward, "Collective Memories," 486. See also David Snow, "Collective Identity and Expressive Forms," in *International Encyclopedia of Social and Behavioral Sciences,* ed. Neil Smelser and Paul Baltes (Oxford, U.K.: Pergamon Press, 2001), 2212–2219.

20. Gongaward, "Collective Memories," 486.

21. Bromley, "Leaving the Fold."

22. See Bryan Taylor, "Conversions and Cognition: An Area for Empirical Study in the Microsociology of Religious Knowledge," *Sociological Compass* 23 (1976): 5–22; Taylor, "Recollection and Membership: Converts' Talk and the Ratiocination of Commonality," *Sociology* 12 (1978): 316–324; James A. Beckford, "Accounting for Conversion," *British Journal of Sociology* 29 (1978): 249–262; and James A. Beckford, "Talking of Apostasy; or, Telling Tales and 'Telling' Tales," in *Accounts and Action,* ed. Peter Abell and Nigel Gilbert (London: Gower, 1983), 77–97.

23. Stephen McNallen, "Asatru Attitudes toward Christianity," *Ásatrú Update,* 2010, available at http://asatruupdate.blogspot.com/2010/05/asatru-attitudes-toward-christianity.html, accessed February 14, 2012.

24. Alfarrin, "Bringing Forth the Gods of My Kin," *The Journal of Hofstadr Hof,* available at http://cauldronborn.blogspot.com/search/label/Criticism%20of%20Christianity, accessed February 15, 2012.

25. Available at "Heathen Humor 'n Stuff" at https://www.facebook.com/AsatruHumor?directed_target_id=0, accessed January 5, 2015.

26. Ephraim Emerton, trans., "Bishop Daniel of Winchester Advises Boniface on the Method of Conversion" (723–724), in *The Letters of Saint Boniface* (New York: Columbia University Press, 2000), 26–28.

27. Alvis (pseud.), interview by the author, October 8, 2004.

28. Brand (pseud.), interview by the author, October 9, 2004.

29. Ivor (pseud.), telephone interview by the author, December 30, 2004.

30. Egil (pseud.), telephone interview by the author, April 13, 2006.

31. Geza von Nemenyi, "Women in Ásatrú," from the *Introductory Booklet of the Germanic Glaubens-Gemeinschaft* (Germanic Faith-Community), an Asatru group founded in Germany in the year 1907. Written by: Geza von Nemenyi. Translation from the German by: Nissa Annakindt available at www.oocities.org/athens/delphi/4452/AsaWomen.htm, accessed January 2012.

32. Alfarrin, "Bringing Forth the Gods of My Kin."

33. VidarsGothi, "New To Ásatrú" at http://vidarsgothi.org/newtoasatru, accessed January 5, 2015.

34. Garman Lord, "The Evolution of Theod Belief, Part I: The Wiccan Years," *Theod Magazine* 2, no. 3 (1995): 19.

35. Garman Lord, "The Evolution of Theod Belief, Part II: The Vitan Theod," *Theod Magazine* 2, no. 4 (1995): 32.

36. Francesca Polletta and James M. Jasper, "Collective Identity and Social Movements," *Annual Review of Sociology* 27 (2001): 285.

37. Ross Haenfler, *Straight Edge: Clean-Living Youth, Hardcore Punk, and Social Change* (New Brunswick, NY: Rutgers University Press, 2006).

38. See Marilynn B. Brewer and Wendi Gardener, "Who Is This 'We'? Levels of Collective Identity and Self Representations," *Journal of Personality and Social Psychology* 71, no. 1 (1996): 83–93; David Snow, "Collective Identity and Expressive Forms."

39. Snow, "Collective Identity and Expressive Forms," 4.

40. David Snow and Peter Owens, "Social Movements and Social Inequality: Toward a More Balanced Assessment of the Relationship," in *Handbook of the Social Psychology of Inequality*, ed. Jane McLeod, Edward Lawler, Michael Schwalbe (Dordrecht: Springer, 2014), 667.

41. Arlie Stephens, "Similarities between Heathenry and Wicca," available at http://www.heathengods.com/library/wicca_comparison/differences_by_stephens.pdf, accessed January 2012.

42. Unni (pseud.), telephone interview by the author, April 9, 2006.

43. Freiwald, "Heathen Stereotypes and Their Interaction on Internet Forums," a topic on the *Germanic Heathenry Forum*, January 12, 2012.

44. Inga (pseud.), telephone interview by the author, April 9, 2006.

45. See Angela Coco and Ian Woodward, "Discourses of Authenticity within a Pagan Community: The Emergence of the 'Fluffy Bunny' Sanction," *Journal of Contemporary Ethnography* 36, no. 5 (2007).

46. Eskel (pseud.), interview by the author, October 15, 2004.

47. Brand (pseud.), interview by the author, October 9, 2004.

48. Alfdis (pseud.), telephone interview by the author, April 27, 2006.

49. Soren (pseud.), telephone interview by the author, February 15, 2006.

50. Jeffrey Kaplan, "The Reconstruction of the Ásatrú and Odinist Traditions," in *Magical Religion and Modern Witchcraft*, ed. James R. Lewis (Albany: State University of New York Press, 1996), 193–236.

51. Alvis (pseud.), interview by the author, October 8, 2004.

52. Ibid.

53. Kathryn Joan Fox, "Real Punks and Pretenders: The Social Organization of a Counterculture," *Journal of Contemporary Ethnography* 16 (1987): 344–370; Lewis Yablonski, *The Hippie Trip* (New York: Pegasus, 1968).

54. Brand (pseud.), interview by the author, October 9, 2004.

55. Valda (pseud.), interview by the author, October 8, 2004.

56. Bromley, "Leaving the Fold"; Rodney Stark and Williams Sims Bainbridge, "Of Churches, Sects, and Cults: Preliminary Concepts for a Theory of Religious Movements," *Journal for the Scientific Study of Religion* 18, no. 2 (1979): 117–133.

57. Thomas Robbins, "'Quo Vadis' the Scientific Study of New Religious Movements?" *Journal for the Scientific Study of Religion* 39, no. 4 (2000): 515–523.

3. NEO-HEATHENS AND RECONSTRUCTIONISTS

1. Wade Clark Roof and William McKinney, *American Mainline Religion: Its Changing Shape and Future* (New Brunswick, NJ: Rutgers University Press, 1987).

2. Karl Seigfried with Josh Heath and Cat Heath, "Heathens in the Military: An Interview with Josh and Cat Heath, Part One," available at http://www.norsemyth.org/2013/01/Heathens-in-military-interview-with.html, accessed January 24, 2013.

3. Ibid.

4. Ibid.

5. Bil Linzie, "The State of Heathenry," *Odroerir* 1 (2011): 8.

6. Heath, "Heathens in the Military."

7. Available at http://theasatrucommunity.wordpress.com/the-asatru-communitys-code-of-conduct/, accessed January 29, 2013.

8. See Reza Szilardi, "Ancient Gods—New Ages: Lessons from Hungarian Paganism," *Pomegranate: The International Journal of Pagan Studies* 11, no. 1 (2009): 44–57; Mariya Lesiv, "Glory to Dazhoh (Sungod) or to All Native Gods? Monotheism and Polytheism in Contemporary Ukrainian Paganism," *Pomegranate: The International Journal of Pagan Studies* 11, no. 2 (2009): 197–222; Kaarina Aitamurto, "Russian Paganism and the Issue of Nationalism: A Case Study of the Circle of Pagan Tradition," *Pomegranate: The International Journal of Pagan Studies* 8, no. 2 (2006): 184–210; and Marlene Laruelle, "Alternative Identity, Alternative Religion? Neo-paganism and the Aryan Myth in Contemporary Russia," *Nations and Nationalism* 14, no. 2 (2008): 283–301.

9. Szilardi, "Ancient Gods."

10. Josh Rood, "Reconstructionism 101" a podcast of *Ravencast: An Ásatrú Podcast,* Episode 47, August 12, 2010. Available at http://www.podcasts.com/ravencast_-_the_asatru_podcast/episode/episode_47_-_reconstructionism_101, accessed January 5, 2015.

11. Erik (pseud.), Facebook exchange with the author, November 2013.

12. Anders Andren, Kristina Jennbert, and Catharina Raudvere, eds., *Old Norse Religion in Long-Term Perspectives: Origins, Changes, and Interactions* (Lund, Sweden: Nordic Academic Press, 2006), 13.

13. Neil Price, "Between Sorcerers and Priests: The Social Construction of Viking-Age Scandinavian 'Religion'" (HESP Symposium, IRMACS Centre, February 15, 2013).

14. Ibid.

15. Josh Rood, "Reconstructionism," *Odroerir* 1 (2011): 12.

16. Seigfried with Josh Heath and Cat Heath, "Heathens in the Military."

17. Rood, "Reconstructionism 101."

18. Available at http://www.asatru.us/junction/thread.php?threadid=942, accessed December 14, 2012.

19. Peter Berger, *The Sacred Canopy: Elements of a Sociological Theory of Religion* (Garden City, NY: Doubleday, 1967), 6.

20. Rood, "Reconstructionism," 12.

21. Berger, *The Sacred Canopy*, 22.

22. Theo Sundermeier, The Individual and Community in African Traditional Religions (Hamburg: Lit, 1998)

23. Ibid., 235.

24. Jan Assman, *The Price of Monotheism* (Stanford, CA: Stanford University Press, 2009), 3–4.

25. Ibid.

26. Bil Linzie, "Reconstructionism's Role in Modern Heathenry," July 13, 2007. Available at http://www.angelfire.com/nm/seidhman/reconstruction-c.pdf, accessed January 5, 2015.

27. H. R. Ellis Davidson, *The Road to Hel: A Study of the Conception of the Dead in Old Norse Literature* (New York: Greenwood Press, 1968), 121.

28. Folke Ström, *Níd, Ergi and Old Norse Attitudes,* The Dorothea Coke Memorial Lecture in Northern Studies Delivered at University College (London: The Viking Society for Northern Research, 1974).

29. Günther Lüschen and Gregory P. Stone, eds. and trans., *Herman Schmalenbach on Society and Experience* (Chicago: University of Chicago Press, 1977).

30. Kevin Hetherington, *Expressions of Identity: Space, Performance, Politics* (Sage Publications, 1998), 99.

31. Egil Asprem, "Heathens Up North: Politics, Polemics, and Contemporary Norse Paganism in Norway," *Pomegranate: The International Journal of Pagan Studies* 10, no. 1 (2008): 41–69.

32. C. Wright Mills, The Sociological Imagination (New York, NY: University of Oxford Press, 1959).

33. Joe Feagin, *The White Racial Frame: Centuries of Racial Framing and Counter-framing* (New York: Routledge, 2009).

34. Michael Strmiska, "Putting the Blood Back into *Blót*: The Revival of Animal Sacrifice in Modern Nordic Paganism," *Pomegranate: The International Journal of Pagan Studies* 9, no. 2 (2007): 154–189.

35. Arlie Stephens, "Similarities Between Heathenry and Wicca," n.d., 2, available at http://www.heathengods.com/library/wicca_comparison/differences_by_stephens.pdf, accessed February 2, 2013.

36. Josh Heath, "Two Yule Rituals: One Heathen's Experience in the Northeast US," *Odroerir* 2 (2012): 104.

37. Edred Thorsson, *Northern Magic, Rune Mysteries, and Shamanism* (St. Paul, MN: Llewellyn Publications, 1998).

38. Thomas A. DuBois, *Nordic Religions in the Viking Age* (Philadelphia: University of Pennsylvania Press, 1999).

39. Sunna (pseud.), Facebook exchange with author, April 2, 2014.

40. Mark Anderson, "Beer and Brewing Culture through the Eyes of a New England Heathen," *Odroerir* 2 (2012): 112.

41. Linzie, "State of Heathenry," 10.

42. Ibid., 7.

43. Commentary by "Odin's Son," available at http://www.norsemyth.org/2013/01/Heathens-in-military-interview-with.html, accessed January 25, 2013.

44. Kathryn Joan Fox, "Real Punks and Pretenders: The Social Organization of a Counterculture," *Journal of Contemporary Ethnography* 16, no. 3 (1987): 334–370.

45. Devo, "Kemeticism is Like a Fandom," *The Twisted Rope*, available at http://thetwistedrope.wordpress.com/2013/01/14/kemeticism-is-like-a-fandom/, accessed January 5, 2015.

46. David Thorne, "Celtic Reconstructionist Paganism," available at http://www.inkspotsandcoffee.com/writer/non-fiction/celtic-reconstructionist-paganism/, accessed January 25, 2013.

47. Andren, Jennbert, and Raudvere, *Old Norse Religion in Long-Term Perspectives*, 13.

48. Steven Abell, "Ritual and Reconstruction," available at http://www.patheos.com/Resources/Additional-Resources/Ritual-and-Reconstruction-Steven-Abell-12-01-2011, accessed January 13, 2013.

49. Cat Heath, "Heathens in the Military."

50. Leon Van Gulik, "On the Pagan Parallax: A Sociocultural Exploration of the Tension between Eclecticism and Traditionalism as Observed among Dutch Wiccans," *Pomegranate: The International Journal of Pagan Studies* 12, no. 1 (2010): 49–70.

51. Tess Dawson (*Wyrd*wulf), available at http://underthewaningmoon.tumblr.com/post/39358895432/reconstruction-revivalism-and-polytheism-often, accessed January 30, 2013.

52. Lynne Hume, "Creating Sacred Space: Outer Expressions of Inner Worlds in Modern Wicca," *Journal of Contemporary Religion* 13, no. 2 (1998): 314.

53. An instance of a bridal blessing can be found in Þrymskviða (The lay of Thrym) in the *Poetic Edda*. See Carolyn Larrington, *The Poetic Edda* (Oxford University Press, 2009).

54. Scott Mohnkern, "The Hammer Rite," *The Modern Heathen*, April 16, 2009, accessed January 15, 2013.

55. Wednesbury Theod, "Sacred Space in the Lore and Modern Paganism," available at http://www.englatheod.org/sacredspace.htm, accessed January 23, 2013.

56. Bil Linzie, "Germanic Spirituality," 2003, available at http://heathengods.com /library/bil_linzie/germanic_spirituality.pdf.

57. Leif (pseud.), telephone interview by the author, April 18, 2006.

58. Devyne Gilette and Lewis Stead. "The Pentagram and the Hammer" (Paper presented at the workshop "Wicca and Modern Heathenism" at the 1994 FreeSpirit festival), http://www.webcom.com/~lstead/wicatru.html, accessed October 15, 2002.

59. Erik (pseud.), Facebook exchange with the author, November 2013.

60. Odinic Rite, "The Nine Charges" The Odinic Rite: Odinism For The Modern World, (May 25, 2009) available at http://www.odinic-rite.org/main/the-nine-noble -virtues-and-charges-of-the-odinic-rite/, accessed January 5, 2015.

61. Seigfried with Josh Heath and Cat Heath, "Heathens in the Military."

62. Brand, interview by the author, 2003.

63. Karl Seigfried, "Sorry, Loki Fans . . . ," *Norse Mythology* Facebook page, January 2013, available at https://www.facebook.com/photo.php?fbid=604461666250172, accessed March 2013.

64. Lokavinr, "On Loki: In Response to Anon," 2012, available at http://lokavinr .tumblr.com/post/23370478446/on-loki-in-response-to-anon, accessed October 15, 2013.

65. Macho Nacho (Original Poster) in *Ásatrú & Heathenry* (Facebook group) January 2, 2013 at https://www.facebook.com/groups/heathenry/permalink/10151393036067612/, accessed January 5, 2013. The group has since been made private.

66. Elizabeth, "A Month for Loki: Day Twenty-Two," *Twilight and Fire: Mysticism, Devotion and Explorations of The Heart*, July 22, 2012, available at http://twilightandfire .wordpress.com/2012/07/22/a-month-for-loki-day-twenty-two/, accessed February 25, 2013.

67. David (pseud.), *Ásatrú & Heathenry* (Facebook group) accessed January 3, 2015 (group now private).

68. Erik, username "Exile_x2," "Patron God(s) and Fulltrui," *Runatyr Kindred Forum,* available at http://runatyrkindred.com/forum/index.php?topic=128.0, accessed February 22, 2013, an exchange among the members of Runatyr.

69. David (pseud.), Ásatrú & Heathenry (Facebook group).

70. Hyrokkin, "Loki," public Yahoo! group *Ásatrú Heathen,* available at http://groups .yahoo.com/group/Asatru/message/1454, accessed February 22, 2013.

71. Josh Rood, *Ásatrú & Heathenry* (Facebook group), January 2, 2013.

72. Elizabeth, "Month for Loki."

73. Raven, "A Formal Introduction," *Hail Loki!: An Account of a Worshipper of Loki and Other Gods,* available at https://hailloki.wordpress.com/about/, accessed January 5, 2015.

4. CYBER *HOFS* AND ARMCHAIR VIKINGS

1. See Christopher Helland, "Religion Online / Online Religion and Virtual Communitas," in *Religion on the Internet: Research Prospects and Promises,* ed. Jeffrey K. Hadden and Douglas E. Cowan, Religion and Social Order 8 (London: JAI Press/Elsevier Science, 2000), 205–224.

2. Heidi Campbell, "Internet and Religion," in *The Handbook of Internet Studies,* ed. Mia Consalvo and Charles Ess (Malden, MA: Wiley-Blackwell, 2011), 236.

3. Lorne Dawson and Jenna Hennebry, "New Religions and the Internet: Recruiting in a New Public Space," *Journal of Contemporary Religion* 14, no. 1 (1999): 20.

4. Campbell, "Internet and Religion," 241.

5. Lorne Dawson, Douglas Cowan, eds., *Religion Online: Finding Faith on The Internet,* (New York: Routledge, 2004), 206.

6. Brenda E. Brasher, *Give Me That Online Religion* (San Francisco: Jossey-Bass, 2001).

7. Knut Lundby, "Patterns of Belonging in Online/Offline Interfaces of Religion," *Information, Communication and Society* 14, no. 8 (2011): 1223.

8. Lundby, "Patterns of Belonging," 1223.

9. Douglas E. Cowan, *Cyberhenge: Modern Pagans on the Internet* (New York: Routledge, 2005), xi.

10. Lundby, "Patterns of Belonging," 1221; Lori Kendall, "Community and the Internet," in *Handbook of Internet Studies,* ed. Consalvo and Ess, 309–325.

11. Denise M. Carter, "Living in a Virtual Community: Making Friends Online," *Journal of Urban Technology* 11, no. 3 (2004): 109–125.

12. Ibid., 109.

13. Barry Wellman et al., "Computer Networks as Social Networks: Collaborative Work, Telework, and Virtual Community," *Annual Review of Sociology* 22 (1996): 213–238.

14. Helen A. Berger, "Contemporary Paganism: Fifteen Years Later," *Alternative Spirituality and Religion Review* 3, no. 1 (2012): 3–16.

15. Some of the many heathen organizations that have risen and fallen are the Ásatrú Free Assembly (1974–1986), Witan Theod (1976–1983), and Angelseaxisce Ealdriht (1996–2004). Many groups experienced schisms, forming splinter groups that themselves later collapsed.

16. The Ásatrú Folk Assembly and The Troth are two of the most influential Heathen organizations with active Facebook pages. The Ásatrú Alliance hosts a purely informational page without a discussion board. Since the Ásatrú Alliance is relatively small, members form individual, private group pages dedicated to their local areas. The Ásatrú Alliance does not play as pivotal a role in ongoing greater community dialogue as do the AFA and The Troth, and although a couple of Heathens have mentioned to me that the AA is "getting better," most of my informants seem to maintain an impression of the AA as an incubator for founder Valguard Murray's especially troublesome racial ideologies.

17. In July 2013 military Heathens won the right to mark their graves with a Thor's hammer. Gina Harkins, "VA Approves Thor's Hammers for Gravestones," *The Marine Times Battle Rattle,* July 23, 2013. Available at http://blogs.militarytimes.com/battle-rattle/2013 /07/23/va-approves-thors-hammer-for-gravestones/, accessed August 28, 2013.

18. Kell (pseud.), telephone interview by the author, March 27, 2005.

19. Dual-trad or dual-tradition practitioners are those who practice two religious traditions simultaneously, most commonly Wicca in combination with some other Paganism. To some who stereotype Wicca as liberal, effeminate "hippie stuff," the conflict with Heathenry is irreconcilable.

20. Stephen McNallen, "Ásatrú Folk Assembly," Facebook status update, January 13, 2013.

21. "The Midwest Tribes," available at http://www.heathengods.com/midwest/index.htm, accessed on January 6, 2015.

22. Cowan, *Cyberhenge*, 262.

23. John P. Hewitt, *Dilemmas of the American Self* (Philadelphia: Temple University Press, 1989), 135.

24. Kell (pseud.), telephone interview by the author, March 27, 2005.

25. Anja (pseud.), "America Online" instant message conversation with the author, June 4, 2004.

26. Ivor (pseud.), telephone interview by the author, December 30, 2004.

27. Mattias Gardell, *Gods of the Blood: The Pagan Revival and White Separatism* (Durham, NC: Duke University Press, 2003).

28. Rod Landreth, "Toward Stronger Healthier Heathen Clergy Resulting in Better Heathenry," available at http://scrwtape.blogspot.com/2013/06/towards-stronger-healthier -heathen.html, posted June 3, 2013, accessed May 8, 2014.

29. Eskel (pseud.), interview by the author, October 15, 2004.

30. Midwest Tribes, "Midwest Tribes—The Midwest Thing," available at http://www.heathengods.com/midwest/, accessed January 6, 2015.

31. Stephen McNallen, *Ásatrú Folk Assembly* Facebook page, available at https://www.facebook.com/Asatru.Folk.Assembly, accessed January 6, 2015.

32. Mark Stinson, during a speech at Lightning Across The Plains, 2012.

33. Hewitt, *Dilemmas of The American Self*, 110.

34. Ibid., 112.

35. Ernst Troelsch, *The Social Teachings of the Christian Churches* (Macmillan, 1931), 744.

36. Leslie Irvine, *Codependent Forevermore: The Invention of Self in a Twelve-Step Group* (Chicago: University of Chicago Press, 1999), 70.

37. Valda (pseud.), interview by the author, October 4, 2004.

38. Signy (pseud.), telephone interview by the author, April 23, 2006.

39. Hewitt, *Dilemmas of the American Self.*

40. Wellman et al., "Computer Networks as Social Networks."

41. Douglass Cowan, "Online U-Topia: Cyberspace and the Mythology of Placelessness," *Journal for the Scientific Study of Religion* 44, no. 3 (2005): 257–263.

42. In 2013–2014 the Facebook group "Do You Even Heathen, Bro?" provided a haven for Heathens entertained by flaming other Heathens. Although the group had only a little over 100 members, it was open to the public and received recognition (through outrage) by cross-posting in other groups. Its main targets were Heathens who positioned themselves as leaders, experts, or academics. The ongoing bullying was frequently misogynistic and racist and often involved screen shots of a person's Facebook activity or a mock-up of a photographic meme, used to discredit, emasculate, and embarrass the target.

43. Eskel (pseud.), interview by the author, October 15, 2004.

44. Jim (pseud.), conversation with the author, June 2007.

45. Dawson and Hennebry, "New Religions and the Internet," 20.

46. George Cheney et al., eds., *Organizational Communication in an Age of Globalization: Issues, Reflections, Practices* (Prospect Heights, IL: Waveland Press, 2004), 369.

47. Wellman et al., "Computer Networks as Social Networks," 221.

48. Einar (pseud.), telephone interview by the author, October 28, 2004.

49. Wellman et al., "Computer Networks as Social Networks," 222.

50. Einar (pseud.), telephone interview by the author, October 28, 2004.

51. Jill J. McMillan and Michael J. Hyde, "Technological Innovation and Change: A Case Study in the Formation of Organizational Conscience," *Quarterly Journal of Speech* 86, no. 1 (2000): 19–47.

52. Stephen McNallen (posted January 13, 2013, on the *Ásatrú Folk Assembly* Facebook page, shortly after the events of Sandy Hook), available at https://www.facebook.com /Asatru.Folk.Assembly/, accessed January 6, 2015.

53. Comments in response to McNallen's post on Gun Control, on the *Ásatrú Folk Assembly* Facebook page, January 13, 2013.

54. Penny Edgell, "A Cultural Sociology of Religion: New Directions," *Annual Review of Sociology* 38 (2012): 250.

55. Mark Stinson, *Temple of Our Heathen Gods*, Facebook page, January 12, 2013, available at https://www.facebook.com/heathengods/posts/10151413933292792, accessed January 13, 2013.

56. Ivor (pseud.), telephone interview by the author, December 30, 2004.

57. Patrick J. Williams and Heith Copes, "'How Edge Are You?': Constructing Authentic Identities and Subcultural Boundaries in a Straightedge Internet Forum," *Symbolic Interaction* 28, no. 1 (2005): 67–89.

58. Eric L Lesser, Michael A Fontaine, Jason A Slusher. *Knowledge and Communities* (Boston: Butterworth-Heinemann, 2000), 184.

59. Eskel (pseud.), interview by the author, October 15, 2004.

60. Einar (pseud.), interview by the author, October 28, 2004.

61. Brandon (pseud.), Facebook conversation with the author, June, 2014.

5. VALKYRIES AND FRITHWEAVERS

1. Hallgerd (pseud.), interview by the author, March 9, 2003.

2. Evelyn Nakano Glenn, "The Social Construction and Institutionalization of Gender and Race: An Integrative Framework," in *Revisioning Gender,* ed. Myra Marx Ferree, Judith Lorber, and Beth B. Hess (Thousand Oaks, CA: Sage, 1999), 14.

3. See Kimberly M. Aronson and Ester Schaler Buchholz, "The Post-feminist Era: Still Striving for Equality in Relationships," *American Journal of Family Therapy* 29 (2001): 109–124.

4. Orit Avishai, "Women of God," *Contexts* 9, no. 4 (2010): 46–51.

5. Helen Berger, "Contemporary Paganism: Fifteen Years Later," *Alternative Spirituality and Religion Review* 3, no. 1 (2012): 5.

6. Ibid.

7. Sally K. Gallagher and Christian Smith, "Symbolic Traditionalism and Pragmatic Egalitarianism: Contemporary Evangelicals, Families, and Gender," *Gender and Society* 13, no. 2 (1999): 211–233.

8. Debra Renee Kaufman, "Patriarchal Women: A Case Study in Newly Orthodox Jewish Women," *Symbolic Interaction* 12, no. 2 (1989): 299–314.

9. Lynn Davidman, *Tradition in a Rootless World: Women Turn to Orthodox Judaism* (Berkeley: University of California Press, 1991).

10. Kaufman, "Patriarchal Women," 310.

11. Ibid.

12. Heathenblogr, "The Standing of Heathen Women," *The Heathen Kinship,* 2010, available at http://www.goheathen.org/wordpress/?p=18, accessed January 10, 2011.

13. Soren (pseud.), telephone interview by the author, February 15, 2004.

14. Eskel (pseud.), interview by the author, October 15, 2004.

15. Brand (pseud.), interview by the author, October 9, 2004.

16. Ivor (pseud.), telephone interview by the author, December 30, 2004.

17. The Standing Stone Society "Understanding Ásatrú," available at http://sites .google.com/site/thestandingstonesociety/home/encyclopedia/asatru/understanding -asatru, accessed February 10, 2012.

18. Vana (pseud.), telephone interview by the author, April 20, 2006.

19. Dave, "Women in Heathenry," *The Urban Ásatrúar,* available at http:// gallowsburden.wordpress.com/2011/05/16/women-in-heathenry/, accessed February 15, 2012.

20. Susan Starr Sered, "Food and Holiness: Cooking as a Sacred Act among Middle-Eastern Jewish Women," *Anthropological Quarterly* 61, no. 3 (1988): 129–139.

21. Judith Halberstam, *Female Masculinity* (Durham, NC: Duke University Press, 1998).

22. Preben Meulengracht Sørensen, *The Unmanly Man: Concepts of Sexual Defamation in Early Northern Society,* trans. Joan Turville-Petre (Odense: Odense University Press, 1983), 17.

23. Grethe Jacobsen, "Sexual Irregularities in Medieval Scandinavia," in *Sexual Practices and the Medieval Church,* ed. Vern L. Bullough and James Brundage (Buffalo: Prometheus Books, 1982), 72–85.

24. Robyn Wiegman, "Unmaking: Men and Masculinity in Feminist Studies," in *Masculinity Studies and Feminist Theory: New Directions,* ed. Judith Kegan Gardiner (New York: Columbia University Press, 2002), 51.

25. Carol Clover, "Regardless of Sex: Men, Women, and Power in Early Northern Europe," *Speculum* 68, no. 2 (1993): 363–397.

26. Gayle Rubin, "The Traffic in Women (Notes on the 'Political Economy' of Sex)," in *The Second Wave: A Reader in Feminist Theory,* ed. Linda Nicholson (New York: Routledge, 1997), 27–62.

27. Clover, "Regardless of Sex."

28. Carrie Praechter, "Masculine Femininities / Feminine Masculinities: Power, Identities, and Gender," *Gender and Education* 18, no. 3 (2006): 253–263.

29. Susan Starr Sered, *Priestess, Mother, Sacred Sister: Religions Dominated by Women* (New York: Oxford University Press, 1996), 4.

30. Sulda (pseud.), telephone interview by the author, July 27, 2006.

31. Lauraine Leblanc, *Pretty in Punk: Girls' Resistance in a Boys' Subculture* (New Brunswick, NJ: Rutgers University Press, 1999).

32. Alvis (pseud.), interview by the author, October 8, 2004.

33. Joan Wallace Scott, "Deconstructing Equality-versus-Difference," *Feminist Studies* 14 (1988): 43.

34. Michael A. Messner, *Politics of Masculinities: Men in Movements* (Walnut Creek, CA: AltaMira Press, 2000), 16.

35. Michael Schwalbe, *Unlocking the Iron Cage: The Men's Movement, Gender Politics, and American Culture* (Oxford: Oxford University Press, 1996), 64.

36. Ibid., 66.

37. Stephen McNallen, "Ásatrú Folk Assembly," Facebook status update, July 31, 2012.

38. Ibid., January 14, 2013.

39. Tony Evans, "Spiritual Purity," in *Seven Promises of a Promise Keeper* (Colorado Springs, CO: Focus on the Family, 1994), 73.

40. *Ásatrú Folk Assembly* Facebook page comments in reply to Stephen McNallen's January 14, 2013, status update regarding gun control.

41. Unni (pseud.), telephone interview, April 9, 2006.

42. Alfdis (pseud.), telephone interview by the author, April 27, 2006.

43. Eskel (pseud.), personal interview by the author, October 15, 2004.

44. Brand (pseud.), personal interview by the author, October 9, 2004.

45. Praechter, "Masculine Femininities," 256.

46. Ibid., 257.

47. Mo. B. Dick, interview by Judith Halberstam, Del LaGrace Volcano, in Judith Halberstam, Del LaGrace Volcano, *The Drag King Book*, (London: The Serpent's Tail, 1998) 259.

48. Inga (pseud.), telephone interview by the author, April 9, 2006.

49. Both Wiccans and Heathens apply the "fluffy bunny" sanction to those Pagans seen as inauthentic. Among Wiccans, the term is often applied to newcomers seen as know-it-alls (see Isaac Bonewits, "Making Fauna Pagans," 2005, available at http://www .neopagan.net/Making-Fauna-Pagans.html, accessed January 8, 2015) or to those whose beliefs or behaviors render their faith "an object of entertainment, trivialized, rendered superficial, fetishized, sentimentalized, and devalued through commodification of tools and practices of spiritual meaning and worth." Angela Coco and Ian Woodward, "Discourses of Authenticity within a Pagan Community: The Emergence of the 'Fluffy Bunny' Sanction," *Journal of Contemporary Ethnography* 36, no. 5 (2007): 480.

50. Thrain (pseud.), telephone interview by the author, April 25, 2006.

51. Cena Bussey, "Lessons for Heathen Women: Part 1," *Wane Wyrds,* available at http://wanewyrds.blogspot.com/2011/10/lessons-for-heathen-women-part-1.html, accessed February 2012.

52. Lynda C. Welch, *Goddess of the North* (York Beach, ME: Weiser Books, 2001), 187.

53. Inga (pseud.), telephone interview by the author, April 9, 2006.

54. Aud (pseud.), telephone interview by the author, July 28, 2006.

55. Leszek Gardela, "'Warrior-Women' in Viking Age Scandinavia? A Preliminary Archaeological Study," *Analecta Archaeologica Ressoviensia* 8 (2013): 273–340.

56. Keneva Kunz, trans. "Eirik the Red's Saga," in *The Sagas of Icelanders*, ed. Ornolfur Thorsson (New York: Penguin Books, 1997), 653–677.

57. Sulda (pseud.), telephone interview by the author, July 27, 2006.

58. Mark Puryear, *The Nature of Asatru: An Overview of the Ideals and Philosophy of the Indigenous Religion of Northern Europe* (New York: iUniverse, Inc., 2006).

59. Puryear, *Nature of Asatru*, 2.

60. Ibid., 8.

61. Jacobsen, "Sexual Irregularities in Medieval Scandinavia," 72.

62. Thomas Mann, Norman Ornstein, *It's Even Worse Than It Looks : How The American Constitutional System Collided With The New Politics of Extremism* (New York: Basic Books, 2012), 179.

63. Juleigh Howard-Hobson, "The Feminine in the Post-modern Age: How Feminism Negates Folkways," *Journal of Contemporary Heathen Thought* 1 (2010): 93, 96.

64. Arlea Æðelwyrd Hunt-Anschütz, "Oðin: Misogynist or Bastard," *Cup of Wonder,* 2000, available at http://www.wyrdwords.vispa.com/heathenry/mysoginist.html, accessed April 15, 2007.

65. Ibid.

66. Tacitus, *The Agricola and The Germania,* trans. Cornelius Tacitus, Harold Mattingly, S. A. Handford (London: Penguin Books, 1970), 118.

67. *Saxo Grammaticus: The History of the Danes, Books I–IX,* vol. 1, *Text,* trans. Peter Fisher, ed. Hilda Ellis Davidson (Cambridge: D. S. Brewer, 1979).

68. Praechter, "Masculine Femininities," 256.

69. Ibid.

70. Swain Wodening, "Women in Ásatrú and Germanic Heathenry," *Swain Wodening's Blog,* 2008, available at http://swainblog.englatheod.org/?p=22, accessed February 2012.

71. Valda (pseud.), interview by the author, October 8, 2004.

72. Brand (pseud.), interview by the author, October 9, 2004.

73. Egil (pseud.), telephone interview by the author, April 13, 2006.

74. Jenny Jochens, *Women in Old Norse Society* (Ithaca, NY: Cornell University Press, 1995).

75. Sered, *Priestess, Mother, Sacred Sister,* 6.

76. In response to the author's query on *Ásatrú Women* Facebook Group, February 4, 2012.

77. Herdis (pseud.), Facebook conversation with the author, February 5, 2012.

78. Jean Baker Miller, *Toward a New Psychology of Women* (Boston: Beacon Press, 1976), 76.

79. Mani (pseud.), personal communication to the author, February 23, 2012.

80. Miller, *Toward a New Psychology of Women,* 76.

81. Inga (pseud.), telephone interview by the author, April 9, 2006.

82. Unni (pseud.), telephone interview by the author, April 9, 2006.

83. Sered, "Food and Holiness."

84. Scott, "Deconstructing Equality-versus-Difference," 43.

85. Ibid.

86. Sulda (pseud.), telephone interview by the author, July 27, 2006.

87. Hilda (pseud.), telephone interview by the author, March 30, 2006.

88. Hallgerd (pseud.), interview by the author, November 9, 2003.

89. Brand (pseud.), interview by the author, October 9, 2004.

90. Scott, "Deconstructing Equality-versus-Difference," 45.

91. Ibid.

92. Carol Philpot et al., *Bridging Separate Gender Worlds: Why Men and Women Clash and How Therapists Can Bring Them Together* (Washington, DC: American Psychological Association, 1997), 24.

93. Cat Heath, "Ásatrú Women," Facebook conversation, January 23, 2012. Reproduced with permission.

94. Christie Ward, "Alcoholic Beverages and Drinking Customs of the Viking Age," *The Viking Answer Lady,* available at http://www.vikinganswerlady.com/drink.shtml, accessed October 31, 2012.

95. Christie Ward, "Women and Magic in the Sagas: Seiðr and Spá," *The Viking Answer Lady,* available at http://www.vikinganswerlady.com/seidhr.html, accessed January 30, 2012.

96. Jenny Blain, *Nine Worlds of Seid-Magic: Ecstasy and Neo-Shamanism in North European Paganism* (Routledge, 2001), 122.

97. The word *Völva* is a derivative of *magical staff,* and is also sometimes called a *spá-kona.*

98. Ward, "Women and Magic in the Sagas."

99. Tacitus, *The Agricola and The Germania,* 108.

100. Cena Bussey, "Lessons For Heathen Women: Part 1," Wane Wyrds, October 7, 2011, available at http://wanewyrds.blogspot.com/2011/10/lessons-for-heathen-women-part-1.html#.VK7lycbUNHs, accessed January 8, 2015.

101. Anthropologist Jenny Blain documents the practice of this magical form among Heathens throughout Europe and the United States, discussing how it has been gendered in a sociohistorical context in the eleventh to the fourteenth century and now. See Blain, *Nine Worlds of Seid-Magic.*

102. Kari Tauring, "Völva Stav," *Kari Tauring, Deep Nordic Roots,* 1999, available at http://karitauring.com/teach-volvastav.html, accessed January 30, 2012.

103. Amy C. Wilkins, *Wannabes, Goths, and Christians: The Boundaries of Sex, Style, and Status* (Chicago: University of Chicago Press, 2008).

104. Mimi Schippers, *Rockin' Out of the Box: Gender Maneuvering in Alternative Hard Rock* (New Brunswick, NJ: Rutgers University Press, 2002), Preface.

105. Leblanc, *Pretty in Punk,* 19.

106. Ross Haenfler, *Straight Edge: Clean-Living Youth, Hardcore Punk, and Social Change* (New Brunswick, NJ: Rutgers University Press, 2006); Wilkins, *Wannabes.*

107. Halberstam, *Female Masculinity,* 347.

6. HONORING THE ANCESTORS

1. Herbert J. Gans, 1979. "Symbolic Ethnicity: The Future of Ethnic Groups and Cultures in America," *Ethnicity & Racial Studies* 2 (1979): 1–20; Mary C. Waters, *Ethnic Options: Choosing Identities in America* (Berkeley: University of California Press, 1990).

2. Gans, "Symbolic Ethnicity"; Hout M. Goldstein, "How 4.5 Million Irish Immigrants Became 40 Million Irish Americans: Demographic and Subjective Aspects of The Ethnic Composition of White Americans," *American Sociological Review* 59, no. 1 (1994): 64–82.

3. Jolanta A. Drzewiecka and Kathleen Wong (Lau), "The Dynamic Construction of White Ethnicity in the Context of Transnational Cultural Formations," in *Whiteness: The Communication of Social Identity,* ed. Thomas K. Nakayama and Judith N. Martin (Thousand Oaks, CA: Sage Publications, 1999), 198–216.

4. White racial identity development models are debated in Wayne Rowe and Donald R. Atkinson, "Misrepresentation and Interpretation: Critical Evaluation of White Racial Identity Development Models," *Counseling Psychologist* 23, no. 2 (1995): 364–367.

5. Janet Helms, "A Model of White Racial Identity Development," in *Black and White Racial Identity: Theory, Research, and Practice,* ed. J. Helms (Westport, CT: Greenwood Press, 1990), 49–66.

6. Monica McDermott and Frank L. Samson, "White Racial and Ethnic Identity in the United States," *Annual Review of Sociology* 31 (2005): 245–261.

7. Margaret Anderson, "Whitewashing Race: A Critical Perspective on Whiteness," in *White Out: The Continuing Significance of Racism,* ed. Ashley W. Doane and Eduardo Bonilla-Silva (London: Routledge, 2003), 20–34.

8. Michael Strmiska and Baldur A. Sigurvinsson, "Ásatrú in Iceland: The Rebirth of Nordic Paganism?" *Nova Religio: The Journal of Alternative and Emergent Religious Movements* (2000): 133.

9. Jeffrey Kaplan, "The Reconstruction of the Ásatrú and Odinist Traditions," in *Magical Religion and Modern Witchcraft,* ed. James R. Lewis (Albany: State University of New York Press, 1996), 193–236. The tumults in the early years of Heathenry as outlined

by Kaplan, with all their organizational drama, have been softened by the increase of women and families in what was a primarily male-dominated and hypermasculine community. Its focus on race has likewise softened as Ásatrú and other Heathen groups quite vocally distance themselves from behaviors or associations that could be perceived as racist or discriminatory. Yet the discussion continues as issues of race follow the greater American trend of color-blind racial politics, complicating members' racial discourse and efforts at boundary maintenance.

10. Jeffrey Kaplan, "The Context of American Millenarian Revolutionary Theology," *Terrorism and Political Violence* 5 (1993): 30–82. See also Kaplan, *Radical Religion in America: Millenarian Movements from the Far Right to the Children of Noah* (Syracuse, NY: Syracuse University Press, 1997).

11. Personal communication from Michael Strmiska, September 2014.

12. Mattias Gardell, *Gods of the Blood: The Pagan Revival and White Separatism* (Durham, NC: Duke University Press, 2003), 165–323.

13. The Southern Poverty Law Center, in particular, has published a few such stories over the years. Ásatrú is mentioned in its articles "New Brand of Racist Odinist Religion on the March," *Intelligence Report* 89 (1998); Heidi Beirich, "Volksfront: The Leadership," *Intelligence Report* 152 (2013); Bill Morlin, "Veteran Skinhead Forms New Racist Club, Peddles T-shirts on Internet" on *Hatewatch,* May 27, 2013 at http://www.splcenter.org/blog /2013/05/17/veteran-skinhead-forms-new-racist-club-peddles-t-shirts-on-internet/, accessed January 9, 2015; and other articles, primarily interested in Ásatrú as a platform for racist extremists. In regard to outlawry, one example is the shunning of Eric James Dokken, an inmate convicted of child molestation. His outlawry was affirmed by sixty-one worldwide Ásatrú kindreds. See: Skip Zumberge, "Announcement of Outlawry," *Ásatrú Heathen* Yahoo! Group, available at https://groups.yahoo.com/neo/groups/Asatru/conversations /topics/5658, accessed January 9, 2015. Additionally, white supremacist David Lane, who died in prison while serving a 190-year sentence for a variety of crimes, invited the media spotlight into the Heathen community because of his affiliation with Wotanism, a case explored in detail in Gardell, *Gods of the Blood*, 191–224.

14. Betty A. Dobratz, "The Role of Religion in the Collective Identity of the White Racialist Movement," *Journal for the Scientific Study of Religion* 40, no. 2 (2001): 287–302.

15. The term and classification *indigenous* in relation to Paganisms came under a spotlight at the Parliament of the World's Religions in Melbourne, Australia, in 2009. Heathens and other reconstructionist Pagans use the word *indigenous* to demarcate Paganisms "associated with a specific culture, ethnicity, and geographical region and which predate the arrival or development of a larger, more 'organized' religion" from other syncretistic Neopagan faith systems. In Heathenry's case the identification is with pre-Christian northern European peoples. See Jason Pitzl Waters, "After the Parliament: Who's Indigenous? Who's an NRM?" *The Wild Hunt*, available at http://www.patheos.com/blogs /wildhunt/2009/12/after-the-parliament-whos-indigenous-whos-a-nrm.html, accessed June 16, 2011.

16. Howard Winant, "Behind Blue Eyes: Whiteness and Contemporary U.S. Racial Politics," in *Off White*, ed. Michelle Fine et al. (New York: Routledge, 1997), 41.

17. Stephen Cornell and Douglas Hartman, *Ethnicity and Race: Making Identities in a Changing World* (Thousand Oaks, CA: Pine Forge Press, 1998), 57.

18. Matthew Frye Jacobson, *Roots Too: White Ethnic Revival in Post–Civil Rights America* (Cambridge, MA: Harvard University Press, 2006).

19. Ibid., 21.

20. Ibid., 23.

21. Cornell and Hartman, *Ethnicity and Race,* 14.

22. Richard Alonzo Schermerhorn, *Comparative Ethnic Relations: A Framework for Theory and Research* (Chicago: University of Chicago Press, 1978), 55.

23. Max Weber, *Economy and Society,* ed. Guenther Roth and Claus Wittich, trans. Ephraim Fischof, (Berkeley: University of California Press, [1922] 1978), 389.

24. Schermerhorn, *Comparative Ethnic Relations,* 55.

25. Gardell, *Gods of the Blood;* Jeffrey Kaplan, "Reconstruction of the Ásatrú and Odinist Traditions"; and Strmiska and Sigurvinsson, "Ásatrú."

26. Drzewiecka and Wong, "Dynamic Construction of White Ethnicity," 206.

27. Timothy L. Smith, "Religion and Ethnicity in America," *American Historical Review* 83, no. 5 (1978): 1161.

28. Kveldulfr Gundarsson, "Race, Inheritance, and Asatru Today," *Mountain Thunder: The Independent Pagan Magazine* 5 (1992): 9.

29. Mark Puryear, *The Nature of Asatru: An Overview of the Ideals and Philosophy of the Indigenous Religion of Northern Europe* (New York: iUniverse, Inc., 2006), 4.

30. Peggy McIntosh, "White Privilege: Unpacking the Invisible Knapsack," in *Race, Class, and Gender in the United States,* 6th ed., ed. Paula S. Rothenberg, 181. Also see Eduardo Bonilla-Silva, *Racism without Racists: Color-Blind Racism and the Persistence of Racial Inequality in the United States* (Lanham, MD: Rowman and Littlefield, 2006).

31. Joe Feagin, *The White Racial Frame: Centuries of Racial Framing and Counter-framing* (New York: Routledge, 2009), ix.

32. Ibid.

33. Stephen McNallen, *Ásatrú Folk Assembly* Facebook page, February 4, 2013, available at https://www.facebook.com/Asatru.Folk.Assembly/posts/428276340581035, accessed January 9, 2015.

34. Stephen McNallen, "Ásatrú—Why We Need to Support Indigenous Peoples," *Ásatrú Update,* February 1, 2012, available at asatruupdate.blogspot.com, accessed February 3, 2012.

35. Thad Horrell, "Heathenry as a Postcolonial Movement," *Journal of Religion, Identity, and Politics,* 2011, available at http://ripjournal.org/2011/heathenry-as-postcolonial -movement/, accessed February 3, 2012.

36. Torsten (pseud.), telephone interview by the author, April 13, 2006.

37. Bonilla-Silva, *Racism without Racists,* 53–102.

38. Kristi Keck, "Students Attend School's First Integrated Prom," CNN.com, April 23, 2007, available at http://www.cnn.com/2007/US/04/23/ turner.prom/index.html, accessed April 24, 2007.

39. Bonilla-Silva, *Racism without Racists,* 53.

40. Ibid., 53–102.

41. Jacobson, *Roots Too,* 67.

42. Gunther (pseud.), interview by the author, March 16, 2006.

43. Goldstein, "How 4.5 Million Irish Immigrants Became 40 Million Irish Americans."

44. Gans, "Symbolic Ethnicity"; M. Waters, *Ethnic Options.*

45. See Joane Nagel, "Constructing Ethnicity: Creating and Recreating Ethnic Identity and Culture," *Social Problems* 41, no. 1 (1994): 152–176.

46. Puryear, *Nature of Asatru.*

47. Spazmonkey, "Essential Reading!!" an Amazon.com review, June 30, 2006, available at http://www.amazon.com/The-Nature-Asatru-Philosophy-Indigenous/product-reviews /0595389643?pageNumber=2, accessed January 9, 2015.

48. Stephen McNallen, "A Down and Dirty Look at the 'Browning of America,'" 2010, available at http://www.newsnet14.com/?p=40702, accessed January 6, 2013. This article is listed as "Not Just Another Immigration Piece" at Newsnet 14, a website devoted to "World News for Europeans World Wide," a white supremacist website that also hosts such titles as "Black Invention Myths" and links to shopping sites such as the white-pride clothing store Aryan Wear. Available at http://www.newsnet14.com.

49. Stephen McNallen, "Wotan vs. Tezcatlipoca: The Spiritual War for California and the Southwest," available at http://www.runestone.org/about-asatru/articles-a-essays/150-wotan-vs-tezcatlipoca-the-spiritual-war-for-california-and-the-southwest.html, accessed January 6, 2013.

50. Mitch Berbrier, "The Victim Ideology of White Supremacists and White Separatists in the United States," *Sociological Focus* 33, no. 2 (2000): 175–191.

51. McNallen, "Wotan vs. Tezcatlipoca."

52. According to Joe Feagin (personal communication), this pattern of reactionary racial politics has been a growing trend since the 1970s. Bonilla-Silva outlines the rhetoric of "color-blind" racist framing as a way of framing racist arguments and ideas without being labeled "racist." For example, Bonilla-Silva argues that "cultural racism" has replaced biological essentialist arguments for the "inadequacies" of nonwhite cultures, while the "naturalization frame" is used to justify existing racial segregation. For more, see Bonilla-Silva, *Racism without Racists*, 2, 28, 39.

53. According to the campaign's website, "The Un-Fair Campaign was developed to look at racism and to encourage a community dialogue about the causes and solutions." For more information and access to the campaign's PSA, see Un-Fair Campaign, available at http://unfaircampaign.org, accessed August 9, 2012.

54. Strmiska and Sigurvinsson, "Ásatrú," 137.

55. Gans, "Symbolic Ethnicity."

56. Richard D. Alba, *Ethnic Identity: The Transformation of White America* (New Haven, CT: Yale University Press, 1990).

57. Gans, "Symbolic Ethnicity," 9.

58. Alfdis (pseud.), telephone interview by the author, Colorado, April 27, 2006.

59. Sulda (pseud.), telephone interview by the author, July 27, 2006.

60. Unni (pseud.), telephone interview by the author, April 9, 2006.

61. Ibid.

62. Bryan Sykes, *The Seven Daughters of Eve: The Science That Reveals Our Genetic Ancestry* (New York: W. W. Norton, 2001); mentioned in Heathen author Diana Paxson's *Essential Asatru: Walking the Path of Norse Paganism* (New York: Citadel Press. 2007), 8.

63. Wayland Skallagrimsson, "Racism in Ásatrú," available at http://www.uppsalaonline.com/uppsala/racism.htm, accessed February 26, 2012.

64. Stephen McNallen, "Metagenetics," 1985, available at http://runestone.org/index.php?option=com_content&view=article&id=143:metagenetics&catid=82&Itemid=571, accessed January 9, 2015.

65. Wayland Skallagrimsson, "Racism in Ásatrú."

66. Ibid.

63. Gardell, *Gods of the Blood.*

68. Signy (pseud.), telephone interview by the author, April 23, 2006.

69. Valda (pseud.), telephone interview by the author, October 8, 2004.

70. Sunna (pseud.), interview by the author, Facebook chat, April 1, 2014.

71. Joe Biden, "Foot-In-Mouth Disease: A Dubious Compliment." *Time*, January 31, 2007. Available at http://content.time.com/time/specials/packages/article/0,28804,1895156 _1894977_1644536,00.html, accessed January 9, 2015.

72. Gunnthra (pseud.), interview by the author, Facebook chat, April 1, 2014.

73. McNallen, "Metagenetics."

74. Mark Stinson, "Heathen Gods," 2009, available at http://www.heathengods.com /learning/heathen_gods.pdf, accessed January 9, 2015.

75. Skallagrimsson, "Racism in Ásatrú."

76. Mani (pseud.), e-mail to the author, March 23, 2012.

77. *Ørlög* is "the root of being; it is the first layer of *Wyrd*" (fate, doom, fortune, destiny) and "shapes all that follows. To be 'without *Ørlög*' is not to exist in any meaningful way. . . . *Ørlög* is that which determines how all of life shall be shaped, from beginning to end: it is the that-which-is, the *wyrd* of the individual." Kveldulfr Gundarsson, *Our Troth: History and Lore* (North Charleston, NC: BookSurge, 2006), 506.

78. Mark Stinson, Facebook conversation with the author, March 20, 2012.

79. David Snow, "Collective Identity and Expressive Forms," in *International Encyclopedia of Social and Behavioral Sciences,* ed. Neil Smelser and Paul Baltes (Oxford, U.K.: Pergamon Press, 2001), 2212–2219; Joane Nagel, "American Indian Ethnic Renewal: Politics and the Resurgence of Identity," *American Sociological Review* 60, no. 6 (1995): 947–965.

80. Nagel, "Constructing Ethnicity."

81. Michael Strmiska and Baldur A. Sigurvinsson, *Modern Paganism in World Cultures: A Comparative Perspective* (Santa Barbara, CA: ABC-CLIO, 2005), 134–137.

82. Cornell and Hartman, *Ethnicity and Race,* 51.

83. Puryear, *Nature of Asatru,* xvii.

84. Chika Oduah, "Are Blacks Abandoning Christianity for African faiths?" *The Grio,* MSNBC, available at http://thegrio.com/2011/10/19/african-religions-gain-following -among-black-christians/, accessed February 26, 2014.

85. Stephen McNallen, *Ásatrú Folk Assembly* Facebook page, February 25, 2014. Available at https://www.facebook.com/Asatru.Folk.Assembly/posts/10202281161365237, accessed January 9, 2015.

86. Drzewiecka and Wong, "Dynamic Construction of White Ethnicity," 201.

87. Bernulf, "Folkish Heathens," available at http://heathenblog.wordpress.com/2007 /01/24/folkish-heathens/, January 24, 2007, accessed March 14, 2007.

88. Gardell, *Gods of the Blood*, 20. See 19–29 for more on the Völkisch movement.

89. Alvis (pseud.), interview by the author, Colorado, October 8, 2004.

90. Valda (pseud.), interview by the author, Colorado, October 8, 2004.

91. Eskel (pseud.), interview by the author, October 15, 2004.

92. Inga (pseud.), telephone interview by the author, April 9, 2006.

93. K. Henderson, "I'll Never Understand Folkish Heathens," *Adventures in Vanaheim: Musings on Vanic Paganism (and Life In General) From a Lesbian Feminist Geek,* October 19, 2012. Available at https://adventuresinvanaheim.wordpress.com/2012/10/19/ill -never-understand-folkish-heathens/, accessed January 9, 2015.

94. Alvis (pseud.), interview by the author, Colorado, October 8, 2004.

95. Heathens Against Hate, available at http://heathensagainsthate.blogspot.com, accessed January 9, 2015.

96. Heathens United Against Racism, available at https://www.facebook.com/groups /344834748939176/, accessed September 8, 2014; personal conversation with the group's founder, September 8, 2014.

97. Northwoods Kindred of Minnesota, available at https://www.facebook.com /northwoods.kindred, accessed August 20, 2012.

98. Boarshead Kindred of Washington, available at http://boarsheadseattle.webs.com /asatru.htm, accessed August 20, 2012.

99. Northwest Arkansas Kindred, available at http://www.northwestarkansaskindred .org/main.asp, accessed April 10, 2011.

100. Gundarsson, "Race, Inheritance, and Asatru Today," 10.

101. Gans, "Symbolic Ethnicity," 12.

102. Drzewiecka and Wong, "Construction of White Ethnicity."

103. M. M. Bakhtin, *The Dialogic Imagination: Four Essays* (Austin: University of Texas Press, 1981), 14.

104. Patricia Anne Simpson, "Tragic Thought: Romantic Nationalism in the German Tradition," *History of European Ideas* 16, nos. 1–3 (1993): 331–336. See also Hans Kohn, "Romanticism and the Rise of German Nationalism," *Review of Politics* 12, no. 4 (1950): 443–472.

105. Skallagrimsson, "Racism in Ásatrú."

106. KazigluBey, "Anti-Racist Ásatrú = Cowards in Denial?" August 3, 2003, available at https://www.stormfront.org/forum/t80610/, accessed January 9, 2015.

107. Skallagrimsson, "Racism in Ásatrú."

108. Gundarsson, "Race, Inheritance, and Asastru Today," 7.

109. Ibid.

110. Gamlinginn, "Race and Religion," in *Mountain Thunder* 8 (1993): n.p., reprinted in C. A. Jerome, *The Orthasafn of Gamlinginn* (Albuquerque, NM: author, 1991).

111. Skallagrimsson, "Racism in Ásatrú."

112. Brand (pseud.), interview by the author, Colorado, October 10, 2004.

113. Smith, "Religion and Ethnicity in America," 1156.

114. Strmiska and Sigurvinsson, "Ásatrú."

115. Ibid., 174.

7. THE LONG JOURNEY

1. Wade Clark Roof and William McKinney, *American Mainline Religion: Its Changing Shape and Future* (New Brunswick, NJ: Rutgers University Press, 1987).

2. Galina Lindquist, "Ethnic Identity and Religious Competition: Buddhism and Shamanism in Southern Siberia," in *Religion, Politics, and Globalization: Anthropological Approaches*, ed. Galina Lindquist and Dan Handelman (New York: Berghahn Books, 2011), 69.

3. Ibid., 69.

4. Kathryn Roundtree, "Neo-Paganism, Native Faith and Indigenous Religion: A Case Study of Malta within the European Context," *Social Anthropology* 22, no. 2 (2014), 84.

5. Rodney Stark and William Sims Bainbridge, "Of Churches, Sects, and Cults: Preliminary Concepts for a Theory of Religious Movements," *Journal for the Scientific Study of Religion* 18, no. 2 (1979): 117–133.

6. James Beckford, *New Religious Movements and Rapid Social Change* (Beverly Hills, CA: Sage Publications, 1986).

7. Lorne Dawson, "The Cultural Significance of New Religious Movements: The Case of Soka Gakkai," *Sociology of Religion* 62, no. 3 (2001): 337.

8. Jeffrey S. Victor, *Satanic Panic: The Creation of a Contemporary Legend* (Open Court, 1993).

9. Michael Strmiska argues that the right wing in Heathenry has been active since the beginning, and that the Left is entirely absent. "The main political spectrum in American heathenry is between the more right-wing, the less right-wing, and those who have no marked objections to right-wing views even if they do not strongly hold them themselves. Liberals and leftists tend to be chased out of the religious movement." Facebook message to the author, September 2014.

10. See Jeffrey Kaplan, "The Reconstruction of the Ásatrú and Odinist Traditions," in *Magical Religion and Modern Witchcraft*, ed. James R. Lewis (Albany: State University of New York Press, 1996), 193–236; Jeffrey Kaplan and Tore Bjørgo, eds., *Nation and Race: The Developing Euro-American Racist Subculture* (Boston: Northeastern University Press, 1998); Jeffrey Kaplan, *Radical Religions in America: Millenarian Movements from the Far Right to the Children of Noah* (Syracuse, NY: Syracuse University Press, 1997); Jeffrey Kaplan and Leonard Weinberg, *The Emergence of a Euro-American Radical Right* (New Brunswick, NJ: Rutgers University Press, 1998); Nicholas Goodrick-Clarke, *Black Sun: Aryan Cults, Esoteric Nazism, and the Politics of Identity* (New York: New York University Press, 2002); and Mattias Gardell, *Gods of the Blood: The Pagan Revival and White Separatism* (Durham, NC: Duke University Press, 2003).

11. Egil Asprem, "Heathens Up North: Politics, Polemics, and Contemporary Norse Paganism in Norway," *Pomegranate: The International Journal of Pagan Studies* 10, no. 1 (2008): 42.

12. Ibid., 44.

13. Michael Strmiska, "On Becoming a Pariah (Personal Reflections on My Ásatrú Research)," Unpublished paper presented in August 2012 at CPASE conference in Stockholm, Sweden, available at http://www.academia.edu/2339326/On_Becoming_A_Pariah _Personal_Reflections_on_my_Asatru_Research, accessed December 17, 2014.

14. See Ross Haenfler, *Straight Edge: Clean-Living Youth, Hardcore Punk, and Social Change* (New Brunswick, NJ: *Rutgers University Press*, 2006).

15. Richard Jenkins, *Social Identity* (London: Routledge, 1996).

16. Kevin Hetherington, *Expressions of Identity: Space, Performance, Politics* (London: Sage Publications, 1998), 62.

17. Ibid., 2.

18. Ibid., 50.

19. Émile Durkheim, *The Division of Labor in Society* (New York: Free Press, 1933), 130.

20. Hetherington, *Expressions of Identity*, 141.

21. Ibid., 22.

22. Ibid., 27.

23. Patrick J. Williams and Heith Copes, "'How Edge Are You?': Constructing Authentic Identities and Subcultural Boundaries in a Straightedge Internet Forum," *Symbolic Interaction* 28, no. 1 (2005): 67–89.

24. Douglas E. Cowan, *Cyberhenge: Modern Pagans on the Internet* (New York: Routledge, 2004).

25. Émile Durkheim, *The Elementary Forms of Religious Life* (New York: Free Press, 1965 [1915]), 10.

26. Haenfler, *Straight Edge*; Patricia Weiser Remington, "Women in the Police: Integration or Separation?" *Qualitative Sociology* 6, no. 2 (1983): 118–135; Amy C. Wilkins, *Wannabes, Goths, and Christians: The Boundaries of Sex, Style, and Status* (Chicago: University of Chicago Press, 2008).

27. Elizabeth Weiss Ozorak, "The Power but Not the Glory: How Women Empower Themselves through Religion," *Journal for the Scientific Study of Religion* 35, no. 1 (1996):

17–29; Sherry Ruth Anderson and Patricia Hopkins, *The Feminine Face of God* (New York: Bantam Books, 1991); Lynn Davidman, *Tradition in a Rootless World: Women Turn to Orthodox Judaism* (Berkeley: University of California Press, 1991); Susan Sered, "Ritual, Morality and Gender: The Religious Lives of Oriental Jewish Women in Jerusalem," *Israel Society for Science Research* 5 (1987): 87–96; Carol Gilligan, *In a Different Voice* (Cambridge, MA: Harvard University Press, 1982).

28. David R. Roediger, *The Wages of Whiteness: Race and the Making of the American Working Class* (New York: Verso, 1991), 13.

29. Alicia Fedelina Chavez and Florence Guido-DeBrito, "Racial and Ethnic Identity and Development," in *An Update on Adult Development Theory: New Ways of Thinking about the Life Course,* ed. Carolyn Clark and Rosemary Caffarella (San Francisco: Jossey-Bass, 1999), 39.

30. Michelle Fine, "Witnessing Whiteness," in *Off White*, ed. Michelle Fine et al. (New York: Routledge, 1997), 214.

31. Chavez and Guido-DeBrito, "Racial and Ethnic Identity," 42.

32. Monica McDermott and Frank L. Samson, "White Racial and Ethnic Identity in the United States," *Annual Review of Sociology* 31 (2005): 245–261.

33. Eduardo Bonilla-Silva, *Racism without Racists: Color-Blind Racism and the Persistence of Racial Inequality in the United States* (Lanham, MD: Rowman and Littlefield, 2006), 5–7.

34. John Dovidio and Samuel Gaertner, "Aversive Racism," *Advances in Experimental Social Psychology* 36 (2004): 1–51.

35. Gary B. Cohen, *Two-Dimensional Man: An Essay on the Anthropology of Power and Symbolism in Complex Society* (Berkeley: University of California Press, 1974), 96.

36. Trinh T. Minh-ha, "Not You / Like You: Postcolonial Women and the Interlocking Questions of Identity and Difference," in *Dangerous Liaisons: Gender, Nation, and Postcolonial Perspectives,* ed. Anne McClintock, Aamir Mufti and Ella Shohat, (Minneapolis: University of Minnesota Press, 1997), 415–419.

37. Herbert Gans, "Symbolic Ethnicity: The Future of Ethnic Groups and Cultures in America," *Ethnic and Racial Studies* 2 (1979): 1–20.

38. Timothy L. Smith, "Religion and Ethnicity in America," *American Historical Review* 83, no. 5 (1978): 1156.

39. See CAORANN (Celtics Against Oppression, Racism, and Neo-Nazism), available at http://www.bandia.net/caorann/, accessed April 5, 2011.

40. Charles Bosk, "The Fieldworker and the Surgeon," in *Forgive and Remember: Managing Medical Failure* (Chicago: University of Chicago Press, 1979), 143.

Glossary of (American) Heathen Terms

Notes: The terms, roles, and definitions of Heathen concepts sometimes vary by region and by cultural origin of Heathen practice. I have made every effort to take possible differences into account and to define each term according to its most common usage/understanding. In order to produce the most concise and most recognized definitions for these terms, I engaged in some virtual crowd-sourcing. I thank the following people for their advice and corrections: Karl Seigfried, Brad Selby, Kari Tauring, Magni Thorsson, Sin Odinsson, Kaedrich Olsen, Rod Landreth, and Jeff Peterson.

Asgard: (Old Norse: *Ásgarðr;* "Enclosure of the Aesir") Asgard is the home of the Aesir (tribe of gods) and is one of the nine worlds of Norse cosmology. The primary source for our knowledge of Asgard is the *Prose Edda* (see *Eddas*).

Blót: (Old Norse: *blót;* pronounced "bloat") The primary ritual of Heathenry, *blót*s vary from private, individual prayers and offerings of food and drink to one or more deities to large-scale community events. The origin of the term *blót* is debated; some scholars and Heathens argue that *blót* is etymologically related to the word for *blood*, while others argue that it simply means "blessing." Some Heathens believe that authentic *blót*s require animal (blood) sacrifice, while others offer sacrifices of mead or sacred objects.

Chieftain: Chieftains are the leaders and lead administrators of kindreds or tribes, chosen or elected by group members. The chieftain is responsible for building consensus and maintaining a working knowledge of a group's *thew*. At multigroup events, chieftains may speak for their entire group and represent them at *things*. In Anglo-Saxon groups, chieftains may be called *Ealdorman*. Other cultural varieties of Heathenry may have different titles, although the responsibilities are the same.

Eddas: The *Eddas* are a major component of "the lore"—the central texts of Heathenry. The *Prose Edda*, compiled by Snorri Sturluson circa 1220, contains the major surviving myths of the Norse gods and goddesses and preserves pre-Christian poems not recorded elsewhere. The *Poetic Edda*, an anonymous manuscript from circa 1270, contains poems composed in the centuries before the formal conversion of Iceland to Christianity in 1000. Because they were recorded by Christian monks, the *Eddas* are widely understood to contain Christian interpolations.

Faining: (Old English *fægen,* meaning "joyful" or "glad") Some Heathens use the term *faining* interchangeably with *blót,* while others (primarily Anglo-Saxon Heathens) distinguish between blood sacrifice (*blót*) and celebrations without blood sacrifice (*faining*). (See also *Blót.*)

Folkish: The term *folkish* derives from the German word *Volk* (English "folk") and corresponds to "people." The term has its origins in the populist Völkisch movement of nineteenth-century Germany. Folkish Heathens often take a variety of positions on sociopolitical issues but may hold one or a combination of the following beliefs: (1) As an ethnic religion, Heathenry should be practiced only by those of northern European heritage. (2) Heathenry is an ancestral/inherited faith that speaks primarily to people of northern European heritage, although others may feel called to the gods. (3) There is something primordial, spiritual, or biologically distinct and unique about each cultural group, and each should pursue its true pre-Christian ancestral faith (sometimes called *indigenous religion* or *native faith*). Heathenry is the native faith of northern Europeans. The Ásatrú Alliance and the Ásatrú Folk Assembly are two organizations that identify as folkish.

Frith: (Old English *friðu,* Old Norse *friðr*) Often translated as "peace," *frith* describes the complex relationship of mutual obligation, commitment, and responsibility that members of a group have toward one another in order to preserve the established social order of a kindred or tribe. Keeping *frith* means obeying the law, keeping *thew,* maintaining loyalty, and adhering to right action.

Gefrain: (pronounced yeh-FRAIN) *Gefrain* is reputation or renown among one's community, often involving popularity and a person's perceived worth to the group. *Gefrain* can be earned through deeds deemed good and worthy and can be lessened by disgrace.

God pole: God poles are a physical representation of a deity. They are most often carved wooden columns erected in or near a sacred or ritual space, with a place for offerings at the base. Heathens use them to venerate the gods and goddesses, ancestors, and other honorable beings. They are often decorated with clothing or other objects associated with the likeness of the god or goddess being honored.

Gothi/Gythia: *Goði* or *Gothi* (plural *Goðar* or *Gothar*) is the Old Norse term for a priest (and chieftain, although some modern Heathens have created separate functions and offices for leaders and clergy). *Gyðja* signifies a priestess. *Gothar* are responsible for spiritual leadership, counseling, conducting *blót*s, and taking care of sacred spaces and are chosen by tribes or kindreds for their knowledge of the lore, wisdom, and leadership abilities. Although there are formal training programs sponsored by national organizations, most *Gothar* receive either lay training from other *Gothar* or are self-taught.

Grith: A *grith* is a temporary peace or truce put into place between individuals or groups for a particular time and place. Maintaining *grith* is in the best interests of those gathered and is enforced by the possibility of ostracism, social sanctions, loss of friendships, and lasting animosity should a person disturb the peace. This is in contrast to *frith,* which is a relationship of obligation and loyalty among members of a tribe or kindred (see *Frith*).

Hamingja: (pronounced ha-MING-ya) *Hamingja* is *luck* as an ancestral energy force that is passed on to subsequent generations. It can be affected through deeds and expectations and success and failure. The lore suggests that it can also be stolen or given away.

Hof: *Hof* is a term used in the Icelandic sagas to refer to Heathen temples or to farm structures in which both sacred and secular activities took place. Contemporary Heathen *hof*s are places of worship that vary greatly in design and material, from small backyard constructions to larger and more permanent structures.

Innangard: (pronounced "INN-ann-guard"; Old Norse *innangarðr*, "within the enclosure") *Innangard* is the "inner yard" or inner circle of a person's family, tribe, or social group. It is the separation between lawfulness, civility, safety, and order and the opposing forces of chaos, destruction, and lawbreaking. It is the collective "we" that works in opposition to the "them"—those outside the yard (*utangard*), those who are rendered "other."

Jotnar: (pronounced "YOT-nar," Anglicized singular *jotunn* from Old Norse *jötunn*, plural from Old Norse *jötnar*) As the first race of beings created, the Jotnar inhabit Jotunheim, one of the nine worlds. Their relationship with the gods is complex, often competitive, and sometimes hostile. They often appear in the lore as giants, but they can also be hideous trolls or beautiful maidens. Jotnar are usually associated with the natural world and often with great wisdom.

Lawspeaker: Also called a *Thule,* the lawspeaker performs the role of rule keeping and judgment within a group (tribe, kindred, and so on), hearing disputes and rendering opinions. In some groups, the lawspeaker is responsible for hearing prospective oaths before their public announcement so as to render judgment about the oath's feasibility and the consequences of failure. The election of lawspeakers in kindreds or tribes is a regional trend, concentrated mostly in the Midwest.

Lore: The term *the lore* is a shorthand Heathen reference to the Icelandic sagas, the Eddic poems, Saxo Grammaticus, and other primary sources of knowledge about Scandinavian and Germanic mythology, legends, and folklore.

Luck: Heathens understand *luck* as the spiritual wealth of a person, family, or tribe rather than simply good fortune. Having good *luck* influences *wyrd* positively, and likewise, bad *luck* influences *wyrd* negatively. *Luck* can also be inherited. *Luck* is earned through right action.

Midgard: (From Old Norse *miðgarðr*, "middle enclosure") Midgard is Middle Earth, connected to Asgard via a rainbow bridge. It is the world inhabited by humans.

Mjollnir: (Pronounced "MYUL-neer," from Old Norse *Mjöllnir*) Mjollnir is the Old Norse name for Thor's hammer and is worn primarily as a pendant by Heathens around the world. The tradition dates back to Bronze Age carvings in Scandinavia. The hammer has a four-thousand-year history as a symbol of protection, blessing, and community.

Ørlög: (Pronounced "OOR-lug"; from the Old Norse words *ór* "out of, from" and *lög* "law") *Ørlög* is accumulated or inherited *wyrd*. It is the summation of the deeds of our ancestors, layers on layers of deeds, words, and outcomes, passed on to us. It can be both positively and negatively affected through our choices, and it influences everything about us. In conjunction with the Norns, we weave the *wyrd* that is becoming. The Norns determine our *Ørlög* or the laws and absolutes of our fate, such as our biological parentage and the circumstances into which we were born (environment, social class and culture). Yet, to a great degree, we are responsible for the *wyrd* that is coming and that will affect the *Ørlög* of our children.

Sagas: The sagas are prose narratives written by Icelandic authors between the thirteenth and fifteenth centuries. Of the many saga genres, those most relevant to Heathens are (1) legendary sagas treating Germanic heroes from before the settlement of Iceland,

(2) sagas of Icelanders dealing with the settlement of Iceland and the early development of its culture, and (3) kings' sagas recording the lives of Norwegian kings. Although they were written well after the conversion to Christianity, they preserve selections of preconversion Heathen poetry and are mined by contemporary Heathens for descriptions of belief and ritual.

Shild: *Shild* is the debt owed for wrongful action against a person or tribe. When a person breaks an oath, he or she must pay *shild* in order to make reparations. *Shild* is determined by those wronged or, in the case of oaths made during *Sumbel,* is predetermined by the lawspeaker.

Sidu: (Old Norse *siðr;* Anglo-Saxon *sidu, seodu*) *Sidu* means "custom." It is the way things are done, a notion of religious practice integrated into everyday life. (See also *Thew.*)

Sumbel (Symbel): *Sumbel* is a social, political, and religious drinking ritual in which those gathered cement bonds of friendship, form alliances between kindreds or tribes, and show respect to one another by public displays of gift giving, toasting, and praises to deity as well as those gathered. During this ritual participants pass a horn of mead around a circle from hand to hand or by way of a cupbearer in three rounds, which can vary according to group and tradition. In round one, the gods and goddesses or spirits or both are hailed. In round two, remembrances of ancestors and heroes are offered. The third round varies but sometimes includes boasts of accomplishment, toasts to gathered friends and hosts, and, more rarely, oaths. Subsequent free rounds can continue for hours. *Sumbel*s can be formal (*High Sumbel*) or informal.

Thew: *Thew* is kindred or tribe norms, values, and customs. (See also *Sidu.*)

Thing: The *thing* was the regional legislative and executive assembly of free men in Germanic antiquity. Today, Heathens across the country hold annual regional *thing*s, or assemblies, attended by kindreds' delegates (usually the chieftain) in order to cement alliances, share accomplishments, and deliberate the troubles or wrongdoings of members. *Thing*s are often held at regional events, for example, the Midwest Thing at the annual event Lightning across the Plains, held in Kansas City, Kansas.

Thule: See also *Lawspeaker.*

Universalist: Different from the universalism of "universal salvation" in Christian traditions, *universalist* is a label, usually derogatory, that Heathens employ to refer to those Heathens with "liberal" political leanings, for whom Heathenry is not necessarily tied to ancestry, and who believe that anyone can be "called" to it by the gods. Universalist Heathens are welcoming of anyone to Heathenry regardless of race, ethnicity, or sexuality. The Troth is the organization most often perceived as universalist.

Unverified personal gnosis (UPG): Unverified personal gnosis is the concept that an individual's spiritual insights (or gnosis) are valid for him or her but not necessarily for others. It is primarily used to differentiate personal experiences, beliefs, or insights from beliefs verifiable in historical or archaeological sources. It is often used in a somewhat derogatory sense to imply that spiritual insight (including visions, dreams, experiences, and intuition) that are not supported by the lore are less authentic than historically minded reconstructionism.

Utangard: (pronounced "OOT-ann-guard"; Old Norse *útangarðr,* "beyond the enclosure") *Utangard* is the space or people outside a group's inner circle. People are labeled *utgard* as a way of marking them as outsiders. See also *Innangard.*

Valkyrie: Observed in *Beowulf* and other early English and Icelandic poems, the serving of ceremonial drink to guests was a sacred task taken up by noble women of rank, whose job it was to cement alliances, preserve the position of their husbands or fathers, establish mutual obligations between ruler and subject, and maintain the social order.[1] Not all Heathen groups observe this role; some pass the horn hand to hand. Some call the servers *cupbearer,* others *Byrele* (Anglo-Saxon, meaning "cup-bearer"), and others *Ealu bora.* To those who observe this role, it is a critical position at *Sumbel.* In ritual, the horn represents the well of *wyrd* (*Urðarbrunnr,* the well of "that which was"), the great depths into which we speak our words, becoming a part of those who partake of the mead thereafter. Women who perform the part experience it as a great honor and deep responsibility.

Wight: (also called *Vaettir,* pronounced "VIT-ir") *Wight* is a general term for sentient spiritual beings that are neither gods nor humans. *Wights* include trolls, dwarves, elves, fairies, or other land spirits that may be found in any feature of the landscape (e.g., rocks, trees, streams, lakes, mountains—*Landvaettir*) and are sometimes, though not always, interested in or kind to humans. Many Heathens believe in house *wights,* or spirits of the home, generally considered to be helpful and beneficial if honored but mischievous if slighted or ignored.

Wyrd: (pronounced "weird") The Old English term *wyrd* derives from a common Germanic term *wurdíz. Wyrd* has cognates in Old Saxon *wurd,* Old High German *wurt,* and Old Norse *urðr. Wyrd* encompasses the sum total of one's actions and decisions, as well as one's predetermined destiny. Because *wyrd* is a web of action, it is fluid and changing—a ripple in a pond, each person affecting others. It can be inherited, improved by honorable action, and worsened by bad choices. *Wyrd* is intertwined with the concepts of *Ørlög* and *luck.* (See *Luck, Ørlög.*)

1. Christie Ward, "Alcoholic Beverages and Drinking Customs of The Viking Age." *The Viking Answer Lady,* available at http://www.vikinganswerlady.com/drink.shtml, accessed October 10, 2012.

Index

Jennifer Snook is an Instructional Assistant Professor of Sociology at the University of Mississippi.